Reconceptualizing Literacy Methods Instruction

For Brenda – Academic
Mother, Soul Sister –
Though it's been a while since
we've traveled these roads
and forests together, you're

ever present in my teaching
& scholarship – The mark of
a great mentor!

Love, Cyn

Studies in the
Postmodern Theory of Education

Joe L. Kincheloe and Shirley R. Steinberg
General Editors

Vol. 28

PETER LANG
New York • Washington, D.C./Baltimore • Boston
Bern • Frankfurt am Main • Berlin • Vienna • Paris

Cynthia McCallister

Reconceptualizing Literacy Methods Instruction

To Build a House That Remembers Its Forest

PETER LANG
New York • Washington, D.C./Baltimore • Boston
Bern • Frankfurt am Main • Berlin • Vienna • Paris

Library of Congress Cataloging-in-Publication Data

McCallister, Cynthia.
Reconceptualizing literacy methods instruction: to build
a house that remembers its forest / Cynthia McCallister.
p. cm. — (Counterpoints; vol. 28)
Includes bibliographical references and index.
1. English teachers—Training of. 2. Language arts teachers—Training of.
3. Literacy programs. I. Title. II. Series: Counterpoints (New York, N.Y.); vol. 28.
PE1066.M35   428'.007—DC20   95-45394
ISBN 0-8204-3082-X
ISSN 1058-1634

Die Deutsche Bibliothek-CIP-Einheitsaufnahme

McCallister, Cynthia.
Reconceptualizing literacy methods instruction: to build
a house that remembers its forest / Cynthia McCallister.
–New York; Washington, D.C./Baltimore; Boston; Bern;
Frankfurt am Main; Berlin; Vienna; Paris: Lang.
(Counterpoints; Vol. 28)
ISBN 0-8204-3082-X

Cover design by Andy Ruggirello.
Cover illustration: "Nonconformist" by Russell P. Orrico, 1996.

The author gratefully acknowledges permission granted to publish excerpts from the following:
Van Maanen, *Tales of the field: On writing ethnography.* Chicago:
University of Chicago Press (1988). Appearing on pp. 231–233.
Power, *Long roads, short distances.* Unpublished manuscript. Appearing throughout the text.

The paper in this book meets the guidelines for permanence and durability
of the Committee on Production Guidelines for Book Longevity
of the Council of Library Resources.

For Gerry and Packie and Fiona

Contents

Acknowledgments

Although I didn't realize it at the time, this book began on the first night I stood before a group of graduate students as their teacher; and since that night all the experiences I've had in the classroom have contributed to its development. I would like to thank the faculty members of the College of Education at the University of Maine who provided me with my first college teaching opportunities. I am grateful to my academic mentors who encouraged me to pursue a relevant question and offered the guidance necessary for me to do so. Special thanks goes to Brenda Power, who has been my friend, advisor, and research subject. Many have asked with skepticism how I could have written an honest, objective study of my mentor's teaching. In response to their questions, "How could you remain objective?," and "Didn't your relationship interfere?" I've often wondered "How could I have done it otherwise?" The bonds that developed as a result of our relationship have, if anything, strengthened my ability to better understand the issues that structured my study. As my advisor, Brenda helped me stay motivated by valuing my abilities while challenging me to grow. She graciously offered time and assistance in order to help me improve my teaching, and she invited me into her methods classroom as an observer. The thoughts and ideas we shared through our ongoing conversations were the inspiration for this study, and the process of talking through wide-ranging research possibilities helped the project develop and take shape.

From the moment she became my supervising editor, Shirley Steinberg has offered enthusiastic support for this project. From her review of my book proposal to her comments on the final draft, Shirley's response to my work has been positive, constructive, and humane, and her suggestions for further reading helped me to expand horizons and grow as a scholar. I carried Ruth Hubbard's voice with me in all of my writing, and for her the text is richer. I am indebted to her for her generous investment of time and energy in reading my drafts and for our many long-distance writing conferences. I always hung up the phone feeling good about my writing and knowing exactly what I could do to make it better. I would like to thank Janice Kristo for her readings of my drafts. Her reminders to clarify and to come back to my original questions served as guide-posts that helped me stay on the right path throughout the writing and revision process. Robert Cobb, the Dean of the College of Edu-cation at the University of Maine, was an enthusiastic and suppor-tive reader whose background as a college administrator helped me see my study from a different perspective. Phyllis Brazee was the first teacher I had as a graduate student. It was she who initially helped me see teaching as a personal and creative act, rather than a technical one—a theme that continues to play itself out in both my teaching and scholarship. Judith Brown was the invaluable friend who carefully and thoughtfully read each chapter and made insight-ful and critical comments.

Throughout the preparation of this book, my family has been my greatest source of support. I am grateful to my mother, Pat McCallister, who, as a single, working mother of five children, re-turned to school to complete a bachelor's and then a master's degree. She has always been my greatest inspiration and my most dedicated fan. Finally, I would like to thank my husband, Gerry, and our children, Packie and Fiona. They are my sustenance. As is the case with so many professional projects, this book would not have been possible were it not for Gerry, my soul mate. He helped me carve out time to write and helped me maintain perspective with his irony and wit. Throughout my graduate program and my first years as a professor, he has been a pillar of support, holding me up and helping me remember the happy larger picture of our life together. Our children, Packie and Fiona, are a constant source of enchant-ment and joy. At my lowest points, when commitments and dead-lines forced me into a state of frantic tunnel vision, Packie and Fiona made me remember my priorities. The days we share, filled with laughter and happiness, always calm and center me and give me strength. I am eternally grateful to my family, and I consider myself blessed to live in their loving company.

List of Tables

Preface

In the modernist school system from which most of us stem, we are products from products of products. Getting there is the nuisance, being there is the desire—as students we were seldom taught to celebrate the process, only the product. Cynthia McCallister has taken up this travesty of education and pulled us back to not only the process, but the inspiration, inception, travel, and exploration of the trip. The destination, or process becomes merely another point on a continuum of learning. Indeed, as Miles Horton and Paulo Freire maintained, "we make the road by walking"—the process is the key. Cynthia walked miles discovering her journey and with humility and scholarship, she reveals her own evolution as a student of teaching and a teacher of students. Never lapsing into trivial self-indulgence, she uses Pinarian autobiography as a form of research which uncovers the layers of social, psychological and academic history that have formed her being. Working with the discovery of self-reflection and theory, she solidly walks alongside of the reader, exploring ways of journeying through literacy.

As a teacher of teachers, Cynthia incants the loving assistance and scholarship of people like Brenda Power and Bill Pinar. The circle of mentoring goes on as she shares her reactions and experiments with suggestions and readings of other scholars. This acknowledgment of mentorship is essential in working in the elastic paradigms of critical literacy. Not citing any one model of literacy, Cynthia eschews dogma. Always relating to literacy as a process, we are able to hear suggestions from both students and teachers—from these examples we are then able to playfully, yet seriously form our own tentative descriptions of literacy.

What a fine book Cynthia McCallister has given us. We are immersed in a rich narrative of theoretical autobiography and given a plethora of examples and vignettes with which to re-write and re-read for our own purposes. Enjoy the forest, and look at the trees.

Shirley R. Steinberg, Adelphi University

Introduction

My brothers and I are again the woodcutter's children. We play under the trees, but even our play is a likeness to work. We construct shelters of rotten logs, thatch them with fireweed, and then invite our parents into the shelters to eat their lunches...

When I think of it now, it is not far from the building of those makeshift shelters to the making of poems. You take what you find, what comes naturally to the hand and mind. There was the sense with these shelters that they wouldn't last, but that they were exactly what could be done at the time. There were great gaps between the logs because we couldn't notch them into each other, but this allowed us to see the greater forest between them. It was a house that remembered its forest. And for me, the best poems, no matter how much order they make, have an undercurrent of forest, of the larger unknown.

To spend one's earliest days in a forest with a minimum of supervision gave a lot of time for exploring. I also had some practice in being lost. Both exploring and being lost are, it seems now, the best kind of training for a poet. When I think of those times I was lost, it comes back with a strange exhilaration, as though I had died, yet had the possibility of coming back to life. The act of writing a poem is like that. It is that sense of aloneness which is trying to locate the world again, but not too soon, not until the voice has made its cry, "Here, here, over here," and the answering voices have called back, "Where are you?"

(Tess Gallagher, 1983, pp. 121-122)

The experiences of exploring and being lost are the best kind of training for teachers and researchers, as well as poets. Journeying through the unfamiliar woods of new theory and practice, exploring the larger unknown forest of experience, feeling completely lost before finding the way home again—these are the elements of a learning odyssey that render the once-familiar home a completely different place. New understandings develop through inquiry and stem from interludes with the larger unknown. In simile, the forest is my professional life as both an elementary and college-level teacher. I have constructed houses, various versions of curriculum, in the manner of styles I admire. The strength of those structures has always depended on the degree to which I understand the forest of my life and experience. The structure is stronger and more meaningful when it is a house that remembers its forest.

The narrative that follows is both a story of my teaching and my research. It is about being lost in the forest and finding my way home. It is also a story about the process of building a house with enough gaps in its structure to force a view of the "undercurrent of forest." Exploring the larger unknown worlds of students, content, and teaching, and the ways those worlds meet and interact, is central to the art of teaching. Yet the nature of their union cannot, in isolation, be taught. Working through all of the phases of my research project—data collection, analysis, interpretation, and composition—has helped me understand that there must always be gaps between the logs of my house that will allow me to see the unknown forest. The gaps are the continual questions I have about teaching, and they always challenge me to continue the process of rebuilding.

My story has its beginnings in my early professional experiences, first as an elementary school teacher and then as a college teacher, when I struggled through new experiences and tried to find my way. During those early experiences I had many questions: "Why didn't that approach or lesson work?," "Why did that child behave the way she did?," "What am I doing wrong?," "What am I doing right?" Those early teaching experiences and the plethora of questions they posed have become the backdrop for my development as a teacher. They have remained with me through my years as a graduate student and helped guide my learning as a new professor. Now those questions, in refined and revised form, provide the structure of this book.

Chapter 1

C'est Moi

Bringing the past to the present by printing it. The words coalesce to form a photograph. Holding the photograph in front of oneself, one studies the detail, the literal holding of the picture and one's response to it, suggestive of the relation of past to present.

(William Pinar, 1994, p. 24)

Uneasy Beginnings

I have a recurring dream, one I know as the *fledgling teacher dream*, in which I stand at the front of a class or a group of students and proceed to screw up. In the dreams, I have no idea what I'm talking about. I am faking my way and making statements that are completely dissociated from the purpose of the presentation—about which, of course, I know nothing. My students look bored and lifeless. The situation proceeds from bad to worse. By the end of the dream, just when I am suffering the worst kind of subconscious angst, I awaken and suddenly feel an exhilarating sense of relief.

The dreams are composed of shards of memories and images of my most anxious teaching moments. They are moments that stand out from others; the stress of an uneasy situation always heightens my senses and leaves me feeling memorably ill at ease. I feel my heart race and my face flush. Confusion replaces clear thinking. My words sound stupid, unclear, inarticulate. I see blank, puzzled, or apathetic expressions on the faces of my students. During these times an oppressive feeling of doubt overcomes me, causing my confidence to collapse.

In the dream, these memories combine to form the worst possible scenario. But as terrible as they are, I believe these dreams are a mechanism to help me cope with the anxiety I experience in new teaching situations—times before the first day of class or a conference presentation when I feel especially uneasy about disclosing myself and my ideas to an unfamiliar group of people. I also believe the dreams symbolize a prevalent theme in my personality that often emerges during stressful situations. Through the process of subconscious rehearsal and reflection, the dream must somehow help me work through uncertainty and insecurity.

I have felt the ups and downs of those experiences many times. In fact, I often feel as if I have been through what seems like a continuous cycle of new and uncertain beginnings. Though I have been teaching in some capacity for nine years, during many of those years I have experienced the familiar anxiety of being a beginning teacher. During my first four years as a teacher, I taught four different grade levels. During the subsequent three years when I struggled to meet the demands of college-level teaching, I encountered a new set of challenges. I often wished for more certainty and predictability while I was learning the art of teaching. It's difficult to develop skill and security in a process that is always changing.

Through the years I've attempted to cope with uncertainty by creating my own "laws" about teaching and learning—a system of rules that guide my actions. I process bits and pieces of information about teaching and learning I acquire through reading, interactions with colleagues, and other experiences in order to assimilate them into my own personal code of practice. These laws govern all facets of my teaching; I draw upon them almost spontaneously and without thought. Often though, just as I have fully implemented one of my laws, a student, a situation, or a new set of circumstances shatters its proof, leaving me where I started. Teachers like myself, whose classrooms are shaped more by the unpredictability of humanity than the predictability of science, can't operate according to a system of concrete laws. That's not to say that theoretical knowledge is not important or that basic research has not had a significant impact on the development of professional knowledge in teaching. However, insights and perceptions that are independent of formal reasoning—hunches or immediate and spontaneous insights—have always been the most potent source of guidance in my practice as a teacher. Even though they will never be as concrete, reliable, or eternal as the laws of nature, my system of writing and revising these laws has been the essence of my professional development. A continual challenge for me in developing my personal professional knowledge has been to try to fully understand who and what contributed to helping me develop my own system of teaching.

For all of its dead ends and disasters, teaching is a career that is also filled with fresh starts and new beginnings. At the start of each term, an unfamiliar group of students gathers and forms the basis of what will become a unique, collective experience for everyone involved. Sometimes I am thankful that teaching is never entirely predictable and familiar. The uncertainty keeps the experience fresh and stimulating. There have been several major phases in my teaching career; these times were occasionally marked by disaster, almost always filled with uncertainty, and often held the promise of a new beginning. These experiences were an important part of my development as a teacher and have shaped the questions I've tried to answer as a researcher within this text.

Reality Shock

The term *reality shock* characterizes my first year as a teacher in a rural Maine school. It was during that year that I discovered that the real world of classroom teaching was far different from the one I had imagined. My idealism collided, head on, with the sobering reality of the classroom. Before that fateful time, I had grand expectations for myself and looked forward to beginning a successful and satisfying teaching career. During the summer months before I was to begin my job, I spent long hours preparing for the year to come. My imagination was active during this time. In my mind I would visualize a classroom in which my students enjoyed school and where learning was interesting, engaging, and fun. I looked forward to establishing strong relationships with my students. Behavior problems never entered my mind. Why should they? Nothing goes awry in Utopia. I was sure I was going to love my job, and I never doubted I would be good at it.

My first day as a teacher took me by storm when eighteen fifth graders entered my room, and I began the uneasy, uncertain job of being their teacher. On that first day I was optimistic, confident, and only a little bit nervous. But just as quickly as the year began, my high hopes were dashed. I recall standing at the front of the class on that first day, beside an overhead projector, demonstrating the process of webbing personal information in preparation for writing personal stories. My students responded to my lesson with boredom and apathy. I wondered what could possibly have been the problem, thinking the negative response to my lesson was a fluke. But in retrospect, their affect was a harbinger of the dreadful year ahead. The situation didn't improve, as I thought it would; instead, the job of teaching became more difficult. I made continual adjustments by rearranging the furniture, readjusting the schedule, or moving problem students. But to no avail. Whatever I was doing, it wasn't working. Things seemed to go from bad to worse; the year continued on a steady downward slide. Sometime during the first week with my students I began to reconcile my images of a Utopia-like classroom with reality. As days passed and things got worse, I couldn't help but compare myself to other teachers in my school who appeared to be enjoying great success. I couldn't determine what qualities separated me from them. It seemed to me that good teaching was shrouded in a kind of mystique. I figured, either you have it or you don't—it seemed *I didn't.*

After several weeks in the classroom, I abandoned any grand, albeit vague, notions I had previously entertained about implementing a holistic, student-centered curriculum that was similar to the ones I had been reading about. I came to terms with my limitations, cut my losses, and began planning my lessons from textbooks. For the most part, the curriculum I followed was straight from the textbook. I felt the pressure of accountability and understood that I needed to cover an approved curriculum. I didn't trust myself to create my own—nor did I have the energy or time. I divided the day into periods of about forty-five minutes according to subject areas. At the start of each period, I directed my students to get into their groups, turn to the assigned page, and read or problem solve their way through the assignment. The predictability and ease of the smooth and linear progression through a textbook lent safety and stability to an otherwise unstable year. I tried my best to incorporate activities into the curriculum. But they were always "add ons" and the first thing to go in a time crunch.

Keeping track of the progress of eighteen students through the pages of five textbooks was itself a seemingly daunting task. Each day, I listed on the marker board the names of students who owed me work. Next to their names I listed the pages they hadn't completed. Record keeping was a messy task, one that required attention several times a day. Students who were regulars to my list often tried, and succeeded, to sabotage my recordkeeping efforts. They erased their names or page numbers. There would be inevitable complaints and disagreements as to whether a certain assignment was turned in. Recognizing my hopeless and chaotic recordkeeping skills, I often gave in. This was a gesture that only encouraged more disagreements. Prior to recess I would announce those unlucky souls who needed to stay in to make up work. These were the children who needed to be out the most. Needless to say, the regular homework debacles didn't contribute to a healthy sense of community within the classroom.

For a number of reasons—inexperience, fatigue, apathy—my first-year classroom altogether lacked a sense of community. Outside of school, I was reasonably welladjusted, so it was easy to see the good in most of the people who surrounded me. But, as a teacher feeling the stress of a new job, in the best cases my relationships with students were less than positive, but in the worst cases they were plainly dysfunctional. Some of my students met all of my teaching efforts with resistance, others tirelessly looked for every fault—and that year there were many. Unfortunately, the prepackaged curriculum presented in the textbooks didn't leave any space for my students' interests or concerns. This factor, I believe, had a negative influence on their attitudes and, consequently, on my relationship with them.

The general emotional and physical strain of the job was getting the best of me. My voice was weak at the end of each day from talking too much and too loudly. At night I sat in my living room correcting my way through mounds of papers or planning for the next day. Over time, I became frustrated and cynical and began to question the career I had chosen. I was irritated at myself for being so naive in the beginning. I began to think of ways out—a job at another school? Another career?

The classroom structures I had devised were work-intensive. All day, every day, I was as busy as a trainer in a three-ring circus with coordinating lessons and activities. My students weren't independent. They never managed to do what I asked. Every activity I assigned required constant attention. I was worn out by the endless work of preparing lessons and correcting student assignments, and overwhelmed with the demands of organizing and implementing a total curriculum.

During that year I felt isolated and uninspired. I was continually inundated with the tedious work of grading papers and writing lesson plans, overcome by behavior issues, and puzzled by learning problems. I internalized my growing anger and frustration, and as a defense mechanism, I saw the difficulties I was experiencing as the fault of others—administrators, my students, their parents. I began to hate my job. But I also began to worry about whether or not I would be lucky enough to have a job to hate the following year if the administration discovered my flaws. What would happen if I lost my job? What would that loss mean for my career? As the year continued, I became more insecure about my ability and my future prospects in the career I had chosen.

I muddled through my first year of teaching, relying on the prepackaged lessons provided by textbooks. I hadn't the energy or the wisdom to think critically about what I was doing in the classroom. I fell into the habit of relying on artificial routines according to the progression of lessons and chapters in textbooks, and the level of enthusiasm in the classroom suffered as a result of the blasé curriculum.

Finally, the year came to a close. On the last day of school, I was happy when I could say good-bye to my students, and, under my breath, good riddance! I packed up my belongings, turned out the lights of my classroom, and retreated to my quiet little home overlooking a peaceful stream and the promise of a tranquil summer without the troubles of students and school. So had passed my first year of teaching—it was a failure, a flop, a bad memory I have since tried hard to forget. I doubt other first-year teachers have perceived their first year to have been such a bust. Perhaps I am too self-conscious, too critical, or have too high expectations. Or, perhaps my perceptions are accurate and my first experience was an aberration—an undeniable failure. I have forced myself to reconsider elements of that year over and over again.

I believe unsuccessful experiences have more to offer in the way of learning than highly successful ones; and so that first dreadful year has been a frame of reference for my professional growth. Supposedly, in every cloud there is a silver lining. Through subsequent years, as painful as it has been, I have used that cloud of my first-year teaching experiences to understand the initially indefinable phenomena known as teaching and learning. That year has long served as a sounding board for any new theories I read or attempt to apply to myself. Though subsequent teaching experiences have added to that base of knowledge, my long year in fifth grade was my point of origin.

Beginning Again

I was happy to be invited back to teach the following year. I knew I was fortunate to have a job and felt lucky that I slipped through the cracks of the gates that kept out incompetents. I figured either they hadn't discovered that I was incapable, or maybe they had simply decided to give me a second chance. But I also felt ambivalent. I had been reassigned to teach kindergarten, and I knew precious little about that age group. In the back of my mind there was a subtle voice complaining, "Not again"! I felt that just as I was beginning to understand the rules of the fifth-grade game, the game was being changed on me. Though it was my second year as a classroom teacher, it would certainly be a new beginning—a new grade level, new colleagues, and a new curriculum. In a way, I was starting over. I didn't have children at the time; preschoolers and kindergartners were as foreign to me as an entirely different species of school children. I was uncomfortable with my new assignment, but I needed a job and decided to make the best of it.

During my first year of teaching, I enrolled in course work that would eventually lead to a master's degree in literacy education. Over that summer I took a writing process course where I focused on emergent literacy in preparation for my new teaching assignment. I learned to recognize signs of emerging literacy in the reading and writing behaviors of young children and became interested in the theories that helped explain literacy development. When school finally began I felt more confident about my teaching ability and more knowledgeable about the abilities of the children I would be teaching. I made drastic changes in the daily routines and underlying structures of classroom life. I refocused the curriculum, implementing instructional practices that were representative of theories about teaching and learning that I was beginning to understand. My revised practices were largely based on knowing each student and being able to address each one's individual needs. Since the focus of the curriculum centered on the students, the personal connections I made with them were more authentic and satisfying. This sense of unity was a positive influence on the classroom community.

During the fall semester of my kindergarten teaching year, I took an ethnographic research course. I conducted my own qualitative research project that focused on the writing of several of my students. As a researcher in my own classroom, I assumed more of a reflective stance in my teaching. The reflective stance helped me understand my students' individual needs, and caused me to observe patterns of learning and development in each student. I was nourished by the process of classroom-based inquiry. Because teacher research provided me with a professional lifeline, I understand its benefits at a personal level. I see that experience as a turning point for me on the road to better teaching, and one that caused me to become interested in the teacher research movement. I have studied the phenomena of increased professional awareness of teachers who engage in researching their own classrooms. My students responded well to my changed program. They seemed to like school. To my relief and delight, I was beginning to feel good about my relationships with my students, and those feelings bolstered my teaching and, as a consequence, my students' learning.

Though I characterize my second year as a teacher as unquestionably more successful than the year before, I had plenty of fledgling teacher dreams, dreams in which I was challenged by parents, colleagues, and administrators. But I was more comfortable in my role as a teacher, more organized, better at communicating with my students, and more understanding of their development. I was gaining skills, knowledge, and confidence, and was beginning to feel successful. Recognizing that good teaching is, in part, a process of learning, I had begun a course of professional development that helped me continue to grow and expand my thinking. I had developed a new identity as an elementary teacher. I was more reflective in my practice and recognized the need to know my students in order to teach them. Though my beliefs were more sophisticated, I hadn't yet recognized the themes that governed my teaching. As I was to find out in my new experience of teaching adults, those important lessons I had learned as an elementary teacher didn't automatically transfer. I had to learn a new set of hard lessons about teaching and to reconstruct a new teaching identity all over again.

Another Transition: Doctoral Studies

Elementary teaching became exciting and challenging when I began to integrate theory into my daily practice. As I moved from kindergarten to first, and then to second grade, I satisfied the course requirements for my master's degree in literacy education. Connecting theory with practice made my job intellectually invigorating. I was increasingly intrigued by the theory/practice connection and began to consider going on for my doctoral degree in literacy education once I had finished my master's. After my fourth year as a classroom teacher, I decided to begin my doctoral studies on a full-time basis at the University of Maine in order to study how to work with pre- and in-service literacy education teachers. This new experience brought with it many uneasy beginnings, more new teaching experiences, and, with them, many more fledgling teacher dreams.

When my husband Gerry and I decided we would both attend school on a full-time basis, we began to make the necessary sacrifices. I quit my tenured job as an elementary teacher in a school that was just a mile away from our home. Knowing we couldn't make house payments on a graduate assistant stipend, we put the house on the market. We had completely renovated our old nineteenth-century Cape Cod—rebuilt it inside and out. I cried when we walked from room to room, saying good-bye to the place we called home and the memories it held.

As I stepped into each empty room, a flood of memories engulfed me. In the bedroom upstairs I could picture myself sitting in the blue armchair near the window during a snowstorm, holding my two-week-old baby in my arms while I watched an otter push its head up from beneath the icy stream below. In the bathroom, I recalled the time I gave my two babies their first bath together, and I could almost hear the echo of their squeals and laughter above the sound of splashing water; and in the front bedroom, I looked one last time at the circle of teddy bears on the wall I had stenciled when I was expecting my first child. The separation was painful, and I questioned our decision to uproot our existence in a community where we had grown quite comfortable. The very day our little Cape was refurbished to perfection, just after we had washed the brushes we had used to apply the final coat of white paint to the bathroom window frames, we said our last good-bye to our home, shut the door on that chapter of our lives, and drove to nearby Bangor to close on the sale of our first home.

That day marked a turning point. Later in the afternoon a new chapter began as we pulled the moving truck up to the residence hall where I had been assigned a graduate assistant position as residence hall director. All at once I felt sad, scared, and uncertain. Our new apartment was small and institutional with industrial quality carpet covering the cold concrete floors. Though we sold most of our furniture to prepare for smaller digs, our apartment bulged with belongings. After a day of sorting, organizing, and boxing junk, we sat exhausted in our new living room, feeling the emptiness of an abrupt ending and waiting uncomfortably for the glad feelings that accompany new beginnings.

After the semester began I was too busy to question the wisdom of our decision. Gerry and I were both full-time students. We shared the responsibility for caring for our one- and two-year-old children, Patrick and Fiona, and took turns doing homework. "Two hours on, two hours off" defined the homework/child-care rotating schedule we shared. Meanwhile I was faced with the challenge of supervising a staff of college-age resident assistants and pulling my hair out over statistics homework. From that first day when we sat in the emptiness of our new apartment, to the day I sat around a table with my advisory committee during my dissertation defense, it frequently occurred to me that the decision to return to school might not have been the right one. I was uncertain of my marketability once I graduated—"Would I get a job?" "Was I cut out for a faculty position?" "Would I succeed?" To compound the insecurity, as each week of each school year passed we were sinking further into debt from day-care and health-insurance expenses. By the end of the first year we had gone through half the proceeds of the sale of our house and had borrowed a substantial amount of money.

It's a cliché to say that in order to grow you need to take risks. Yet when I look back on the decision to return to school, I see it is true. I am happy at where I am in life now—I look forward to beginning my new faculty job, teaching college students, and doing research. But the risk I had to take in order to return to school was great, and it didn't always seem to be the right choice, especially when I found myself in new and difficult situations. The most formidable new experience of my doctoral program was the process of developing as a college teacher.

My long-term goal when I entered the doctoral program was to eventually become a professor. The importance of having college-level teaching experience was something my doctoral advisor, Brenda Power, explained to me early in my program. She arranged for me to teach a graduate-level literacy education course during my first year as a full-time student. I trusted her advice and felt a certain sense of satisfaction that stemmed from her confidence in me. It was an overload assignment, on top of an already overloaded life as a mother, wife, student, and graduate assistant. Because I needed the benefits of a live-in position as a resident director in order to cover living expenses for my family, I was never able to take a teaching assistantship. But it was important to include teaching as part of my preparation. So from that second semester until the last, I taught courses while I directed a residence hall.

The first course I taught was entitled Reading and Writing Across the Curriculum. I had taken plenty of undergraduate science courses and was interested in theories having to do with integrating the elementary school curriculum. I selected an assortment of texts ranging in focus from basic principles of literacy instruction (Atwell, 1987; Routman 1991) to examinations of social contexts of literacy (Fishman, 1988; Heath, 1983). I sought feedback and advice from instructors who had previously taught the course, and they supported my approach. After heavy preparation, the semester finally began.

I vividly recall the first class meeting. After going through the syllabus, I remember standing at the front of the class, at the overhead projector, talking about shifting paradigms and newer perspectives on teaching and learning. I have only vague memories of the activities and presentations I organized that semester—selective amnesia, I suppose. My more vivid recollections involve my own feelings and perceptions about how I was doing as an instructor. I approached that semester feeling secure and confident, as I had initially felt as a new fifth-grade teacher.

But just as it had been with that first unpleasant year as an elementary teacher, my first college-teaching semester went from bad to worse. After the first five minutes in front of my class, I began to feel insecure and quite certain my students were becoming suspicious of my credentials and my ability. The gestalt of my first experience with a new class, whether positive or negative, for me is invariably an indication of the experience to come. If I begin a new situation with confidence and security, I build on my strengths and experience success. On the other hand, if I start poorly, feel insecure and incompetent in those critical first moments, I never gain the necessary momentum to carry me successfully through the course of the term. For me, the launching stage of a new experience is critical. The self-awareness, knowledge, and skill I feel during those initial moments seems to influence the course of my success.

As the semester proceeded I became paranoid and insecure. I approached each class with hesitation and ambivalence. Just as it had been when I ended my first year as a classroom teacher, it was a happy moment when I had collected the last of the end-of-term evaluations and turned out the lights on the classroom. After the semester ended, my family and I headed to Ireland where we spent the summer. My relationship to school that summer was a comfortable distance—I was separated by a wide ocean and distracted by pub life, friends and family, and the beauty of the Irish landscape.

Reality eventually struck when I returned to Maine where my first set of college teaching evaluations awaited. As plain as ink on paper, they revealed the uncomfortable truth—one I had accepted with minimal concern due to a blissful break abroad—that I was not a natural-born college teacher. In fact, I was clumsy, amateur, and average. I tried to reevaluate that experience and concluded that I had been unsuccessful for several reasons: I was uncertain as to how I should interact with my students; I lacked confidence in my knowledge of the field; I was overextended by my other obligations; I felt my elementary teaching experiences were inadequate compared to some of the students I taught; and I was overwhelmed at the amount of time required to plan a college course. I had muddled my way through, and my evaluations showed it—some of my students had considered my course a *good* experience, but there were just as many who ranked it below average. Though I was mildly disappointed that I had not been capable of modeling excellent teaching to my students, I convinced myself that the mediocre evaluations stemmed from teaching the course for the first time. With the benefit of a learning experience behind me, I felt confident I would be more successful the next time around. I was assigned to teach the same course during the upcoming semester, so I revamped my syllabus, revitalized the curriculum, changed some texts, and planned interesting speakers. I felt ready to go and certain to succeed.

An Uneasy Second Try

It was the beginning of a new fall semester, and again I found myself standing at the front of a new group of students. It was an Indian summer evening. The late afternoon sun glared through the wall of windows into the classroom. Sweat dampened my blouse and the heat reddened my face as I stood in front of another new class. Again, I stood at the overhead projector, talking to the class about emergent literacy while putting up overheads of examples of young children's writing. The heat was intensified by the glaring light of the antique overhead projector.

As I stood there, flushed in the face and preoccupied with the heat, I suddenly felt every trace of confidence I'd managed to muster up for the occasion fade away, leaving me nervously stuttering and stammering. I couldn't concentrate or effectively communicate my ideas. A student asked a question. I drew a complete blank and couldn't answer. At that moment I convinced myself I had lost credibility with my students. The first class finally ended, but that was just the beginning of the end.

The semester brought other problems that stemmed from my instructional approach. I had never been a firm believer in lectures, especially for an applied discipline such as teaching. Long before I began teaching college courses I believed that learning experiences should be active and experiential. My own experiences had confirmed this: as an elementary teacher I improved my practice dramatically when I shifted my focus of teaching from the perspective of trying to help my students master a body of knowledge to a more child-centered, constructivist approach. But beliefs and practices don't always mesh. In reality I didn't have the slightest idea how to modify my approach to teaching adults in order to reflect the constructivist and social-learning theories in which I believed. Though I incorporated activities and group work, most of my classroom structures remained teacher-directed. During that semester I spent hours combing through texts, familiarizing myself with theories, and planning presentations. Week after week I came to class wellprepared and loaded with materials, including overheads, charts, and handouts. But in spite of how much I prepared, each class limped along.

As a result of whatever it was that I was doing wrong, the classroom climate suffered. In all of my planning, it never occurred to me that I would need to take deliberate actions to establish and nurture a positive community in the classroom. I simply accepted that college students, being adults, were capable of attending to curriculum and content without attention to, what seemed to me then, peripheral issues concerning classroom community.

I dreaded each class and found my confidence and self-esteem shrink away to nothing. Eventually I avoided talking in front of the class, and when I did, my words sounded phony and stilted. I forfeited leadership of the class and allowed it to steer its own course, out of my control. My relationships with some of my students descended to new depths. As a new college teacher, I navigated my way to setting and enforcing standards and expectations; as a result, I bumped heads with several of my students who probably thought I was misguided and dogmatic. While I was trying to establish my own understanding of standards and expectations as a college teacher, some of my students were equally committed to the notion of being liberated adults who should have the final word on the quality of work and what should be acceptable. I discovered factions had developed between myself and several of my students when I heard reverberations of their complaints to their advisors who were faculty members in the college. I began the semester lacking confidence, and, with the passing of each week, I grew less confident, more disheartened, and more depressed.

During that semester I was taking an advanced educational psychology course. In that course I remember learning about the theory of self-efficacy and its influence on the learning process. This psychological construct explains that self-perceptions are important to the learning process—the better you feel about your ability, the more confidence you have, and the better you perform. Once any factor begins to inhibit self-confidence and positive self-perceptions, efficacy is diminished and, as a result, performance suffers. As I read about the self-fulfilling prophecy of self-efficacy, I began to see and understand the inevitability of my own failure as a teacher. In fact, I served as my own metaphor for self-efficacy principles.

I finished the semester. I had been a failure. I knew this had been my second chance, and I had blown it. I awaited confirmation of my worthlessness as a college teacher in the form of my course evaluations. But at the same time I had to prepare for my third college teaching experience. This time it would come in the form of a six-credit undergraduate integrated reading language-arts methods course. It was a big course to prepare. And unfortunately, at that point, teaching was the last thing I wanted to do.

Toward the end of the semester break I began checking my mailbox for the dreaded evaluations. Each day, twice a day, I checked to see if the packet had arrived. Finally, after three weeks, the large manila envelope appeared in my mailbox. I pulled it out and held it for a moment. The envelope contained the formal measure of my success. It represented my second chance, my opportunity to try the same course again, to improve the curriculum, delivery, and evaluations. These evaluations were an indication of how well I modeled the practices I taught. I knew I couldn't fail this time—and if I did, I knew it would be an indication that there was no hope for my future as a college teacher. The evaluations would either vindicate me and confirm my rightful place among the ranks of other teacher educators, or they would reinforce the doubt and suspicions about my ability that already contaminated my sense of professional self-worth.

I stood there in the lobby of the education building, holding the envelope that contained my fate, feeling only trepidation. Believing my second chance at teaching the course had been even worse than the first, I opened the package. Inside there was a stack of twenty or so questionnaires upon which my class of graduate students from the previous semester had penciled in their responses to questions about my teaching; questions such as how organized I was, how worthwhile my class was, and how well I knew the content of my specialty. My hands trembled as I sorted my way through the pile. Eventually, I came to the most important paper in the stack, the page of statistics.

For each set of evaluations, the university compiles combined results of individual responses to each question so that the instructor can understand her teaching averages. These statistics are printed out on large green and white computer paper. Adding to the humiliation I was already feeling as a result of having had a bad teaching semester, I was now confronted by the realization that two semesters of statistics had not been enough to make me statistically literate. Though I knew the averages weren't good, I didn't know exactly what they meant either. I thought, perhaps, there could be some good news couched in the pages of numbers, some indication that I did something well.

Moments of truth such as these have always made me uncomfortable. As one who sometimes lacks confidence, I often try to steer my way clear of any circumstances in which I might risk being told how far I fall short of expectations. When I began studying for my master's degree and was taking a course on the writing process, I dreaded hearing responses to my writing. The dread I felt in sharing my work lurked in my mind as I wrote, inhibiting my creative process. I believed that problems with a piece of my writing meant I was a bad writer. It was difficult to separate the parts from the whole, to understand that writing isn't ever categorically bad or good, but that any piece of my writing had an array of qualities, each of which could be given attention and improved. Subjecting myself to hearing a response about a piece had the effect of confirming what I already knew to be true—that my writing was terrible.

As a teacher who thought her writing was poor, who was also a graduate student In literacy education, I felt like a fraud. Many of my fellow graduate students wrote beautifully, read widely, and had obviously chosen their rightful calling. And then there was me, often bothered by the hypocrisy of my evolving role as reading/writing teacher who does both poorly. I felt those familiar doubts as I stood in the office holding the stack of teaching evaluations that indicated I was a mediocre teacher, and one who, of all things, was training to be a teacher educator.

I felt overcome by a sudden wave of hopelessness; I needed to talk to someone who could help. I headed to Brenda's office and was glad she was there. Probably noticing something was troubling me when she saw me at her door, she asked, "What's wrong?" I handed over the evaluations. She read the statistics silently, and as she did, her glance shot systematically to what I know now to be the key questions, the ones I now look at first with every new set of evaluations: number 13, "Overall, how would you rate the instructor?" and number 22, "What was your overall rating of this course?"

"They aren't very good," I mumbled.

"No, they aren't," she agreed.

I think I already knew the answer when I asked, "How will they affect my getting a job?"

Brenda responded: "You won't get a job with evaluations like these." Those words still burn in my memory. I was glad she was honest, but her comments were painful to hear. The irony of this situation was that I had been taking on a teaching overload in order to increase my job prospects after graduation, and after great effort it appeared that my evaluations would be the factor that would limit my job prospects. Suddenly I remembered the sacrifices. I thought of my kids and my husband and felt guilty and ashamed that I might fail them. After all this, after giving up so much and working so hard, I was faced with the prospect that it might not have been worth the risk. Reflecting on my experiences that had to do with my growth as a teacher, I recognized that I had to take risks, and that they were essential to my development. But this time I had risked, and the situation backfired.

I stayed in Brenda's office and talked briefly about the last semester and the challenges I had with my course. More importantly, we discussed the coming semester. She insisted, "Your teaching has got to be a priority." She advised me that everything else should take a back seat to my teaching. Then she arranged a time when we could meet to plan for the six-credit course I would begin teaching the following week.

I left Brenda's office feeling like I knew what I had to do—I needed to let go of the last semester in order to develop some self-confidence. But at the same time I had to use it as a learning experience. I needed to systematically change aspects of my teaching that hadn't worked in the past. As I walked home, a dense cloud of depression closed in on me, the kind I knew would take a long time to work through. In fact, it would be another entire semester before I would have another chance to prove myself. Facing a new semester of teaching, a six-credit course I had not taught before, on top of my assistantship as a resident director, I realized the difficulty of what I had to do, and I doubted my ability and courage to meet the challenge of a third chance.

A Leap of Faith

To improve as a teacher—this emerged as a primary goal during my doctoral program. Since I was preparing to help pre- and in-service teachers improve their teaching practices, it seemed essential that I develop exemplary teaching practices. So, in order to improve, I took every opportunity during my doctoral program to teach, and I found the process of learning to teach at the college level to be the highest hurdle of my doctoral experience.

Joann Curtis writes, "Learning to teach is a process of casting and recasting images of what it means to teach" (1995, p. 4). Recalling the ways I interacted with my students in some of my earliest teaching experiences reveals the image I had cast. In nearly each situation, I would stand in front of my students, overhead projector at my side, imparting knowledge. I had studied teaching and learning enough to know this wasn't the position I wanted to take. In that assigned role of all-knowing authority, I felt terribly inadequate, even fraudulent. As a result, I found myself recoiling from the role of a directive teacher, with no alternative to fill the void; my teaching suffered, and so did my self-concept as a teacher.

I began to wonder if I was a lost cause. Would I ever master the art of good teaching? Brenda believed that serving as a teaching mentor was part of her obligation to me as my advisor. She proved her commitment to the cause of helping me out of my slump by setting aside time to help me plan the course I would begin teaching the following week. The question haunted me, "Is it worth it?"

Several days later when we met, Brenda asked, "OK, how are you going to begin the class?" I offered the obvious answer, relying on the images of the teacher I had constructed. I told her I would approach the course from a developmental perspective and begin by discussing emergent literacy and the processes that young children go through as they acquire print and oral language.

"No," she said, "you need to get them writing—first thing." Brenda then went on to tell me how she always begins her undergraduate classes with a writing or reading workshop. This is a block of time set aside for students to read, write, and respond to their peers. She shared a method she commonly uses to get the class started writing: "Tell them to take out a piece of paper and begin writing—they can write about anything. You can give them a prompt by asking them to think of an early memory they have of learning to read or write. Have them write silently for ten minutes, then have each student reread their piece, underlining the passage they would like to spend more time on. Then, have them pair up and alternate reading their pieces aloud to a partner. The listeners respond to the piece. The author shares the part she underlined, then asks what part the listener would underline." I took copious notes, and several times asked Brenda to repeat directions so I captured each step. Admittedly, at the time I didn't really get it. How could I justify wasting precious class time on a writing activity? After all, my students were with me to learn something. Didn't that mean I should provide them with information? However, in my state of panic and desperation, with only one week to go before classes started, I didn't question the rationale. Having already withstood the painful blows of two sets of low teaching evaluations, I figured trying a new approach could do no additional harm.

It was at that moment, after Brenda had offered her simple piece of advice, that I decided I couldn't risk another failed semester. I wanted a tried and true approach, one that was likely to work. I wanted to succeed. Admitting to myself that I was incapable of creating a curriculum, I adopted every approach she shared. For the first several weeks of the semester I was hanging around Brenda like a puppy at mealtime, asking for advice, materials, and tips on how to conduct the course. I often called her several times a day in order to ask countless questions. I was determined, even desperate, not to fail a third time.

I began to recognize that the approaches Brenda shared were compatible with theories about literacy learning in which I believed and, as a methods instructor, touted. These methods follow the reasoning that if educators are to be effective reading and writing teachers, they must themselves be readers and writers (Murray, 1991; Nathan, 1991). Moreover, these approaches centered on the writing and reading workshop, an instructional approach that put experience and activity before theory. At that time the whole idea of engaging in a workshop as a means to teach theoretical perspectives on literacy acquisition and instruction was new to me. In adopting these approaches, I was taking a big risk. While I felt comfortable talking about theories of teaching and learning, demonstrating them was an entirely different matter. After all, I had been away from the classroom for a couple of years; moreover, I left the classroom partially because I felt I still had a lot to learn about developing my teaching. Expecting myself to act as a reading and writing teacher, demonstrating the very practices we would be studying, proved to be very challenging.

I took a leap of faith, and incorporated new approaches into my course, including reading and writing workshops and daily informal assessments, and began my third semester as a college teacher. Initially, I was paralyzed with the fear of failing. During the first few weeks I felt uncertain and awkward. My students didn't balk when I asked them to read and write; in fact, some seemed to enjoy it. I persisted. I successfully hid my nervousness from my students. Once the semester was well underway, after I was comfortable with the structure and rhythm of the course, I began to feel comfortable with new approaches. I could begin to make improvisations on Brenda's suggestions. Eventually I felt confident enough to plan my own course of action.

I felt good about the fact that I was asking students to be active readers and writers, thereby helping them to better understand the processes of writing and reading instruction. From this foundation of active involvement, we could explore the theoretical underpinnings of the practices we used. It seemed like such a sensible and obvious approach that I wondered why I hadn't thought of doing it earlier. This approach was revolutionary in its simplicity. But often the most basic changes in routines and habits involve exceptional self-awareness, self-confidence, and creativity. The new role I was assuming in the classroom challenged me to alter my prior conceptions about what a teacher was supposed to do—to recast those traditional images in favor of a different role for myself as teacher. This new role forced me to hand over the responsibility for learning to my students. On the first days of class, instead of standing in the front by the overhead projector, I sat next to my students, participating in their learning.

I had begun previous classes less in tune with my students' perspectives and more focused on my own. This new role allowed me space to reconsider the content I was covering with my students. As a result, I simplified my expectations for my students and myself. Without realizing it, previously I had put my own questions at the center of the course agenda; I was less aware of my students' needs than I should have been. Child psychologist Margaret Donaldson (1978) provided an insightful critique of Piaget's stage theory of child development when she pointed out that the limitations that are often attributed to children's intellectual development have, in many cases, been due to flaws or limitations in the design of experiments intended to test their thinking. She points out that it is important for the researcher to decenter from her own perspectives in order to view the world from the child's terms. Ultimately, this changed perspective will lead to better, more accurate, research conclusions. To borrow Donaldson's terminology, I wasn't *decentering* in my own teaching. Because I was blindly bound to my own perspective, I wasn't able to accommodate for the specific needs of my students. My understanding of what they knew and needed to learn was restricted by my perspectives as a graduate student and former teacher. I hadn't built procedures into my teaching procedures that forced me to assess their needs and build my courses accordingly. To a degree, it is inevitable that every beginning teacher fails to decenter as much as necessary. Only with time and experience does one learn to acknowledge the questions, needs, and concerns of students, allowing them to become the framework for curriculum.

As I considered my relationship with my students, I was reminded of a summer course I once took in cabinetmaking. As an emergent antique connoisseur a decade ago, I decided to enroll in a weeklong furniture conservation course taught by a well-respected furniture conservator. My project for the course involved restoring a nineteenth-century mahogany shaving stand. It needed new legs and a touch-up job on the finish. My teacher, Merv Martin, was well regarded in the United States and abroad for his skill in furniture conservation. He was regularly hired to work on museum-quality pieces in some of the finest collections of early American furniture. His knowledge of furniture periods and styles was vast, and he was highly talented in all facets of his craft—from basic construction to elaborate carving. However, I came to appreciate him not so much for his impressive credentials as a craftsman and artist, but more for his patience, advice, and skill as a teacher. In spite of my limited understanding and appreciation for Early American furniture, I had no sense of what style of legs my stand required. Worse still, I hadn't a clue as to how I would begin to carve them out of a solid block of mahogany. I could count on one hand the number of times I had sawed, filed, or sanded a piece of wood. I was a complete novice without any prior experience in cabinetmaking. Yet, in spite of my lack of ability, Merv was able to guide me through the most basic steps without causing me to feel like a fool. He helped me maintain enthusiasm while I conquered the challenges of my project.

The experience of my week as a fledgling cabinetmaker helps me reflect on and better understand the experience I had as an emerging college teacher. As a doctoral student interested in cutting-edge theory in my field, I was involved with the theoretical and philosophical issues—those that are currently shaping the development of knowledge in literacy education. Early in my teaching I allowed my perspectives to shape the curriculum; I knew no alternative. I focused on the tensions that seemed to me to be at the center of debates that engaged me the most. My personal agenda took priority; but my students needed a different kind of guidance that focused more on understanding the practical issues in literacy instruction. In retrospect I realize I hadn't provided enough of those basics—the experiences that would enable my students to understand and master the basics of implementing an effective literacy curriculum. For my students, my courses were probably built like castles of sugar. Certainly to me they appeared grand, pristine, elaborate, and based on lofty and respectable theoretical constructs. But from my students' perspectives, I'm sure they dissolved too easily, offering little that could readily be applied to their own classrooms. The castles I tried to help them build were insufficient to withstand the steady rains of classroom reality. Without attention to practical knowledge, I couldn't offer my students a foundation from which to explore some of the key theoretical issues of literacy instruction and program implementation.

As I began to acknowledge the importance of an experience-based curriculum, I realized I was becoming more like my cabinetmaking teacher, Merv. While I was growing as a scholar and theorist through my graduate studies, these weren't the accomplishments that seemed to be helping me most as a teacher. Instead, my developing ability to observe, assess, and respond to my students seemed to be making the biggest difference. As I learned to design and incorporate activities that allowed my students to assume the roles of readers and writers in class, I was increasingly more successful at helping them link their experience to the theories and practices we were reading about. As the end of the semester approached, I was feeling good about my teaching. I had developed positive relationships with students and felt good about the experiences I was providing. After having suffered the slow and excruciating decline of two bad teaching semesters, I was allowing myself to savor the pleasure of success. I asked for written feedback after every other class, and the comments were positive. Some of my students had suggestions, and some even had complaints. I considered both in my attempts to modify my instruction. The occasional critical comment was balanced by positive ones; positive comment gave me confidence enough to confront the weak points in my teaching. Still, I remained tentative, unwilling to label this experience a success based exclusively on my subjective perceptions. I needed good evaluations to lend objectivity to the definition of my success. I needed my teaching to be validated by the authority vested in the form of evaluations.

When the course finally did end, and I had collected the last set of evaluations, I felt lighthearted and optimistic. For the next several weeks, as I had after the close of the previous semester, I nervously approached my mailbox twice a day, awaiting the familiar yellow package. Finally, my optimism was confirmed several weeks later when the results of my course evaluations appeared in my mailbox. This time I tore open the envelope without trepidation. I scanned the page, deliberately looking for the results of those most important questions, numbers thirteen and twenty-two (added proof that meaning and relevance enhance learning—even in statistics). I was nearly giddy after I read the results.

Question thirteen: "Overall, how would you rate the instructor?" Sixteen students labeled me excellent, eight above average, and only one said average.

Question number twenty-two: "What is your overall rating of the course?" Fourteen said it was excellent, nine said above average, and only two said average.

The teaching evaluations showed that it was a good semester for my students and, as a result, for me too. I was elated by the results, and I was proud of myself. I went to find Brenda to share my good news. She scanned the pages, surveying my results. "These are really good," she said.

Those words still ring in my memory, almost loudly enough to drown out her words of concern when my evaluations hadn't been so good. The experience of learning had become memorable for my students and the course content had been put into a context that had immediate relevance. The semester had, after all, ended on a positive note. Finally! I was triumphant—I was gaining competence as a teacher and felt more certain about the career path I had chosen.

Researching Teaching

Individual intellectual movement occurs in relation to others—those present physically as teachers and other students—and through print in books and other artifacts. This movement occurs in the context of individual life history; when it occurs it is educational experience. In this sense we research the role of curriculum in educational experience.

(William Pinar, 1994, p. 91)

Through the ups and downs of my college teaching experiences, Brenda had become my mentor—my audience and my source of guidance. I adopted her syllabus, texts, and routines for use in my own course; together we talked over issues of concern as they arose in my teaching, and we frequently discussed our beliefs and philosophies about teaching and learning. Initially I felt a little guilty at having to rely so completely on someone else's suggestions. I expressed those concerns to Brenda, explaining how my reliance on her advice made me realize I wasn't skilled or knowledgeable enough to create my own program. But she reassured me, "Everything I do is based on what my past teachers taught me. Nothing you're doing is really mine." She explained that

her teaching was directly influenced by her former teachers—
Donald Graves, Tom Newkirk, and Donald Murray, among others. As
a student herself, Brenda was invited to explore a body of
knowledge about teaching handed down to her by her teachers. She
adopted the practices they used, adapted them to better meet her
needs, and incorporated additional strategies and approaches over
time. In the field of teacher education, this kind of knowledge is
sometimes known as "teacher lore." In relation to literacy
instruction, North (1987) describes lore as "the accumulated body of
traditions, practices and beliefs in terms of which Practitioners
understand how writing [and reading] is done, learned, and taught"
(p. 22). Teacher lore has existed for as long as there have been
teachers; but only recently have the research and scholarship
produced by teachers earned a place within the educational
research establishment.

Most students of teaching have probably read countless
research reports that make various claims about how teaching is
performed, learned, and taught. These contributions, generally
offered by university researchers, tend to come in the form of
generalizations or abstract principles. Of course, this knowledge is
important and relevant. But often the words of fellow colleagues,
those people who are in tune with the specifics of our particular
situation, are most helpful. I recall, as a beginning teacher
challenged by the immediate demands of the classroom, that I
always benefited most from the opportunity to discuss my particular
problems and receive immediate and specific feedback. That is not
to say that the theoretical knowledge I encountered in my graduate
course work didn't inform me or help me improve my teaching. But
as a beginning teacher I practiced something akin to knowledge
triage—I sorted out helpful sources of advice and counsel to
determine priority. I had only so much time and energy to devote to
my professional development, and advice from colleagues familiar
with classroom situations and predicaments that mirrored my own
were always given the first priority.

Bill Ayres has written, "The secret of teaching is to be found in
the local detail and the everyday life of teachers; teachers can be
the richest and most useful source of knowledge about teaching;
those who hope to understand teaching must turn at some point to
teachers themselves" (Schubert and Ayres, 1992, p. v). As I approached the completion of my years as a doctoral student, still
developing as a college teacher, I understood that the richest and

most potent source of knowledge about college teaching had come to me as a result of observing the actions and heeding the advice of my mentor. At that point it became important for me to do more than simply borrow the practices suggested by others. Experiencing success with my college-level teaching bolstered me with feelings of confidence and satisfaction, but it also brought about new questions: "What were the elements of my success?" "How could I understand them better in order to continue to grow as a teacher?" A new learning agenda began to emerge for me. I wanted to observe the local detail of everyday life in Brenda's classroom. I wanted to examine how Brenda conducted the instructional practices and approaches that had been so helpful to me.

As I grappled with questions relating to my own beliefs about teaching and learning, I began to plan a research project that would allow me to study Brenda's approaches to literacy methods instruction. I saw the opportunity to observe her course as a rich and intense research experience that would allow me to formally explore the lore that directly influenced my teaching, an experience which would allow me to more systematically explore the course content and teaching techniques of an instructor whose approaches I respected. I designed a qualitative study of literacy methods in-struction at the college level—a case study of one class of students and their professor, Brenda, framed within the larger context of the development of college teachers, myself among them. The study is based on the theoretical premise that in order to help preservice teachers acquire a practical teaching pedagogy and a foundation of knowledge, they need experience-based learning opportunities within the college classroom. As an observer and researcher in the undergraduate literacy methods course that Brenda would teach the following fall semester, I would attempt to answer these questions:

1. What principles of teaching and learning are at work in Brenda's literacy methods classroom?

2. What course structures provide the framework for learning?

3. How are curriculum and content addressed in the methods course?

4. What instructional strategies are in place that promote the development of the classroom

community? How does the classroom community foster learning?

In her essay, "Confessions of a Biographer," Phyllis Rose (1995) discusses the presence of *self* in scholarship. Explaining how the act of writing biography has helped her explore her own life issues, Rose amends Oscar Wilde's aphorism, "Criticism is the only civilized form of autobiography," to her own, "Biography is the only civilized form of autobiography." Rose explores the relationship between her own life and the lives she chronicles, explaining how the act of biography is a variation on autobiography. Research and scholarship are, to varying degrees, subjective. Pursuing a research interest can be a way to impose sense and meaning on existence, and to answer personal questions. The scholar is drawn to questions that are personally engaging, to which she can find a connection. Rose says that in every book, for her "there is some personal involvement, a psychic nurturing, the nature of which is not clear until after the book is finished" (p. 74).

My motives for conducting my research study and the questions I set out to answer have been singularly personal; they were linked with my own development as a teaching professional. In this way, the context for my study was completely autobiographical. Because of the nature of my research questions, for me autobiography was the only civilized form of research. Just as Rose uses the art of biography to make meaning of her own life, I have employed the method of qualitative research analysis to study exemplary teaching practices in an effort to understand the many questions I have concerning the art of teaching. These questions have become the basis of my research and are defined by the unique experiences surrounding my teaching. In an effort to emerge from the fog of life as a novice teacher, I set out to systematically study the teaching practices of the one who was most influential in helping me improve my own teaching.

Rose echoes the theme of subjectivity again when she borrows Flaubert's statement, "Madame Bovary, c'est moi," (Madame Bovary, that is me) and adapts it for herself in order to explain the relationship between herself and her subjects. She writes "Jane Carlyle, c'est moi. George Eliot, c'est moi. Harriet Taylor, c'est moi. And Charles Dickens, c'est moi aussi" (p. 73). As a struggling new college teacher I sought help from my mentor, and at the close of my first successful semester, after the practices suggested actually worked, I emerged from that experience with a new perspective as a teacher. Through the process of researching Brenda's teaching I made discoveries that taught me about myself. Rose's comments spoke to my experience as a researcher. My adaptation on Rose's words were "Brenda Power, *c'est moi.*" Brenda Power would likely modify that statement for herself to something like, "Donald Graves, *c'est moi.* Donald Murray, *c'est moi.* Ruth Hubbard, *c'est moi.*" I believe the more I understand the lineage and traditions that shape my mentor's teaching, the better I understand myself. And the better I understand myself, the more power I have to improve my teaching.

The remainder of this book can best be understood as an apprentice's study of her mentor. It is a comprehensive study of Brenda Power's literacy methods course. But this study also serves as a context for self exploration, a place where I strive to untangle the intricate web of theories and ideas that have played a significant role in influencing my personal teaching pedagogy. As I examine Brenda's teaching practices and beliefs, I do so partly as a means to understand the philosophies, theories, practices, and traditions that undergird my personal system of teaching. My observations and interpretations filter through my experience as a teacher. I have shared some of these in the previous pages. In the next chapter I'll introduce you to the literacy methods course—a place where the future teachers begin the process of reinventing their understandings of teaching and learning. In chapter 3 I'll provide an overview of theoretical perspectives that are relevant to Brenda's teaching approaches. Chapters 4 through 6 address the questions outlined above, and they are organized around the themes of classroom structures, course content, and classroom community.

As teachers, we embody the legacies of others—past teachers we have had or colleagues who have shared their insights and wisdom. These legacies are passed on as we share our own brand of practical wisdom with colleagues. We continue to change and develop professionally as we try on various teaching approaches, strategies, and practices for personal fit. We keep some and discard others. Most of our learning takes place within a community of colleagues. We give and take, adopt and adapt, listen and learn. Our learning is not linear and predictable, rather it is situation specific and results from personal responses to immediate needs and concerns. This book is a more formal account of the processes of professional development that most of us engage in through the days and weeks and years of our professional lives—the process of learning more about our own system of teaching through personal experience and interaction within a larger society of teaching colleagues. There are several plots in this research chronicle—my story, Brenda's, and those of her students. I invite you to borrow from this body of teacher lore and to become a part of the story.

Chapter 2

Reinvented Teaching: A Literacy Methods Course

Welcome to ERL 313-318—Literacy Methods for Elementary Teachers. This six-credit integrated reading/language-arts methods course is offered twice each semester and is a requirement for all elementary education majors and certification students at the University of Maine. It is designed to help them prepare to teach reading and writing in the elementary classroom. You're joining us as Cathy, a nontraditional student, is reading aloud to the class from a paper she wrote. It is her first draft of a personal narrative in which she describes a fond memory of her mother washing her hair over the kitchen sink. She reads, "Then, my mother would nestle my head on a big, thirsty towel. As she massaged my scalp with the shampoo and warm water, my mother would sing a song or we would talk about what was happening in our lives."

You may ask what Cathy's memory of this event has to do with learning about literacy development and methods of instruction? For Cathy and her fellow classmates the two are closely linked. From the very first assignment, a short personal narrative, students are invited to use autobiographical writing in order to explore both personal literacy and the elemental principles of literacy instruction. Cathy chose her topic because it was meaningful to her. For several subsequent class meetings, she brought drafts of her piece and during the first half hour of the class she wrote silently, read drafts to classmates, and made revisions until the piece was finally finished.

From the first day, students use classtime to read and write. This involvement provides the basis for exploring the role of the literacy teacher in the classroom. It helps students reconstruct their understanding of what it means both to be literate and to be a teacher concerned with her students' literacy. In the pages that follow you will see how the students in this class are immersed in classroom experiences that require them to be readers and writers, helping them develop simultaneously theory and practice. As students read and write, they construct personal understandings of what it means to teach and learn.

Figure 2.1. Methods Course Introduction

Literacy Methods for Elementary Teachers

Literacy is something bigger and better than mechanical skill in reading and writing. Literacy is a potent form of consciousness. Once possessed, it makes us productive. It gives us power for good and ill—more often for ill in proportion as we misunderstand it. I hope by understanding it better, we may finally have more of it.

Robert Pattison, on Literacy

This course will introduce you to current literacy instruction methods through your own literacy. You will understand how to teach reading and writing as you explore how you learned to read and write, and what engages you now in texts. We will also visit exemplary classrooms from kindergarten through eighth grade, by way of books, videotapes, and discussions with students and teachers. As we consider best practice in literacy instruction, we will examine the theories that undergird the work of fine teachers. We will pay special attention to the issues of multiage classrooms, assessment, and multicultural instruction.

Source: Excerpt from ERL 313-318 course syllabus, Brenda Power, Instructor, University of Maine, September 1994.

This chapter is a survey of Brenda Power's literacy methods course. It will include an explanation of the daily schedule, routines, and course components; a description of assigned texts; an overview of the curriculum; and a discussion of the theoretical rationale for the course structure. It will also serve as backdrop to the themes of classroom structures, course content, and classroom community that will be described in detail in subsequent chapters.

Course Components–Connecting Theory and Practice

> [S]ince the last century, "teaching" in North American classrooms has
> consisted only of providing tasks and assessing individual development.
> This must be changed: Students cannot be left to learn on their own;
> teachers cannot be content to provide opportunities to learn and then as-
> sess outcomes; recitation must be de-emphasized; responsive, assisting
> interactions must become commonplace in the classroom. Minds must be
> roused to life.
>
> Teaching must be redefined as assisted performance. Teaching con-
> sists in assisting performance. Teaching is occurring when performance is
> achieved with assistance.
>
> (Roland Tharp and Ronald Gallimore, 1988, p. 21)

Since learning is essentially a social process and knowledge is
personally constructed, the literacy methods course should provide
learning experiences for future teachers that mirror these principles.
The literacy methods course should serve as a learning environment
that emphasizes the collaborative and social nature of learning
(Vygotsky, 1978), it should provide authentic opportunities for
learning (Dewey, 1944), allows students opportunities to construct
their conceptions of teaching and learning (Champagne and
Klopfer, 1986; Piaget, 1926), and provides continual opportunities
for students to reflect on their thinking process (Schon, 1991; Pollard
and Tann, 1987). Although social learning and constructivist viewpoints dominate current research literature in the field of literacy
education, preservice teachers come to the methods classroom with
a personal schema of teaching based on past school-related experiences that usually contradict those perspectives. For most methods
students, teachers from their past hold places of prominence in
their conception of the teacher's role in the classroom. And in all
probability, most of those teachers embraced perspectives on
curriculum that mirror the technical or scientific management
theoretical models that have dominated the curriculum field for
most of this century. Any new ideas about teaching and learning
introduced in the methods course have to compete with an existing
schema of teaching and learning, probably shaped by traditional
influences that contradict progressive perspectives on curriculum.
Therefore, preservice teachers need to do more than become
familiar with current theories of literacy development and instruction, they need classroom-based experiences that epitomize them.
And as they experience an alternative curriculum, they need assistance in developing their own critical stance toward a range of

approaches to curriculum. Because Brenda believes that adult learners need social, experience-based learning opportunities as much as children, she incorporates many hands-on learning opportunities in her course.

In this overview of the course components, I will describe how principles of literacy instruction widely promoted for elementary classroom instruction are applied to the literacy methods course. Methods students have active, social, and reflective learning opportunities in order to help them build a personal understanding of what it means to be a literacy teacher. The class is structured so that students have a range of experiences to help them develop their own teaching pedagogy. The excerpt from the course syllabus featured in Figure 2.2 shows how the biweekly, three-hour block is organized. The following description is intended to be a brief overview. The components described will be discussed in greater detail in the chapters that follow.

Figure 2.2. Overview of Class Routine

Our class meetings will be structured to include three elements: a literacy workshop, a presentation, and reading discussion groups. Typical meetings will follow this format:

First hour—Literacy Workshop
Opening of class with student reading (three to five minutes)
Silent writing or reading (ten minutes)
Small response groups for drafts and literature response (twenty-five minutes)
Whole class sharing (twenty minutes)

Break

Second hour
Presentation on a theme by instructors

Break

Third hour—Reading Seminar
Discussion of readings and related activities
Close class with student reading (three to five minutes)

Source: Excerpt from ERL 313-318 course syllabus, Brenda Power, Instructor, Fall 1994

Opening Reading and Closing Reading

Stephen Nachmanovitch (1990) writes that a ritual is an act that transforms an otherwise ordinary activity into something special, sacred, or intense. The methods class began and ended with the ritual of an oral reading. Students signed up to bring in a children's book, short excerpt, or a poem and read it aloud to the class. As well as being an important ritual that provided introduction and closure to the class period, opening and closing reading also demonstrated the importance of finding time during the school day for shared literature. The many benefits of reading aloud to children came up frequently during the semester both in the assigned readings and during class discussions, and the opening and closing readings served as the collective class experience that helped bind the practice of reading aloud to the related theory.

Literacy Workshop

On the second day of class, after a brief discussion about writing leads and ten minutes of silent writing, Brenda reviewed the routine of group conferences she had established during the previous class. She then asked students to form groups of six and left the room to get some materials. I sat observing the mild chaos and confusion that always seems to result when a class of students, strangers to one another, are asked to form groups. A young woman passed me, commenting to her friend with an upturned lip, "This is strange." I chuckled to myself when I heard her comment, and I thought that in a way she was right. At least that was my reaction when Brenda had first explained her approach to me. The idea seemed strange and foreign to my understanding of what a college course should be about. All those years of sitting in class and writing intently whatever information the lecturer transmitted had solidified in my mind a certain image of what a professor should be like. For me, transforming that image took a great deal of courage, effort, and experience. This experience probably was strange and disorienting for a student who has been accustomed to taking a passive role in predominantly lecture-based, teacher-directed college classes. With all its bustle and apparent chaos, the workshop provides a realistic glimpse of the reality of classroom life—one that mirrors the kind of interactions that will take place in the elementary classroom.

As strange as it might have initially seemed, the writing workshop became an accepted and comfortable routine. The literacy workshop occupies the first forty to sixty minutes of class. These workshops provide an experience-based framework for class discussions on writing and reading instructional principles. Literacy workshops incorporate elements of the writing workshop (Graves, 1983), the reading workshop (Atwell, 1987), and procedures for literature discussion groups described by Regie Routman (1991). Each day of class, Brenda gives a brief presentation about a writing technique or element of craft (described in greater detail in the following section). After these "minilessons" (Calkins, 1986), the class participates in a period of silent writing followed by small- and large-group sharing or conferences. During these workshops students work in small- and whole-class response groups where they work on drafts of assigned papers, give and receive feedback on their writing, and read and respond to children's literature. The workshop process helps students explore theories of literacy development and instruction while they develop and strive to understand personal literacy. Students were assigned three two- to three-page papers during the semester, including a personal narrative, a reflective essay about something they learned over the semester, and a free-choice piece. With the exception of reading workshops when students participate in literature circles, this time is used to work on writing assignments. For the first ten class meetings, as an introduction to workshop practices, students participate in writing workshop (Graves, 1983). Midway through the semester the class is introduced to reading workshop (Atwell, 1987), for which each student has the opportunity to assign literature response activities to their group members and facilitate a literature circle (Harste and Short, 1991). During the final weeks of the course, the morning workshop evolves into an integrated reading/writing block. Students make decisions about what to work on and with whom they will work.

Brenda's role during workshop is both to facilitate the experience and to participate with her students. During silent writing or reading, Brenda does as her students, silently reading or writing. During small response groups for drafts or literature responses, she circulates among the students do, responding to the texts that are being shared. During whole class sharing Brenda occasionally comments or offers some information about teaching, but most of the time she prompts responses from class members and hands responsibility for carrying the discussion over to class members. On several occasions Brenda read drafts of the book she was working on at the time and asked for feedback from the class.

Examples of the relationship between workshop practices and associated theories appear in Figure 2.3. In the left-hand column are the tips or strategies Brenda suggests to her students. The right-hand column contains the theories or rationale that justify them. This is a good example of how teacher lore plays a role in the methods course. Brenda shares knowledge she has acquired through her experience as a writer, a writing teacher, and a student of writing.

Figure 2.3. Experience-Based Connections to Theory and Practice

Workshop Experience	**Connected Theory/Practice**
Students are asked to work in groups of three instead of pairs.	Groups of three work better than pairs because there is a greater likelihood that more will be accomplished.
Students are asked to do some freewriting.	Freewriting is uncensored writing. It allows the writer to lower her standards enough to become involved in the writing process.
Students are asked to stop writing, even if they are in the middle of a sentence.	Stopping mid-thought forces the reader to get back into the piece.
Students underlined their favorite part.	Strategy for setting the conference agenda.
A student has difficulty remembering a word.	A tip from journalism: use "TK" in place of the word you can't remember.
A student commented that the first part of the narrative is weak and repetitive.	The beginning of a piece is usually the worst written. Revising the beginning is hardest because there is always more to do.

A student commented that the response from the group helped her see what was good about the piece.	Writers don't need critics, they need support.
A student has difficulty focusing on another student's writing.	If you "space out" in a conference, try a "tell me" question.
Students are encouraged to read their piece during optional whole-class share.	Brenda stressed the importance of taking risks in teaching.
Students are assigned their first two- to three-page paper. They are told the objective is to work on revising the piece.	Emphasis on the process of writing and not just the final product.

Experience-Based Learning in the Workshop Current teaching methods based on the sociallearning and constructivist perspectives include process instruction and workshop approaches (Graves, 1983), whole language instruction (Goodman, 1986a, 1986b), and reader response theory (Harste and Short, 1988; Rosenblatt, 1991), among others. These instructional models are more complicated than skills-based approaches that come in the form of prepackaged textbooks with accompanying workbooks and lay out specific steps the teacher can follow. On the part of the teacher, newer approaches presume a practical understanding of cognitive development (Piaget, 1926), an awareness of the importance of the student's perspective to the learning situation (Donaldson, 1978), and an understanding of the social nature of learning (Vygotsky, 1986). However, preservice teachers come to the methods course with a limited theoretical knowledge base. Just as it had been with me as a beginning teacher, their image of teaching often means standing in front of the class and telling students what they should know. Because of their own past experiences in school, most preservice teachers view learning as a teacher-directed endeavor and see the role of the student as passive and receptive rather than active. This presents a challenge to the methods instructor who is charged with teaching the complexity of present-day literacy instructional methods and helping students learn how to apply them. By having students experience literacy, rather than having them read about it or listen to a lecture about it, Brenda is helping students build a base of literacy-related experience.

In order to be successful, education should be based on personally meaningful and relevant experiences (Dewey, 1944). Incorporating literacy workshop and reading seminar as course components helps infuse the learning experience with personal meaning and relevance. Because they are actively participating in the workshop process, students better understand that learning is an active process.

The importance of literacy teachers being readers and writers themselves is a point that arises repeatedly in Brenda's methods course, and will be addressed in greater detail in subsequent chapters. Brenda wants her students to have an implicit understanding of what it is they hope to bring about in their students. But many teachers don't understand the importance of writing themselves. Ruth Nathan (1991) suggests that only after you yourself have attempted to get an idea on paper does the difficulty inherent in the process of writing become obvious. A similar understanding is required of the reading teacher; unless she is a reader herself and understands the value of the literary transaction, the requests she makes of her students will be artificial exercises (Rosenblatt, 1938). The "zone of proximal development," defined as the distance from a child's actual level of development and the level at which a child can function in an instructional social interaction with a more capable person (Rogoff and Wertsch, 1984), is more easily navigated by the teacher when she intimately knows the zone. The ability to serve as the "more capable other" in social learning situations requires the teacher to have an ability to assess the child's current development as well as an understanding of where and how the child should proceed. A teacher must understand the activity well enough to understand the child's development in relative terms. This empathy will allow her to respond more specifically to her students' needs. Through reading and writing workshops, preservice teachers begin to understand the art of reading and writing and the complexity of current instructional theories.

Response in the Workshop

> I've never called myself a whole language teacher, and process teaching really doesn't explain what I do either. "Whole language classrooms" and "process workshops" operate on many of the principles I believe and practice, but the terms mean such different things to different teachers. I think of what I do as response-based teaching, or responsive teaching. I've seen these terms in the literature, but they aren't known enough to be in the lexicon of most educators. Response to students is at the heart of what I do. My students need immediate, specific and thoughtful response to their needs.
>
> (Brenda Power, 1995, pp. 14-15)

When learning is viewed as a social construction, the role of the more capable adult in the learning situation is significant (Vygotsky, 1986). Honest, direct, and explicit teacher feedback helps a learner understand exactly what can be done to improve subsequent performance or products (Weiner, 1986). This is why response is at the heart of the teaching process, and teachers need to know how to give meaningful and relevant responses to their students (Graves, 1983). Response giving is an acquired skill; it comes with practice and a thorough knowledge of the subject at hand. But like anything else, skilled response giving takes time and practice. That's why it's important for methods students to have time to practice giving response. During writing workshop, students have the opportunity to hear their peers' and teachers' feedback to their pieces, and they can use that feedback to improve their writing. As apprentice teachers, they experience the value of effective feedback. During the course, when reading and writing conference principles are discussed, the importance of skilled response is made more tangible as a result of workshop involvement.

During writing workshop and throughout the semester, the methods students have many opportunities to practice responding to other writers. During reading workshop, they have an opportunity to experience and analyze the phenomenon of constructing personal meaning from a text. They learn a range of possible ways to respond to texts in personally meaningful ways while they enjoy the satisfaction of talking about books with their peers. Following a line of reasoning established by social and constructivist learning theories, due to these reading and writing experiences the methods students' teaching schemas are enriched and broadened. The workshop experiences serve as a foundation for exploring the theoretical components of the course.

Minilessons

Brenda frequently gave a minilesson which had the dual purpose of covering information on the craft of writing or the experience of reading and prompting students to think about literacy learning issues. Through demonstrations the methods students were able to see how minilessons are structured and presented. Figure 2.4 includes some of the minilessons presented during the course. These will be more fully described in subsequent chapters.

Figure 2.4. Minilesson Topics

September 12	Writing Leads
September 14	The importance of routines to the writing process; developing good routines
September 19	Qualities of good writing/strong verbs
September 21	Goal Setting
September 26	Mechanics Issues
September 28	Finding the shape of your writing
October 5	Vocabulary Development
October 12	Titles

Presentations

The second hour of class is reserved for presentations by Brenda, the instructor, or Janice, the assistant instructor. Brenda's goal for this segment of class is to introduce her students to important theories and practices by showing them a wide assortment of real-life models and techniques. In her own words:

> This is the part of the class where I give presentations. I'll give you information, show overheads, but I won't recapitulate information found in the text. I want to expose you to new ideas and information. (Excerpt from Field Notes, September 12, 1994)

Either Brenda or Janice organized brief presentations and demonstrations to extend the students' understanding of literacy development and instruction. During the presentations, questions and discussion are encouraged. Often, the presentation involves hands-on activities. For example, students were assigned to interview elementary students, friends, and family in order to find out about others' literacy perspectives. They then returned to class to analyze and discuss the interview results (see chapter 5 for a discussion on teacher-research methods presented to the students). During other presentations students had the opportunity to see real-life examples of classrooms through videotape clips (See Whitney, Hubbard, and Miller, 1988) and classroom visits, which were later discussed in class. When the class explored emergent literacy and writing development, Brenda showed overheads of children's writing samples and prompted students to explain what they observed about the children's development, as well as where they would go next with instruction.

Learning occurs vicariously, through observation (Shunk, 1991), as well as enactively, through involvement and activity. Presentations provide learning experiences that combine these learning modes. They are mediated learning opportunities in which students are introduced to new concepts and practices with Brenda's assistance. With the aid of the instructors' experience and expertise, presentations bring the students to higher levels of understanding and critical thinking. A list of presentation topics appears in Figure 2.5. Dates for which special events were scheduled, such as field trips to public-school classrooms, do not appear on this list.

Figure 2.5. Presentation Topics

September 12	Discussion of workshop principles; *Time and Choice* video (Whitney and Hubbard, 1988)
September 14	Emergent literacy
September 19	Reading interview and discussion—students work in groups to categorize their responses to the interview questions. They are asked to create a diagram of their findings. The class discusses both their group process in creating the diagram as well as the findings of the survey.

September 21	Classroom organization/student responsibility; *One Classroom: A Child's View* video (Whitney and Hubbard, 1988)
September 26	Written language stages
September 28	Working with students with special needs: new perspectives
October 5	Analysis of student interviews (methods students visited pen pals at an elementary school for the previous class)
October 12	Conference principles; classroom reading/language arts schedules
October 17	Literature circles—organizational principles and planning
October 19	Models of reading instruction
October 26	Nonfiction and cross-cultural literature
November 2	Basal readers
November 7	Role plays
November 14	Reading process; cueing systems
November 16	Reflective teaching process; teacher research
November 21	Social issues in education; integrated learning—showed the Nova program: *Can We Make a Better Doctor?*
December 7	Theoretical orientation to teaching; beliefs continue

Reading Seminar

During the last segment of the class, students worked in their reading seminar groups. Unlike the reading workshop, where children's literature is the focus of discussion, reading seminar is the forum for critical discussion of literacy instructional issues addressed in the assigned texts. Students are assigned to write a one-page, single-spaced, typed response to one of the assigned readings for each class session (see Figure 2.6 for reading response guidelines handed out with the syllabus). Students make enough copies for every person in their group, as well as copies for Brenda and Janice. The first ten minutes of seminar are spent reading group members' papers. The remaining time is spent discussing papers and issues that arise from the readings.

The process of writing personal reactions to the readings provide a way for the students to translate their thoughts into words and to structure their own meaning. In this way, they were writing to learn (Emig, 1977). Like children, adults learn from the exchange of ideas with their peers. The process of discussing reading responses provides an avenue for social learning (Vygotsky, 1978).

Phenomenological perspectives on human development emphasize that behaviors and beliefs are shaped by experience (Bernstein, et al. 1994). In respect to teacher development, individual theories about teaching and learning arise through one's own personal experiences. Students need to have opportunities to investigate how new ideas influence their thinking. This is an important force in changing and transforming beliefs. Responding in personal ways to new theories encountered in the text helps students uncover and analyze their personal teaching biases. Writing personal responses also gives students the opportunity to construct new teaching beliefs that are compatible with current theories of how children learn and should be taught. The daily opportunity to discuss how the readings were personally relevant allows each student to connect new theories to existing ones. Guidelines for reading responses appear in Figure 2.6.

Figure 2.6. Reading Response Guidelines

Reading Responses

You are required to write a one-page, single-spaced, typed response to one of the assigned readings for each class session. These written responses will serve as a starting point for class discussion, and they will also help you think harder about what you are reading in our class. Some of the ways you may choose to respond include:

Quoting or pointing out: Quote a part of the book you feel is an example of good writing—a sentence, a paragraph, a long passage (cite only, don't write it out), or a phrase. What do you like about this writing?

Asking questions: What confuses you? What don't you understand? Why do you think the author did something in a particular way?

Sharing experiences/memories: Does the writing remind you of anything? What comes to mind as you are reading this book? Write about those experiences or memories. What made you think of them?

Reacting: Write about your reactions to the book, giving examples and reasons for your reaction. Do you think the author was hoping you'd have this response?

Connecting: How does the article or book relate to other things we've already read? How do you predict you will use it in the future. What will it mean for your teaching?

This assignment should be considered a series of focused, thoughtful responses to the topics in our readings. You must bring five copies of your work to each class session for small-group work.

Adapted from Rief, 1992

Source: Excerpt from ERL 313-318 Course Syllabus, Brenda Power, Instructor, Fall 1994

Assessment

Assessment and instruction are closely linked. Assessment should be a reciprocal process between teacher and student, helping students understand where they are in relation to community standards, as well as helping the teacher to understand how well she is meeting her instructional goals. In the methods class, instructional plans are based on the assessed needs of students, and Brenda adjusts her teaching in order to meet individual needs.

Sometimes the learner-centered curriculum is misinterpreted to mean that "anything goes" and that there are no collective standards. This interpretation is problematic. It is important to recognize that methods instructors fulfill an obligation to school children when they maintain standards in the methods classroom. These standards help ensure that only competent new teachers will enter the work force. That's one reason why maintaining high standards is a function of evaluation in the methods course. Brenda began to set the standards on the first day of class when she discussed her expectations. Figure 2.7 shows an excerpt from the course syllabus which explains the grading process. In quantifiable and concrete terms, the grading system lets students know what will be expected from them for the extent of the course.

Figure 2.7. ERL 313-318 Grading Criteria

Short Papers (15%)

You will be required to complete three short (two to three-page) papers. You will have opportunities to work on·these papers during our weekly writing workshops.

Reading Responses (30%)

You need to spend time reflecting upon the assigned readings for small group work (see attached sheet for more information).

Regular Attendance and Participation (20%)

Attendance in this class is very important. Your classmates will depend upon you for help in small groups. Two absences are allowed during the semester. After two absences, your grade in this category will automatically be reduced by one full letter grade per absence.

Weekly Literacy Assignments/Projects (30%)

You will complete regular assignments as part of our whole-class internship in Jane Doan's and Penny Chase's multiage classrooms and in response to the readings and class discussions.

New England Reading Association Conference (5%)

We are very fortunate to have the annual NERA conference in Portland this year in late October. Attendance at **one day** of this conference will be required.

Source: Excerpt from ERL 313-318 Course Syllabus, Brenda Power, Instructor, Fall 1994

As well as maintaining standards, assessment practices in the methods course also serve as a mirror for the students. Through a range of self-assessment strategies, including the act of goal setting, midterm self-evaluations, and participation in peer response groups, students are guided to reflect on their accomplishments and helped to measure themselves against the set standards.

Yetta Goodman (1978) coined the term "kidwatching" to emphasize the importance of watching for signs that reveal what children know as well as signs of growth. Brenda assumes a role of "student watcher" in the class, continually assessing needs and adapting the course to meet the changing needs of students. In order to more accurately watch her students, Brenda frequently assumes the role of participant. She continually works with groups of students, responds to their writing, discusses assigned texts, and answers questions. She is involved in the learning process and consequently is able to gauge what her own next steps should be. One method that helped her monitor the pulse rate of the class was through the *dialog journal*. Brenda introduces dialog journals on the first day of class as follows.

> Write five minutes in a journal response to me. If you're an early bird, do it first thing. Some prefer writing them at the end of the class. I'll bring the journals to class early. Put your name at the top. What you're going to read in books is that journals are great. But as a student, I got journaled out. They're good if they're used in the right way. They aren't effective if someone doesn't respond to them. So at some point during the class, I want you to write me a brief note. Today I'd like you to write a brief response to class—what you liked, didn't like, any questions you have. Write a line down the center. You write on the left, and I'll write on the right. It's called a dialog journal. (Excerpt from Field Notes, September 7, 1994)

Brenda read these journals each day after class in order to assess what students were thinking and what concerns they had. Dialog journals help her know what works, what doesn't work, and what students would like to learn more about. In subsequent classes she addresses specific questions and concerns. Ongoing assessment, such as dialog journals, serve a purpose that extends beyond the semester. The feedback Brenda gets in the methods course helps her modify instruction in future courses, and it also contributes to her developing a professional knowledge base which she continually draws from in order to improve her teaching.

Brenda meets with each of her students individually five times throughout the semester in short out-of-class conferences. She explains that the first conference is set up "to learn names, answer questions, get to know you" (excerpt from Field Notes, September 7, 1994). The conferences serve different purposes throughout the semester. During midterm evaluation conferences, students discuss their progress with Brenda. Students bring completed "Midterm Evaluation Conference" forms to the meeting (see chapter 4 for a description of the midterm evaluation process). Final conferences are oral or written, depending upon the student's preference.

Textbooks

Brenda doesn't assign traditional textbooks for her undergraduate students. Instead, she prefers to use texts that are written by practicing teachers and represent a practitioner's point of view. Survey or research-oriented textbooks are often sold back to the bookstore by students at semester's end, but texts that offer personal accounts of classroom teachers and have a practical orientation often remain on students' shelves through their transition into the classroom (Power, personal communication, November 1993).

Brenda's choice of texts represents her ideology of teacher empowerment, believing that teachers' voices should command the respect and authority that has, until recently, been solely reserved for academic scholars and researchers. This ideology guides her to select literacy instructional trade books that are written by teachers. Some of these are as follow.

In the Middle (1987), by Nancie Atwell—*In the Middle* won the 1987 Mina P. Shaughnessy Prize awarded by the Modern Language Association as well as the NCTE's 1990 David H. Russell Award. "The author, an eighth-grade English teacher in Boothbay Harbor, Maine, when she wrote the book, provides a convincing model of what classroom research can accomplish...Atwell details her own process of discovery about what's wrong with how writing and reading are typically taught, then offers extensive discussions of how (and why) to establish the classroom as a workshop for writers and readers." (Heinemann, 1995, p. 53)

Joyful Learning (1991), by Bobbi Fisher—*Joyful Learning* "is written to assist kindergarten and other pre-primary teachers in developing whole language programs to match their own teaching styles and school cultures, to meet the needs of their student and parent populations, and to satisfy the curriculum goals of their school systems." (Heinemann, 1995, 1995, p. 113)

Invitations (1991), by Regie Routman—"This complete text provides in-depth information and support for putting whole language theory into practice, as well as step-by-step demonstration lessons for [a wide range of topics]." (Heinemann, 1995, p. 2)

Full Circle (1994), by Penelle Chase and Jane Doan—The authors team teach a multiage class in a rural Maine elementary school. In their book they "describe their classroom, discuss both the philosophy and practicality of multiage grouping, trace the history of the multiage concept, and illustrate how multiage principles have been adapted to address the needs of learners today." (Heinemann, 1995, p. 124)

Walking Trees (1990), by Ralph Fletcher—*Walking Trees* is the author's story of his year spent in New York City schools as staff developer for the Teachers College Writing Project. This "book offers an authentic portrait of the life in the city's schools... *Walking Trees* recreates a world in which all of us who have ever spent time in a school setting will instantly be able to recognize ourselves." (Heinemann, 1995, p. 131)

Literacy in Process (1991), edited by Ruth Hubbard and Brenda Power—Though her selection of texts emphasizes practical applications of exemplary practices, Brenda recognizes the need for teachers to understand theory. *Literacy in Process*, by Ruth Hubbard and Brenda Power, "is an anthology of thirty-two selections by major theorists and practitioners in the field of Literacy Education. It represents the best current thinking in holistic theory and practice and conveys the broad range of voices from teachers and researchers. Here are essays, research reports, interviews, and extracts from books by writers whose work has done so much to change the process of education and to redirect classroom practices toward child-centered teaching." (Heinemann, 1995, p. 55)

Making Elementary Classroom Connections

As a researcher in the methods classroom, I limited my observations to campus-based class meetings. I did not travel to local area schools for scheduled field trips. Consequently, a thorough description of the field experience component and an adequate exploration of its influence is beyond the scope of this study. But field experiences were an integral part of the methods course and deserve a brief overview. Brenda read a number of drafts of this book and offered comments throughout its preparation. But it wasn't until she read the final draft that she made the following comments to me.

> As I read it, I felt that something was missing. I couldn't quite put my finger on it. Then it occurred to me that you don't include references to any of the field experiences to Jane and Penny's class. That is one of the most

important aspects of the course, and a lot of the discussions in class refer
to those experiences. (personal communication, 4/25/95)

Providing the methods students with an opportunity to observe
literacy learning in an elementary classroom is an essential part of
Brenda's methods course. On the first day of class, Brenda explains
to her students that two field trips to regional area classrooms will
be required. This semester Brenda has arranged for her students to
visit the classroom of Jane Doan and Penelle (Penny) Chase, who
team teach a kindergarten through grade two multiage class.
Brenda's relationship with Jane and Penny extends back several
years to their enrollment in the masters degree program at the
University of Maine; Brenda was one of their professors. Jane and
Penny have collaborated professionally with Brenda a number of
times since they graduated from the program. They have regularly
presented at national and regional conferences and have taught
courses at the University of Maine. Moreover, Jane and Penny are
the authors of one of the books used for the course, *Full Circle*
(1994), which originated as a project in a literacy seminar course
Brenda taught in 1992. Brenda's professional relationships with
classroom teachers, such as Jane and Penny, serve as valuable links
to real classrooms where students can observe exemplary teaching
practices.

The methods students became pen pals with Jane and Penny's
students and corresponded regularly throughout the course. When
the "pals" eventually met during their first field trip, methods
students interviewed and observed their counterparts. Toward the
end of the semester the elementary students came to the University
of Maine for a field trip where they were taken on campus tours by
their college-age pals.

There are frequent references to Jane and Penny's classroom
and pen pals within my data. For example, many of the discussions,
conversations, and activities that took place in the methods course
referred to experiences in their classroom. Serving as a frame of
reference for theoretical and practical information, the elementary
classroom experiences provide an important means of
contextualized learning.

Summary

The approaches taken in the methods course incorporate elements
of constructivist, social-learning, and autobiographical theoretical
perspectives. They emphasize the centrality of the student,

acknowledging that learning results from student initiative. But, at the same time, the instructor plays an instrumental role in guiding students toward experiences that promote learning. The methods course is designed to guide students to reinvent their conception of the role of the teacher. Fischer and Bullock (1984) explain the term *guided reinvention* in a manner that bears particular relevance to our discussion of curriculum in the methods course.

> [Guided reinvention] acknowledges the social learning theorists' insistence that social guidance is ubiquitous. It also acknowledges, however, the Piagetian insight that to understand is to reconstruct. Thus, guided reinvention elaborates the theme that normal cognitive development must be understood as a collaborative process involving the [student] and the environment. (1984, pp. 112–113).

Through active, assisted involvement in reading and writing activities, students in the literacy methods class are guided to reinvent their understanding of teaching and learning. They write and respond to texts as a method of exploring issues relating to the teaching and learning of language. As their instructor, Brenda is determined that her students' newer inventions of the teacher's role in the classroom will be compatible with current theories of teaching and learning similar to those you are about to read about in chapter 3. Brenda hopes the course experience will stay with her students through their first years of teaching, helping to set the course for their professional development. Not satisfied with helping them make theory-to-practice connections, she hopes her students will acquire a passion for teaching. She writes.

> My hope is that my students will leave with some of the same loves I have for structure, response, and surprise. But I also know they will leave with many other loves borne of the unique passions and experiences they bring to the craft of teaching…
>
> English Professor Peter Biedler may have said it best, "We've got to get our students to the point where they stop asking, 'Will this be on the test?' and start asking, 'Will this be like falling in love?'" As my students start learning from each other, start dialogues with me, start engaging with the texts, they begin to fall in love with all kinds of things— themselves as literate beings, as newly sighted kidwatchers, as humane members of a classroom community. For many, it's the first time they've framed the value of a course in terms other than a grade…
>
> When you love something, you invest a lot of energy in it. Passion drives people, and there is no time of more energy and intensity than those first weeks or months when you are falling in love. When I evaluate what I do, the thing I most value is helping students fall in love with

teaching. And watching them fall in love makes me fall in love all over again, every semester, with the joys and challenges of this profession.

(Brenda Power, 1995, pp. 35-37)

Chapter 3

Practical Theories

> The distinction between theory and practice has disappeared...In the contemporary [curriculum] field, theory and practice are often regarded as embedded in each other.
>
> (Pinar, Reynolds, Slattery, and Taubman, 1995, pp. 55–56)

There is nothing as practical as a good theory. But theory in isolation from practical experience is meaningless. The two go hand-in-hand: experience helps confirm, refute, or extend the theories we rely on to guide our actions, and theory provokes our thinking (Pinar, Reynolds, Slattery, and Taubman, 1995, p. 8). Future teachers need learning experiences that will help them develop more sophisticated insights about teaching and learning, and simultaneously they need to be familiar with the theories that explain literacy development and instruction.

The previous chapter featured an overview of the methods course components. Before venturing further into an interpretation of those components, in this chapter I will focus on the theoretical perspectives that undergird the literacy methods course. What follows is an overview of the theories that shape contemporary, progressive instructional approaches; these theories apply to adults as well as children and form the basis of curriculum and instruction in Brenda's methods course. Even the most sophisticated knowledge of theory is of no use unless it is applied in the classroom. This chapter concludes with a discussion of how progressive learning theories are beginning to transform college-level classrooms. These changes in college methods courses provide future teachers with a frame of experience from which they can construct theoretical understandings that will more likely influence the way they practice as beginning teachers. As you survey these theories, keep in mind how they relate to the course components described in the previous chapter. Think about how the structures Brenda builds into the daily class routines support student learning according to theoretical perspectives. Consider how the content and curriculum of the methods course parallel the practical theories discussed.

The Traditionalists and the Traditions of School

For most of the twentieth century until the 1970s, the dominant paradigm in the field of curriculum was a brand of technical, scientific reductionism based on the mechanistic principles of classical physics. These ideas influenced other fields as well. Philosophers, researchers, and scholars in the natural sciences, the social sciences, and the humanities relied on the principles of physics to explain and understand phenomena. The intellectual historian Richard Tarnas (1991) writes:

> For as reductionism was successfully employed to analyze nature, and then human nature as well, man himself was reduced. With science's increasing sophistication, it seemed likely, perhaps even necessary, that the laws of physics were in some sense at the bottom of everything...The Cartesian program of mechanistic analysis thereby began to overcome even the division between *res cogitans* and *res extensa*, thinking subject and material world, as La Mettrie, Pavlov, Watson, Skinner, and others argued that as the universe as a whole could be best comprehended as a machine, so too could man. Human behavior and mental functioning were perhaps only reflex activities based on mechanistic principles of stimulus and response, compounded by genetic factors that were themselves increasingly susceptible to scientific manipulations. Ruled by statistical determinism, man was an appropriate subject of the domain of probability theory.
>
>   (Richard Tarnas, 1991, pp. 331-332).

The paradigm of reductionism manifested itself most evidently in the approaches of the social efficiency educators, who began their reform efforts during the first decades of the twentieth century. According to Kliebard (1985), the social efficiency educators believe that the curriculum exists as a means to prepare every student for the social position he or she will assume in society (I will use the term *traditionalists* to refer to the social efficiency educators and others who share their perspectives). Thus, the curriculum is objective-oriented and takes the form of a series of steps, each of which is specifically designed to meet the stated objective. Pedagogical traditions, practices, and beliefs of the traditionalist model emphasize efficiency, control, and economy. The curriculum is based on simplicity, specificity, and the principles of scientific management. The traditionalists have enjoyed wide popular and

political appeal because their approaches have always been promoted as scientific and, therefore, reliable. According to the traditionalist perspective, the teacher's role is to efficiently and effectively cover the curriculum, and because of the pressure put upon
teachers to be accountable, curriculum has tended to be broken into
small instructional units (Eisner, 1985). Traditionalists believe that
only the essentials should be taught, and the definition of what core
ideas deserve to be considered essential is continually in debate
and usually defined by the dominant social and political forces.

Since the mid-twentieth century, the Tyler Rationale (Tyler,
1949) emerged as a dominant framework for curriculum planning
and development. In fact, most traditionalist teachers at all levels
continue to rely on the principles of the Tyler Rationale to implement curriculum in the classroom. The Tyler Rationale emphasizes
four central principles that stem from the following questions: (a)
What educational purposes should the school seek to attain?
[Objectives], (b) What educational experiences can be provided that
are likely to attain these purposes? [Design], (c) How can these
educational experiences be effectively organized [Scope and
Sequence], and (d) How can we determine whether these purposes
are being attained? [Evaluation] (Tyler, 1949: quoted in Jackson,
1992, p. 25). The terms objectives, design, scope and sequence, and
evaluation have held a time-honored place in the lexicon of most
teachers, and these terms continue to define what many teachers do
and how they do it. The influence of the social efficiency educators
can still be detected in the typical American classroom, where
instruction continues to be teacher-centered and instructional
practices based on the scientific-management model of instruction
still dominate (Goodlad, 1984).

Traditionalist Perspectives in Literacy Teaching

> My thesis is quite simple: the majority of teachers have accepted,
> unquestioningly, a set of beliefs about learning which had its origins in
> what Arthur Koestler once called "the Dark Ages of psychology." [W]hile
> they continue to hold these beliefs, they will continue to organise their
> teaching behaviour in ways which reflect them.
>
> (Brian Cambourne, 1988, p. 17)

The beliefs and practices that originated from "the Dark Ages of
psychology" are based on the assumption that in order to learn to
read and write, a child must simply acquire mastery over the sub-

skills of each process. According to this belief, the only way to help a child master a given set of behaviors is through drill exercises and recitation. Cambourne (1988) poses the rhetorical question, "What is this theory or model of learning which has imprisoned the majority of teachers?" And he answers, "Effective learning is the establishment of 'good' or 'desirable' habits and the prevention of and/or elimination of 'bad' or 'undesirable' habits. Habits are formed through association between stimuli and responses... repetition strengthens the associative bond between stimulus and response" (p. 18).

The habit-formation view of learning, with its emphasis on the acquisition of skills and core academic knowledge, has served as the theoretical basis of basal reading and language arts textbook programs since their origin (Shannon, 1990). While the reconceptualist theories of teaching and learning that stem from a newer paradigm dominate the research and pedagogical literature, the transformation hasn't taken hold in the typical American classroom. Principles of the Tyler Rationale play a significant role in the reading curriculum of the typical American classroom where skills-oriented programs and instructional approaches rely on drill and memorization to achieve learning objectives. Proponents of the traditionalist model believe

> [Reading instruction consists in stressing the] utility of skills, and standardization of practice... the use of standardized tests to determine students' competence, and the scientific development of curricular materials that would lead students from novice to expert levels of competence without allowing gaps in their knowledge of decoding and comprehension skills. If teachers would follow reading experts' directives, science would serve as the arbiter of which skills were necessary to learn to read and which methods were the most productive.
>
> (Patrick Shannon, 1990, p. 12)

Challenges to the Traditionalists

The traditionalists have always had their critics, and throughout the twentieth century those voices have challenged their practices and perspectives. The child-centered developmentalists, who recognize that play and activity are important dimensions of learning, were especially vocal during the early part of the twentieth century. They attempted to create a curriculum that corresponds to the child's nature and takes advantage of natural curiosity as a means to teach formal concepts (Kliebard, 1985). This movement evolved into what would be called the activity curriculum or the experience curriculum, which after years of subjugation to the traditionalists, has most recently enjoyed renewed popularity in the era of reconceptualism (which will be described below).

Dewey (1933) challenged the traditionalist perspective when he criticized schools for their tendency to judge "education from the standpoint of external results, instead of from that of the development of personal attitudes and habits" (p. 65). He believed the underlying premise of this approach to education was wrong and that education should concern itself with the "formation of wide-awake, careful, thorough habits of thinking" (p. 78). He wrote:

> [The] tendencies toward a reflective and truly logical activity are native to the mind, and that they show themselves at an early period, since they are demanded by outer conditions and stimulated by native curiosity. There is an innate disposition to draw inferences, and an inherent desire to experiment and test. The mind at every stage of growth has its own logic. It entertains suggestion, [sights] them by observation of objects and events, reaches conclusions, tries them in action, finds them confirmed or in need of correction or rejection. (Dewey, p. 83)

The educational philosophy articulated by Dewey is closely related to phenomenological/humanistic perspectives of learning psychology. These perspectives view children as willing participants in their own education, and emphasize the importance of meaningful and relevant learning experiences. Children naturally assume responsibility for their own learning. The teacher has the responsibility to help children draw on their emotional as well as intellectual faculties. Newer perspectives on learning that draw from phenomenological, humanistic, progressive, existentialist schools of thought—for which I will subsequently refer to as *reconceptualism*—differ from the behaviorist perspective in the following ways.

> Unlike theories that emphasize the instincts and learning processes that humans and lower animals seem to have in common, the phenomenological approach focuses on mental qualities that set humans apart: self-awareness, creativity, planning, decision making, and responsibility... In short, phenomenological theorists emphasize that each person actively constructs his or her own world. Humans, they say, are not merely passive carriers of traits, crucibles of intrapsychic conflict, or behavioral clay that is molded by learning. Instead, according to the phenomenological approach, the primary human motivator is an innate drive toward growth that prompts people to fulfill their unique and natural

potential. Like the planted seed that naturally becomes a flower, people
are inclined toward goodness, creativity, love, and joy.
                    (Bernstein, Clark-Stewart, Roy, Srull, and Wickens, 1994, p. 504)

Reconceptualist theories of learning emphasize the fact that people
actively shape and construct their own perceptions of reality—that
the student is at the center of the learning phenomenon. Through a
process of individual interpretation of the world, every learner has a
unique perspective about the world which is continually being
shaped by experience. Learning is cyclical and spiral; what is known
and seen influences what is learned, and what is learned influences
what is known and seen. The influence of this new perspective on
learning has dramatically influenced the way literacy teaching and
learning are explored and understood.

Figure 3.1 summarizes several educational philosophies and
related instructional approaches that might help distinguish the
educational perspectives discussed here. According to these definitions, the traditionalist curriculum is based on essentialism and
behaviorism. The reconceptualized curriculum, which will be described below, is based on progressivism and existentialism.
Reconceptualism's philosophical heritage includes other influences that will be described in the next section.

Figure 3.1: Four Philosophies of Education

Essentialism: The physical world is the basis of reality, and people
learn through empirical reasoning. There is a core of academic
subjects that all students should learn. The primary method of
instruction is the lecture...[The objective] is to prepare students to
be intelligent problem solvers in order to compete in the modern
economic world.

Behaviorism: The physical world is the basis of reality, and humans
are shaped by environmental influences. Free will does not exist.
Learning is a physiological response to stimulus, which is
facilitated by positive reinforcement for desired behavior. The
curriculum is determined by school authorities [and enacted
through programmed instruction]. The teacher... is the expert who
understands how to apply techniques of behavioral engineering.
The aim of behaviorist educators is to produce students who will
think and act in ways that are congruent with the school's
objectives.

Progressivism: The physical world is the basis of reality. People learn best through meaningful experience, social interactions, and scientific experimentation. [The curriculum]... includes integrated study of the academic areas around activities that promote reflective thinking and problem solving. Students learn by doing. The teacher acts as guide or director. Teaching is a creative process...based on finding integrated learning activities that have meaning for individual students. [The objective] is to help students become intelligent problem solvers who enjoy learning and can live comfortably in the world while, at the same time, helping to reshape it.

Existentialism: Reality is whatever each student determines it to be. People shape their perspectives in accordance with free will. Each student determines how she learns best. Emotions are an important aspect of learning and decision making. Each student determines the pace and content of learning. The teacher's role is [to create] a free, open, and stimulating classroom environment... [The goal] is to help students accept personal responsibility for their lives and to be happy with their unique individuality.

Source: Sadker, M. (1991). Teachers, schools, and society (2nd ed.). NY: McGraw-Hill (pp. 422–423).

Reconceptualism: A New Paradigm

In education, as in other fields, the tenets of logical positivism and the primacy of science as an objective method have been called into question (Phillips, 1985). As the intellectual historian Richard Tarnas explains, many have begun to criticize the assumption that reducing all reality to the smallest observable or measurable components will necessarily reveal fundamental or universal truths. He writes, "The reductionist program, dominant since Descartes, now appeared to many to be myopically selective, and likely to miss that which was the most significant in the nature of things" (1991, p. 357). Over the past twenty-five years, methods of inquiry and practice in many fields of study—including the natural and social sciences, humanities, and professional studies, such as education—have undergone a period of reconceptualization as researchers, scholars, and practitioners in the various fields have responded to changes in the dominant philosophical paradigms (Schubert, 1989). In the field of education the reconceptualization has been addressed in teacher education, curriculum theory, and historical, philosophical, and social foundations of education (Schubert, 1989). In relation to the field of curriculum theory, the term reconceptualization has been used to describe profound changes in the field's "primary concepts, its research methods, its status, and its function in the larger field of education" (Pinar, Reynolds, Slattery, and Taubman, 1995, p. 12).

With its repudiation of universals and its intention of finding strategies that will preserve pluralism (McGowan, 1991), reconceptualism in education is distinctively postmodern in its philosophical orientation. McGowan (1991) explains how postmodern ideas generally reject the dimension of humanism that emphasizes "the construction of a unified individual identity that assures the self's power to act autonomously" (p. 20). He goes on to explain the tensions between the ideals of modernity and postmodernism.

> The suppression of women and of minority groups within the society and of non-European races wherever they were encountered must be read as the outcome of the West's obsession with identity, singleness, and purity, with its belief that only unified, homogeneous entities (be they selves or states) can act effectively. Postmodernism finds in the modernist drive for autonomy another version of Western reason's obsession with integrity and insists that this obsession has drastic political consequences, in both the oppression of women and minorities and in the establishment of hierarchical orders that must threaten the egalitarian distribution of power (as capacity to engage in and influence the social processes of decision making) espoused by democracy. Only by abandoning this traditional form of reason and by accepting the fact of heterogeneity could a different politics, a different understanding of how societies are constituted and what they could strive to achieve, be reached. (1991, pp. 20-21)

The modernist emphasis on autonomy is viewed as exclusionary and repressive by postmodern thinkers. In the process of establishing a singular, autonomous definition or identity, heterogeneous elements of the entity are overlooked or marginalized. The resulting effect is to "threaten the self's sense of unity," causing dire political and social consequences (McGowan, 1991, p. 20).

Within a postmodern perspective on education, curriculum is understood as the lived experience of the participants of school. In an effort to achieve balance and unity within the school experience, the multiple realities of all the participants are acknowledged. In order to understand curriculum, one should examine it from the perspective of those who experience and live it. Curriculum theory might best be understood as various discourses, each of which center on a particular set of personal, social, or political concerns.

Within this framework curriculum might be read as *racial text, political text, gender text, autobiographical text,* or *theological text,* among others (Pinar, Reynolds, Slattery, and Taubman, 1995). This approach to curriculum takes into account the wide range of perspectives of the participants of school rather than as a set of universal procedures and principles that apply in the same manner to everyone. Moreover, in an effort to move away from broad definitions and generalizations, reconceptualists address "why" problems, unlike the traditionalists who address "how to" or "technical" problems (Pinar, Reynolds, Slattery, and Taubman, 1995).

Research in the Age of Reconceptualism

If "the Dark Ages of psychology" dominated instructional approaches in the past, then educational psychology has undergone a veritable Renaissance. No longer does the behaviorist-oriented perspective dominate the journals of the professional educational associations. Since the cognitive revolution in psychology, phenomenological research and scholarship have begun to influence education, examples of which are studies with social learning and constructivist theoretical perspectives. Moreover, learning is no longer considered solely a psychological phenomenon. Research in education, once the sovereign domain of educational psychologists, has in recent years become well-charted territory for anthropologists and sociologists.

In an intellectual era that rejects the notion of totality, adherence to metanarratives, and the belief in universal ideals, the reconceptualists have drawn from the ideas of poststructuralism, deconstruction, phenomenology, existentialism, psychoanalysis, feminism, neopragmatism, semantic holism, and contemporary Marxism, among others (Pinar, Reynolds, Slattery, and Taubman, 1995). These intellectual traditions tend to emphasize the importance of variation, diversity, plurality, and multiple perspectives. Truth, meaning, and knowledge are viewed as being culturally constructed and can only be understood within the context from which they originated.[1]

---

[1] A more thorough explanation of the philosophies that have influenced reconceptualism is beyond the scope of this text. For a thorough discussion on the philosophical influences on reconceptualism, see Pinar, Reynolds, Slattery and Taubman (1995). Tarnas (1991) offers a provocative and coherent survey of the western philosophical tradition, providing a good backdrop for an exploration of modern curriculum theory.

Instructional Approaches of Reconceptualism

Increasingly, reconceptualism is working its way into the classroom. The instructional approaches described in this text align with the reconceptualist theories described above; they recognize that knowledge is a personal construction and occurs within the social milieu. The students' individual perceptions and experiences are understood as channels of learning. While every person is born with an original nature, it is continually being shaped and changed through interaction with the environment. The role of the teacher is to continually assess the patterns of culture and social interaction in the classroom, to strive to understand how students act within the classroom, and to understand how, through time and experience, each learner constructs and modifies ideas, concepts, and self image.

In a reconceptualized role, the teacher strives to understand and respond to the complicated, multifaceted, multidimensional workings of the classroom. According to this paradigm, which recognizes that the learning process for each individual child is self-directed and will take its own course, the notion of being in control of students' learning—a distinctively traditionalist pedagogical notion— is abandoned for a more relevant, distinctively postmodern conceptualization of the teacher's role, which is to help students participate in the running of the unique and independent course of their learning. Reconceptualist educators strive to find the right balance between structure and freedom, a balance that helps create a learning context where students can grow and develop to their potential. Holistic, child-centered approaches to literacy instruction now advocated by the major professional organizations (e.g., National Council of Teachers of English, Association of Supervision and Curriculum Development, and the International Reading Association) can be located in the realm of reconceptualism.

The Social and Autobiographical Nature of Learning and the Method of *Currere*

In [the manner of reconceptualism] the curriculum can be seen to evolve, since with its focus on the learner, it acknowledges the student's search for meaning as an interactive and reflective process undertaken in a social milieu. It is further argued that autobiography as writing the self, as a method of reflecting on and grounding the self in lived experience, comes

closest to hand as the prime candidate to accomplish such a task of reconceptualization.

(Robert J. Graham, 1992, p. 27)

Because knowledge is understood as being personally and socially constructed, learning is necessarily an autobiographical phenomenon. The teacher has the responsibility of helping children bridge the abstract—new concepts and ideas—to the personal realm of lived experience.

Personal narrative can be a tool for raising self-awareness. In fact, it is a recognized means of psychological therapy. The psychologist/therapist George Kelly (1955) emphasized that one's personal view of reality is shaped by her expectations, and those expectations form personal constructions of reality. People behave and act according to their personal constructs. For Kelly, a person's development consists of a search for constructs that will help explain and predict personal behavior—the behavior of others. Our searches are self-directed, whether we fully understand them or not. The act of autobiography—the intentional consideration of lived experience—brings the self's hidden intentions to a higher level of awareness. It helps heighten one's understanding of the constructs that are used to make sense of the world. In my case, reflecting on uneasy beginning teaching experiences set me on a search to find answers to my own teaching dilemmas. Autobiographical writing helped me to understand the educational experiences more critically so that I was then able to determine more thoughtful courses of action in my teaching and research.

The method of *currere*, or the autobiographical approach to the study of curriculum, offers a possibility for helping students explore past educational experience and to reconstitute them in more appropriate, less contradictory ways. According to Pinar (as described in Pinar, Reynolds, Slattery and Taubman, 1995), the process of *currere* is fourfold and includes these stages: (a) *Regressive*, in which the student recalls and recounts past educational experience, making free associations in order to generate "data." This process helps the student "enlarge—and thereby transform—one's memory." (b) *Progressive*, in which the student "looks toward what is not yet the case, what is not present." This enables her to imagine the possibility of the future. (c) *Analytical*, in which the student examines the past and the future simultaneously. This stage is "like phenomenological bracketing" and allows one distance from the past and the future in order to be free of the present. (d) *Synthetical*, in

which the student "re-enters the lived present," putting all elements of the experience together with the effect of heightened
awareness (p. 520). The authors describe *currere* in the following
way.

> [*Currere*] seeks to understand the contribution academic studies makes to
> one's understanding of his or her life. The student of educational experi-
> ence takes as hypothesis that at any given moment he or she is in a
> "biographic situation" (Pinar and Grumet, 1976, p. 51), a structure of
> meaning that follows from past situations, but which contains, perhaps
> unarticulated, contradictions of past and present as well as images of
> possible futures (p. 520) ... *Currere* focuses on the educational experience
> of the individual, as reported by the individual. Rather than working to
> quantify behaviors, to describe their surface interaction or to establish
> causality, *currere* seeks to describe what the individual subject him or
> herself makes of these behaviors... Husserlian phenomenology
> undergirds the method of *currere*, particularly the emphasis upon the
> reciprocity between subjectivity and objectivity in the constitution of
> experience and meanings. *Currere* shares phenomenology's interest in
> describing immediate, preconceptual experience, and then makes use of
> the phenomenological process of "distancing" and "bracketing" required
> to do so. (p. 414)

There were many occasions for autobiographical inquiry in the
methods course. One particularly relevant assignment asked students to write personal narratives in which they recollected a past
learning experience. This process is discussed in chapter 5.

Constructivist Learning Theory

> Thus man does not receive all his knowledge from experience, but his
> knowledge in a sense already introduces itself into his experience in the
> process of cognition.
>
>   (Richard Tarnas, 1991, p. 345)

It sounds like a simple proposition: we construct our own understandings
of the world in which we live. We search for tools to help us understand
our experiences. To do so is human nature... Each of us makes sense of
our world by synthesizing new experiences into what we have previously
come to understand. Often, we encounter an object, an idea, a relationship, or a phenomenon that doesn't quite make sense to us. When confronted with such initially discrepant data or perceptions, we either interpret what we see to conform to our present set of rules for explaining and
ordering our world, or we generate a new set of rules that better accounts

for what we perceive to be occurring. Either way, our perceptions and rules are constantly engaged in a grand dance that shapes our understandings.

(Jacqueline G. Brooks and Martin G. Brooks, 1993, p. 4)

Every learner attempts to make sense of the world by integrating new information into an already existing mental schemata, modifying or reconstructing present understandings. Because she is involved in a process of constructing knowledge, the learner is an active participant in her own learning process. This active, logical, and self-initiated learning process is driven by a need and desire to understand new information and ideas. The constructivist theory of learning is largely based on the ideas of Jean Piaget (1952). According to Piaget, children progress through stages of development by a process he calls equilibration. As they encounter new information, children experience cognitive disequilibrium. They must either assimilate new information by integrating it into their present understandings, or reorganize their present understandings in order to accommodate new information. Once a new concept is understood, the child reenters a stage of equilibrium until faced with another new concept. Thus, from a Piagetian perspective, knowledge is personally constructed. Contemporary theoretical perspectives on literacy development reflect an active role for the child in the construction of knowledge about the nature and function of oral and print language (e.g., Clay, 1991; Goodman, 1986a and 1986b, Rosenblatt, 1978; Smith, 1985; Temple, Nathan, Burris, and Temple, 1988). The constructivist perspective has influenced how teachers instruct and assess children in the classroom, focusing on the individual learning processes as opposed to arbitrary goals and outcomes. For example, Susan Sowers (1991) studied young children's "invented spelling" and determined that children draw from their existing knowledge base about how print works as they engage in writing. She found that children's spelling errors, or "invented spellings," are systematic and logical. "Invented spellings" provide a window into the thinking process of young writers, reflecting their judgment and tacit knowledge about how print works. Because children naturally "practice and drill themselves at a pace and a level of difficulty appropriate to their skills," teachers can't provide more appropriate instruction than a child can (p. 175). Sowers stressed that it is more effective and efficient for teachers to provide opportunities for students to write, instead of prescribing instruction based on diagnosis of writing difficulties. The teacher should focus her efforts on assessing the developmental level of each student and provide strategies to help the student move to the next level of development.

The idea that meaning is personally constructed is a theme that also dominates contemporary reading theories. For example, reader response theory, or the transactional model of reading comprehension, emphasizes the central role the reader has in constructing a personal composition of meaning from text. According to this model, a reading *transaction* occurs between the reader and the text (Rosenblatt, 1978). This transaction is the result of the reader bringing meaning to the text at the same time she derives meaning from the text. A reader's interpretation of the meaning of a text, what Rosenblatt calls *the poem*, results from the unique and personal interaction between the reader and the text. Based on this definition, comprehension is unique and individual—no two people who read the same text compose the same poem.

Constructivist theories of learning aren't confined to the education of young children. Champagne and Klopfer (1986) report that a large body of research conducted on students, young and old, has convinced psychologists and science educators that learners have already constructed individual theories, called *naive theories*, about scientific phenomena before they receive any formal science instruction. Naive theories are the unproven, often mistaken conclusions we draw about phenomena in the world around us. I will illustrate a common naive theory by asking a simple question: "What causes winter?" Think for a moment before you read on. If you're like many people, you might have answered that winter occurs when the earth is at its furthest point from the sun as it travels in an elliptical pattern. And, like most people, you are mistaken. Yes, in spite of what your third-grade teacher might have told you, the earth is never far enough from the sun during any course of its travel to warrant such extreme changes in temperature. Instead, winter occurs when the area of the earth we inhabit tilts away from the sun due to the earth's axis. The southern hemisphere experiences summer while the northern hemisphere experiences winter. We cling to our naive theories with such strong tenacity that even after we have successfully completed formal science instruction that repeatedly contradicts our naive theories, we persist in believing them.

Constructivist theory is influencing science instructional methods at all levels. For example, my husband recently took a college-level physics course at the University of Maine in which he learned concepts through experience-based explorations of scientific phenomena (University of Maine, 1995). A semester-long assignment required him to go outdoors to take sun plots at certain times during the day. He was doing them with such regularity and frequency that even our children got involved in his learning. Each time we left our apartment our son would ask: "Daddy, aren't you gonna measure the sun?" This experience-based course was vastly different from the science courses I had taken that embraced a traditional textbook-centered approach. Through direct experience combined with assisted instruction, my husband was finally able to acquire an understanding of the manner in which the earth moves around the sun. Students need repeated experiences such as these in which they encounter and ponder the phenomenon under question.

Formal concepts should be taught in conjunction with experiences that reinforce those concepts. This belief permeates the perspectives of educational researchers and practitioners. In one study, Roth and Roychoudhury (1993) examined the development of scientific thinking skills of twelfth graders in an open-inquiry laboratory setting. They found that students develop higher-order thinking skills through nontraditional laboratory experiences that allow for experiments of personal relevance in authentic contexts compared to traditional methods of instruction in which integrated thinking skills are taught in isolation. As you read about the approaches to methods instruction throughout the book, you will notice how formal concepts are introduced first within a context of immediate experience. Students engage in reading and writing activities as they learn about the theories that support them. In this course, theory is embedded in practice.

The constructivist perspective emphasizes the teacher's responsibility to identify the student's actual developmental level in order to structure a learning situation that will build from that place. That is, in order for the teacher to be able to help a student construct knowledge, she must have an idea of where the building process must begin. Essentially, the teacher acts as a guide in the construction process, facilitating growth through appropriate instruction. Champagne and Klopfer (1986) stress the importance of understanding the student's "naive theory" that governs the phenomenon under investigation, and then plan a course of instruction that takes the naive theory into consideration. Assessment is a critical first stage in the instructional cycle of a new concept. Without prior knowledge of the nature of a student's understanding, instruction is bound to be misguided.

Social-Learning Theories

> [T]he cognitive and social development of the child proceeds as an unfolding of potential through the reciprocal influences of child and social environment. Through guided reinvention, higher mental functions that are part of the social and cultural heritage of the child will move from the social plane to the psychological plane, from the intermental to the intramental, from the socially regulated to the self-regulated. The child, through the regulating actions and speech of others, is brought to engage in independent action and speech. In the resulting interaction, the child performs, through assistance and cooperative activity, at developmental levels quite beyond the individual level of achievement.
>
> (Roland Tharp and Ronald Gallimore, 1988, pp. 29-30)

Throughout life, the interactions a learner has with people in the context of various social worlds stimulates thought and behavior. Social interactions have an essential role in stimulating intellectual development. From historical-cultural and social-learning perspectives, learning is essentially a social process, and interactions with others are at the center of intellectual development (Dyson, 1988; Heath, 1983; Vygotsky, 1986). From their perspectives, literacy development occurs when one interacts with more experienced members of the culture in a social setting, and development is dependent upon and shaped by social interactions. Consequently, it is important for teachers to understand how learners use their social worlds to develop literacy understandings and to structure productive social worlds in the classroom.

Brian Cambourne (1988) elaborates on how novice members of a culture seem to naturally learn dauntingly complicated new things, such as language. He writes:

> [F]ortunately, over the millennia, a pedagogy has been developed which maximizes the probability that the task will be successfully completed by the overwhelming majority of the community. This pedagogy is one which perfectly matches the contours of the contexts in which the learning takes place, i.e. it fits in with the social, physical and emotional parameters of what could be called the "family unit." Although the family unit differs from culture to culture and has differed from age to age, there are certain core features which seem to be constant across time and cultures. (p. 32)

Cambourne identifies these "core features" and describes their interrelationship. He explains how the core learning features relate to literacy learning, whereby a child is immersed in a culture of written and oral language users. The learner continually experiences demonstrations of the process of language use by others in her social worlds. There is an expectation from those around her that she, too, will eventually use language, both written and oral, in conventional ways. She is encouraged to continually use language in functional ways for authentic purposes, first orally, then in writing; first by primitive approximation and gradually, over time, in conventional ways. Initially, her gross approximations are accepted and intended meaning is the basis of response. Over time she assumes more responsibility for achieving meaning and gains proficiency in all facets of language use. As skill and competence develop, the gap between intention and approximation begins to close.

Reconceptualism acknowledges the interrelationship between the learner and the social context. These interactions are nowhere more obvious than in the play of students of all ages. Doll (1993) writes "play deals not with the present and foundational but with the absent and the possible. Its very nature invites dialogue, interpretation, interaction. Its free-flowing form encourages participation. All of these activities are essential to meaning-making" (p. 286). Therefore, play is defended as a sound and productive element of the curriculum. Instead of discouraging play, teachers strive to assess and interpret occasions for learning within the context of children's play.

Vygotsky and Reconceptualism

The Soviet psychologist Lev Vygotsky (1978) differentiated between a child's actual developmental level and potential developmental level. The actual developmental level is defined as "a child's mental functions that have been established as a result of certain already completed developmental cycles," while the potential developmental level is that which a child can do with the assistance of others (Vygotsky, 1978, p. 85). Vygotsky termed the distance between a child's actual and potential development as "the zone of proximal development" (Vygotsky, 1986). The zone of proximal development has also been described as the distance from a child's actual level of development and the level at which a child can function in an instructional social interaction (Rogoff and Wertsch,

1984). Children can perform at different places within the zone depending upon the level of adult support. Through the process of social interaction, a child's (or learner's) naive process of reasoning is reconciled with the more experienced and logical perspective of the adult (or teacher), and through the process of interacting with adults, the weaknesses of a child's spontaneous, impulsive reasoning strategies are strengthened with the aid of an adult's more systematic logic (Vygotsky, 1986). Over time, children are socialized through human interaction to be able to use effective and conventional ways of communicating. Vygotsky's ideas offer a powerful theory of learning and acquisition (Glick, 1995).

The metaphor of the zone of proximal development can be applied to several instructional frameworks that emphasize varying levels of expert assistance in the learning situation. Within these frameworks the learner takes on increasing levels of responsibility in the learning situation. She can work independently at a level close to her present developmental level or at levels well above her actual developmental level with the assistance of a more knowledgeable guide. In any given learning situation, the teacher gradually gives over responsibility for learning to the student. Learning situations that are initially highly supported by the teacher give way to opportunities in which the learner can increasingly manage the task with independence.

The ideas of Vygotsky are an extension of Soviet ideology and the ideals of modernity. That is, they emphasize the progress of the state over the well-being of the individual, economic development and industrial progress over human and environmental ecology, and the notion that people can be taught to perform jobs that fulfill specific needs in society. But since the early 1970s, when his work was finally translated and became accessible to Western scholars, it has become clear that Vygotsky's work is also relevant to the concerns of postmodern educators for a number of reasons. His frameworks allowed for an understanding of cognition and speech as cultural and social phenomena rather than processes that occur in autonomous individuals. As Panofsky explains, in behavioral and cognitive psychological studies the unit of analysis had traditionally been the individual; but with the introduction of Vygotsky's ideas, activity became the central unit of analysis. This new orientation demonstrated a break from the individualism and mentalism of cognitive psychology and opened a more comprehensive model of learning within which the discourses of race, gender, power, conflict, and class could be incorporated (Panofsky, 1996). Aligning with the concerns of postmodernism, scholars who apply Vygotskiian perspectives to contemporary educational issues realize the need to help students develop strategies to resist pervasive social pressure to assimilate (Rogoff, 1996). Vygotskiian ideas have the potential to be as powerful in advancing a critical theory of culture as they have served as a powerful developmental theory of acquisition (Glick, 1995).

Scholars of cultural-historical perspectives and activity theory maintain that Vygotskiian ideas have the potential to address the problems we face in the postmodern era. First, with Vygotsky we have a powerful theory of acquisition that might be used to develop other useful theories. For example, by modifying Vygotsky's ideas, we might develop an equally powerful theory of resistance (Glick, 1995), one that would enable students to retain self determination over the processes of enculturation and assimilation, thus promoting the postmodern ideals of plurality, diversity, and individuality. Second, the field of education to this point has failed to develop a comprehensive theory that accounts for the failure of learning to occur (Panofsky, 1996). Vygotskiian ideas, which offer a comprehensive theory of acquisition, might be used as a starting place to develop such a theory.

Activity theory and literacy instructional approaches. Contemporary literacy instructional approaches recognize that literacy acquisition is largely a social process that centers around the activities of reading and writing. Activity theory is the basis for several effective instructional approaches currently used in increasing numbers of classrooms. I will briefly describe several of those approaches here. More elaborate examples will be offered throughout the book.

Reading Recovery is an instructional program developed by New Zealand educator Marie Clay (1987). It is a theoretically based program in which the lowest achieving first-grade readers are given daily, one-on-one, thirty-minute lessons with a trained teacher for twelve to twenty sessions (Ohio State University, 1996). Since Reading Recovery was introduced to the United States in 1985, approximately 326,000 children have been served; 83 percent of whom have become independent readers (Ohio State University, 1996). Elements of shared, guided, and independent reading occur in the Reading Recovery lesson format, which includes the following components.

Figure 3.2. Reading Recovery Lesson Format

Lesson Format

Each day, the child moves through a lesson sequence that includes:

- reading several familiar storybooks
- reading independently a book that was introduced and read once the day before while the teacher observes and records the student's behavior
- writing a message or brief story and working with a cut-up sentence
- reading a new, slightly more challenging book that will be read independently the next day

Source: New York University Reading Recovery Project. (1995). Program Description. (p. 2). School of Education, New York University, Author.

The same framework of activity, including shared, guided, and independent components, can be applied to writing instruction (Routman, 1991). Children need to have writing demonstrated to them (writing to children), they need to have mediated opportunities to write (writing with children), and they need independent writing opportunities (writing by children). The writing process (Graves, 1983) incorporates these components through lessons and demonstrations of writing, writing in a social context, and whole-group, small group, and one-on-one writing conferences. The writing process will be referred to repeatedly throughout this book.

Practical applications of social learning theory aren't limited to young children. In fact, social interactions in the methods course can serve as potentially powerful learning experiences for future teachers. For example, Andrews (1990) traced the effects of the language arts methods course into her students' student teaching and first-year teaching experiences. She found that participation in student learning teams helped promote a general willingness to try new instructional strategies. Power (1995) describes how two students' involvement in large and small writing response groups influenced their developing images of themselves as teachers and writers. The students reacted and responded to comments and suggestions from their peers, modifying their writing and thinking as a result. Chapter 6 offers a discussion of the power of the social worlds of the methods classroom in shaping learning for students. Within social learning models of instruction, the teacher is perceived as one who is responsible for staging an environment that facilitates growth, allowing the learner to reach ever-higher levels of understanding. While the model recognizes that in the end it is the learner who constructs personal understandings, there is also a recognition that the social environment serves as the reality base from which personal understandings arise.

The New Literacy

The focus of literacy instruction in school has undergone a dramatic shift since the 1970s. The traditionalist approach to literacy instruction—a teacher-directed process aimed at helping children master core academic knowledge and print language skills, such as decoding and encoding—has been replaced by holistic, child-centered instructional approaches during the era of reconceptualism. Willinsky (1990) uses the term *The New Literacy* to identify progressive approaches in literacy instruction such as whole language, the National Writing Project, writing across the curriculum, writing process, and reader response theory. Within these frameworks the learner is viewed as an active participant in the construction of personal literacy. By definition, these approaches are autobiographical because they encourage the student to work from a personal realm of experience in order to develop skill, proficiency, meaning, and understanding.

Elementary literacy instructional models that could be located in the territory of The New Literacy and which embrace a social-learning perspective include shared, guided, and independent reading (Holdaway, 1991; Mooney, 1990; New Zealand's Department of Education, 1985). These opportunities provide the student with reading experiences at varying levels within her individual zone of proximal development (Vygotsky, 1978). In shared reading, the adult carries most of the load, allowing children to participate in reading challenging texts with strong support. In guided reading situations, the adult offers less assistance, but still provides necessary support to help the reader navigate through moderately challenging texts. In independent reading situations, the child carries total responsibility for reading the text. Children need to have opportunities to be read to, read with, and to read by themselves in order to develop proficiency as readers (Mooney, 1990). Providing a range of opportunities such as these ensures that a child will have reading experiences that will challenge her at varying levels of difficulty, thereby facilitating growth. The manner in which preservice teachers are introduced to The New Literacy will be described throughout the next three chapters.

Reconceptualism and Teacher Research

Reflective practice is a term used to describe instructional methods that are based on a teacher's personal assessment and subsequent responses to individual circumstances in the classroom. When teachers adopt a reflective stance, their instruction is more responsive to the individual needs of students. Dewey (1933) elaborates on the value of reflection in teaching. He writes:

> Education that takes as its standard the improvement of the intellectual attitude and method of students demands more serious preparatory training, for it exacts sympathetic and intelligent insight into the workings of individual minds and a very wide and flexible command of subject matter—so as to be able to select and apply just what is needed when it is needed. (p. 65)

The reflective stance calls on teachers to integrate their knowledge of theory, individual student development, the classroom context and community, and perceived goals. Schon (1983) describes a model of self-evaluation and professional development in which the reflective practitioner "reflects-in-action," thinking about what she is doing while engaged in the act. She draws from her knowledge base, applying "theories-in-action," to the particular circumstances of the classroom. She then reflects on the actions taken, considering at once the process of action taken and possibilities for future actions.

A thinking process that causes a teacher to assess and address the unique and individual needs of each student should be an integral part of the teaching process. Dewey (1933) explored the essence of reflective thinking when he compared "routine action" with "reflective action" in the teaching process. According to Dewey (1933), a teacher's routine actions are based on habits, traditions, institutional authority, and expectations. Reflective action, on the other hand, is based on a more flexible and responsive approach to teaching. It can be characterized as a process of continual self- and student-appraisal resulting in a specific and responsive course of action. Reflective teachers respond to specific conditions of the classroom. Reflective teaching emphasizes the connection between the assessment of students and the instruction provided to them.

This approach is based on a spiraling cycle of assessment, response, and action. Pollard and Tann (1987) explain how the reflective teaching cycle moves through a number of phases, including planning, making provisions for instruction, acting, collecting, analyzing and evaluating data, reflecting on the preceding teaching process, and beginning the cycle again.

Dewey (1933) described a related approach to reflective teaching that follows a similar course: the teacher considers a problem of teaching/learning; she considers a sequence of possible solutions that initiate and guide classroom actions and observations; and then determines the success of the approach either by overt or imaginative action.

Inquiry-based teaching resolves the practice/theory dichotomy because it presumes that teachers engage in a cyclical process whereby they ground practice in theory and derive theory from practice. As Short, Willis, and Schubert (1985) explain, teachers develop "the responsibility to ask fundamental curriculum questions about his/her own growth and its consequences for the growth of others that reconceived the theory into practice problem as practice and theory embedded in one another" (p. 66).

Reconceptualism and Teacher Education

In order to help future teachers avoid being imprisoned by Dark Age learning theories, methods instructors need to help their students challenge long-held assumptions about the nature of teaching and learning. Methods instructors need to assist future teachers in reinventing their beliefs about teaching and learning, helping them construct new pedagogical frameworks that are compatible with contemporary learning and teaching theories. In order to help pre-service teachers begin their professional careers as reflective practitioners who are responsive to the varied needs of their students, the methods course should incorporate many opportunities to allow them to practice the art of reflective thinking. Also, teacher-education programs should incorporate opportunities for problem solving, decision making, and complex thinking in order to give students a better idea of what their role will be in the classroom. An inquiry-based, experience-based model of teacher education is compatible with models of literacy instruction where teachers are expected to integrate knowledge about general and individual student development with theories about how children learn. This integrated knowledge becomes the basis of student assessment and instructional decision making.

There are many signs that college-level teachers are attempting to reconcile their own classroom practices with new paradigm theories. For example, Brazee and Kristo (1986) recognized the importance of experience-based learning and implemented a whole-language methods course. This allowed their students to experience whole-language learning as they explored the accompanying theory. Bean (1989) used dialog journals with preservice, content-area teachers in order to help them integrate theory and action. Through a workshop approach, Tomkiewicz (1991) structured an integrated science/reading/language-arts methods course around apprenticeship learning experiences, including classroom observations, supervised teaching opportunities, and classroom-based interactions with students. The course incorporated writing to learn activities that helped students to confront their self-concepts in each discipline. Reflective writing activities in the course helped students acquire teacher perspectives.

Active learning experiences help future teachers develop the skills they will eventually use in future classrooms. Anderson (1989) reviewed three instructional models that incorporate the learning principles of modeling, coaching, scaffolding, articulation, and reflection—Reciprocal Teaching, Reading Recovery, and Kamehameha Early Education Program (KEEP). He explains that through videotape technology, students are able to reflect on teaching, share ideas, and gain insight about teaching. The methods professor's theoretical contributions have more meaning in contextualized situations. He suggests that these approaches might be incorporated into methods courses in order to help close the gap between the talk of good teaching that is a feature of most preservice teacher-education courses and the actual skills and problem-solving expertise that characterize good teaching.

Summary

Researchers, theorists, and practitioners in the field of literacy education routinely use the terms *whole language*, *constructivism*, *process instruction*, and *social learning theory*, among others, to describe a reconceptualized literacy curriculum that is vastly different from the traditionalist model that has dominated education at all levels since the institution of public school originated. While a survey of the journals and position statements of professional organizations may indicate that the reconceptualists have won the paradigm wars (Gage, 1989), the reality in the trenches of the typical American school still sees many teachers holding fast to a traditionalist approach to curriculum and teaching. A familiarity with reconceptualist theories and instructional approaches might help beginning teachers better meet the individual needs of learners and better understand how the social worlds of the classroom influence learning. With this awareness, it will be more likely that the pedagogical schemas that serve as the theoretical framework for their practice during the first years of teaching will incorporate a broader range of strategies and approaches.

The remainder of this book offers a more thorough presentation of what I learned as an observer in Brenda's classroom. It is a record of how the college-level methods course is structured, an explanation of the content covered in the course, and an examination of how the relationships between individuals function to promote learning. Within the following three chapters, under the themes of *classroom structures, course content,* and *classroom community,* the manner in which Brenda guides her students through the process of reinventing the teacher's role will be discussed in detail. Some questions will be helpful to keep in mind as you read the remainder of the book: What opportunities are there for reflective thinking? How does the curriculum take into account the fact that learning is largely a social process and knowledge is personally constructed? How are Brenda's teaching methods related to the method of *currere* discussed in chapter 3? What elements of this course experience place its curriculum within the reconceptualist stream of curriculum theory?

Chapter 4

Building a House:
Classroom Structures in the Methods Course

The first house my husband and I bought had the basic requirements: for the most part, it was structurally sound; it was within our price range; and it was a New England Cape, a style I loved. We could afford the mortgage payments and keep a roof over our heads. But aside from that, our little house left a lot to be desired. After we moved in, we began to realize just how much renovating was needed. At first the job seemed impossible. Neither of us knew the slightest thing about plumbing, wiring, or construction. Fortunately, we found ourselves among kind neighbors who were prototypical self-sufficient, rugged, independent New England types. There was nothing they didn't know or couldn't do when it came to renovating a house. For the next several years, one of our neighbors would pay an occasional visit to do some wiring, plumbing, or complicated carpentry work, or give us some advice about what kind of materials we should buy and how we should tackle the next job. Then they would leave us to it. Over time, with the exception of the structural beams, we rebuilt our house by replacing walls, wires, flooring, and plumbing; we installed windows and doors, bathroom fixtures, and a new kitchen. It took a long time, but we did it little by little with the expert help of our neighbors. Over those years we observed, participated, and had the benefit of living within a house that *we* transformed. With that experience, we have a much clearer concept of all the planning and skill that goes into building a house. Sadly, we had to sell our house. But we will eventually buy again, and next time we'll be more aware of what it means to renovate a house.

My first home-owning experience comes to mind as I try to understand the experience Brenda's methods students go through. Building a classroom is, in many ways, similar to building a house. Planning, skill, and a lot of hard work go into the process. For a novice, it's important to have an experienced classroom builder close at hand. I think of how helpful it was to have our neighbors, Pete and his father Walt, nearby. They frequently stopped by for a friendly, helpful visit, giving us tips and strategies for the next stages in the renovation process, and occasionally coming in to do a complicated job themselves while we stood close at hand. Like Pete and Walt, Brenda provided a range of building experiences for her students. She assumed the role of "expert neighbor," offering tips, strategies, procedures, and expertise. In my role as an observer in the methods classroom, Brenda also helped me build a house of meaning for my teaching. I moved in with the class and throughout the semester constructed my own professional understandings.

My husband and I expected to stay in the house we rebuilt, and our neighbors offered advice within that context. They never said, "The next time you rebuild, remember not to buy that kind of window" or "The angle on this staircase is kind of steep. Next time you plan to put in a staircase, allow for more area." Brenda's role was different because she offered information and advice for students about how they should build their next classroom. Their houses weren't for keeps, but built for the purposes of learning.

In the chapter that follows I will explain what structures are featured in Brenda's methods classroom and how those structures functioned to extend student learning. As you read, keep in mind possible connections to the practical theories surveyed in chapter 3: Is the learning experience social? Does it allow students the opportunity to construct personal understanding? Does it foster reflective thinking? Is the instructional approach compatible with reconceptualist perspectives?

Experience and Classroom Structures

> Structure ignites spontaneity...Limits yield intensity. When we play... by our self-chosen rules, we find that containment of strength amplifies strength.
>
> (Stephen Nachmanovitch, 1990, pp. 82-84)

Through an invitation to engage in writing and reading through literacy workshops, Brenda involves her students in the construction of their own classroom. As they build classroom structures together, she helps them understand their function and importance. This is an excerpt from one of Brenda's reading responses. It reveals some of her beliefs about the importance of classroom structures. Recall from chapter 3 that the final hour of class is spent in a reading seminar. During this segment of class, students silently read each of their group member's one-page responses to the assigned readings. Brenda regularly distributed her response to every class member. This response articulates her beliefs about the importance of structure in the classroom:

> The best-laid plans go awry. It rains, there is no field trip. The response to the reading is in a book bag at home. What is a teacher to do?
>
> I think back to our [field experience class] meeting on Monday. When students from our class interviewed teachers about how they planned, many in effect said they "wing it." This is true, and it isn't true. You could say that today is an example of winging it. But there are things at work beneath the surface that can lead to some good learning.
>
> We have the structure of the small group responses. Over time, the power of these groups builds. This was clear from your written critiques of your learning that you've been presenting in the evaluation conferences. Someone once said that all you need for learning is time, talk, and texts. I would also argue that you need a structure. Within the structure, there is lots of room for winging it. But good things need to be in place, so that the learning can build...
>
> I think good teaching is improvisational, but improvisational in the way that blues and jazz riffs are improvisational. There is lots of room for individual difference and artistry. But the player still knows that there are structures and constraints within each solo, no matter how free it appears. Twelve-bar blues are different than other forms—there are notes, you aren't allowed to hit because they will sound flat or off or cold. You only know as a listener when the wrong note is hit because it sounds wrong. But the player knows what they are avoiding as they play. (Brenda Power, excerpt from response to *Invitations*, November 2, 1994)

Through reading, writing, small- and large-group discussions, and a variety of activities, most of the learning that takes place in Brenda's methods course happens in the *here and now* of experience. Especially in the early weeks of class, students are involved in hands-on, interactive activities that help them build their own understandings about literacy learning and teaching. As an observer in Brenda's classroom, I took scores of pages of notes on what I heard and saw. As I analyzed my field notes I looked for examples of classroom interactions and instructional content that had to do with issues of classroom structure. I then coded each excerpt according to the following categories:

"H"— If the reference point was embedded in the *Here and Now* of experience.

"**B**"— If the learning situation was an experience-based *Bridge*, having one reference point in the here and now of experience and another in the abstraction of a future classroom.

"**C**"— When the reference point was an abstraction, made to a *Classroom* of the future.

Figure 4.1 reveals the pattern of structure-oriented learning experiences throughout the methods course. These are excerpts from the field notes of large-group discussions. Notice how nearly all of the references to structure in the early stages of the course are made in the context of some experience or activity. There are several bridging experiences throughout the course. And toward the end of the course most of the learning situations refer to the abstract world of students' future classrooms. The instructional pattern of introducing concepts in the context of the here and now, then gradually connecting the concrete with the abstract, illustrates the essence of a constructivist learning experience. Learning experiences that are initially imbedded in the "here and now" of existence gradually give way to abstractions. This concrete to abstract and practical to theoretical model of instruction has many parallels to constructivist, social-learning models of instruction that were discussed in chapter 3. In the following sections, I will describe some of the methods classroom structures that serve as experience-based learning opportunities. These experiences serve as the foundation of ideas upon which teaching concepts are built in the methods course.

Figure 4.1. *Structure Domain* **(coded by reference to learning context and subcategory)**

H	Structure:	p. 1.	Work in groups of three
B	Structure:	p. 4.	Chores (where students are assigned daily chores)
H	Structure:	p. 6.	Conference procedures; set agenda as writer
H	Structure:	p. 7.	Conference guidelines; modeling how to give feedback
H	Structure:	p. 7.	Conference guidelines; let the group respond
H	Structure:	p. 7.	Challenges—force yourself to write 2-3 pages (Sept.16)
H	Structure:	p. 8.	Explains the part of class when she gives presentations
H	Structure:	p. 9.	Procedure for reading response groups

H	Structure:	p. 11.	Natural learning—inaccurate term—lots of structure
H	Structure:	p. 12.	Importance of routines
H	Structure:	p. 12.	Grading system, evaluation challenge to do quality work
H	Structure:	p. 12.	Habits and the importance of lower standards
H	Structure:	p. 16.	Challenge to write two to three pages
H	Structure:	p. 18.	Response groups, don't' need to be rigid, underline part
H	Structure:	p. 19.	Assignments
H	Structure:	p. 20.	Always start with the people you didn't get to last class
H	Structure:	p. 22.	Gather up your courage to share
H	Structure:	p. 27.	Goal setting, worksheet and group discussion
H	Structure:	p. 30.	Chores, make sure you pick one you haven't done
H	Structure:	p. 31-32.	Know when structures don't work
H	Structure:	p. 33.	Can you capture images using strong verbs?
B	Structure:	p. 44.	Interview the teacher about how she planned (open)
C	Structure:	p. 51.	Conferences, "few stock questions"
C	Structure:	p. 52-53.	Conference principles, role of teacher
H	Structure:	p. 53.	Integration
H	Structure:	p. 58.	Literature circle handout; "How will you structure group?"
B	Structure:	p. 59.	Lesson plans
H	Structure:	p. 60.	Evaluation, midterm conference
C	Structure:		(Brenda's response Oct. 17) Find structure that works
C	Structure:	p. 64.	Time spent in text versus activities
C	Structure:	p. 66.	Real classrooms, schedules
C	Structure:	p. 66.	Warning against too many activities versus observation
B	Structure:	p. 74.	Planning, "winging it"
C	Structure:	p. 77.	Round robin reading versus other approaches
C	Structure:	p. 79.	Tendency to over plan by new teachers
C	Structure:		November 2 response by Brenda
H	Structure:	p. 88.	Goal setting, structure to work independently
C	Structure:	p. 107.	B's "minimalist" beliefs

Writing Workshop: Living the Structure

Brenda introduces the framework of the writing workshop on the first day of class. The experience is an initiation when the routines that will serve the class for the rest of the semester are established.

After the preliminary introductions of herself and her assistant teacher, Brenda explains the importance of prioritizing daily reading and writing in the classroom:

Field Notes excerpt, 9/7/94

Brenda: I like to start the course by reading or writing. As a teacher you need to make sure you have time for reading and writing. Take care of other details later. The recommendations from all the major professional associations is that students write each day. The trend in the field now is that teachers are allowing the time daily for writing, but that's it...just time and little else.

Beginning on the first day of class, Brenda sets in place the structure for the remainder of the semester. Though these structures change subtly over time, they serve the class for the duration of the course. On the first day of class, within the first fifteen minutes, Brenda's students were involved in a writing activity, and within the first hour they had written independently and responded to their peers' texts in small and large groups. "The first day is the most critical," Brenda explains. Everything builds from that, and from these beginnings the routines of the semester were established.

Reading, writing, and responding to texts are at the center of Brenda's methods course. In this course the literacy workshop functions as an important opportunity for emerging teachers to engage in the dual activities of practicing literacy and teaching literacy. As readers, writers, and speakers, students are urged to develop their skill in these domains through practice. By responding to other readers and writers in the class, they have opportunities to improve their skill at responding to students and developing teaching techniques. Methods students need to have hands-on experiences that help them replace their preconceived notions about learning, which in many cases means learners are viewed as passive recipients of new knowledge, with more theoretically tenable perspectives, where students are active participants in their own knowledge making. Guided experiences through writing activities, such as those done in the methods course, help emerging teachers see new possibilities for structuring learning in the classroom.

On the first day of class, Brenda asked her students to draw a floor plan of a place they remember. She asked them to list related ideas in the margins of the page. The class then wrote about the memory for ten minutes. When they had finished, Brenda gave specific procedures for sharing their writing. This procedure helped the class begin a process that would eventually become familiar.

Field Notes excerpt, 9/7/94

> Brenda: Stop writing. If you're writing, the best thing to do is to stop right in the middle of the sentence—that way when you return you're forced to reread and that gets you back into your piece. Reread and underline the part you like. Could be a sentence, phrase, or paragraph.
>
> Listening is the hardest skill you'll learn as a teacher. Studies show that physiology alters as people are involved in active listening. When you find yourself wandering during a conference, a sure way to get back on track is to try a "tell me" question.
>
> Share your piece. Read orally, don't skip anything, and don't pass your piece on to another to read. Simply tell what part you underlined. Then ask which part your partner would have underlined and why.

The initial step-by-step procedure Brenda gave for writing sharing on the first day of the workshop was specific. On the second day of class her directions served to take the class to the next step. This time she simply reminded them to keep the same format of listening to their peers' writing and responding to it.

Field Notes excerpt, 9/12/94

> Brenda: Last class I gave you an artificial way to begin— where you underlined your favorite part and got a response from your group about their favorite part. You don't have to do that today. You do have to keep the same format of listening to writing and responding to it. What you'll do as a writer is set the agenda for the response you'll get. Let the listener know what you need. Join with the two others who were in your group, then join with three others from another group who will form your writing group for this class. Before you share, think for a moment about the kind of response you'll want. Reform into larger groups of six.

Following small-group responses, the class participates in a large-group sharing of students' writing. After her students had a chance to respond in small groups, Brenda asked who would like to share their writing with the whole class. Brian volunteered to read. But before he did, Brenda asked, "How would you like us to respond?" Brian explained.

Field Notes excerpt, 9/12/94

Brian: It's something I started in my journal. I just want to see how it makes people feel. I'll read it and you'll see.

(Brian read his piece about racing, in which he used metaphor and description. It was exciting and fast paced. When he finished he began to fill the uneasy silence with the following words.)

Brian: I like to start my writing like, clueless, so that no one knows what I'm writing about. I doubt that any of you knew what...

Brenda: But wait. Your first reaction is to keep talking, to fill the silence because you're nervous. Let the group respond to your writing.

With these kinds of comments, Brenda subtly guides her students through the process of group sharing. Her comments are frequent and explicit on the first days of workshop. After the class has had several opportunities to participate in guided sharing experiences, her role shifts from guide to participant. In fact, by the fourth day of class her role is minimal and by the third week of class her guiding comments were limited to brief tips to get the groups started. For example:

Field Notes excerpt, 9/19/94

Brenda: We have about twenty minutes or so for small groups. And you should start with the people you didn't get to on Wednesday. Always start with the people you didn't get to last time.

Six weeks into the semester Brenda changed the focus of workshop time from writing to reading. At this point the class had participated in a dozen writing workshops. They were aware of group-work expectations, and they had already formed new response groups. Once again Brenda assumes a stronger role in order to establish a new procedure. This time, her guidelines for literature circles came in the form of a handout that appears in Figure 4.2. She explained to the class that in the past she had assigned activities, but this semester she wanted to give students a chance to plan and do activities and then analyze them for themselves. She asked her students to think about how they would organize their literature circles.

Field Notes excerpt, 10/17/94

> Look at one book a week and decide as the leader how you want to structure the groups—will you bring in questions? Will you ask people to do activities outside the group? Take twenty minutes or so to talk as a group and decide how you will use this time.

Figure 4.2. Literature Circles Handout

Literature Circles

During the next five class sessions, you will be organizing and running your own literature circles. This is not an activity I would expect you to hand over completely to students, but it is appropriate for you folks. You are both students and teachers, and you will feel yourself moving between these roles in the next few weeks.

You must get through all the books in our Caldecott pack during these literature circles. You will have a half-hour in your small group, with some sharing during the whole group of what you did. For this activity, one member of your group must be responsible each week to lead the group. This person will be responsible for any instruction that takes place during the group, as well as leading the discussion.

During this first meeting time, decide how you want your group to work—who will be responsible for what book each week, what you hope to accomplish, and your own personal goals for the activity.

The person responsible for leading the literature circle each week must submit a plan for the circle, including a reference to where the activity comes from, as well as a one-page, single-spaced typed analysis of what went well during the circle, and what you would do differently if you had the chance to lead again. The plans and the analysis are due at the class session following the circle you lead.

There are many ideas for literature circles within *Invitations* and the chapter on these circles in *Literacy in Process*. This is your chance to do some planning and take a few risks as a teacher within a small group of supportive peers.

Dates for Literature Circles:
- Wednesday, October 19
- Wednesday, October 26
- Monday, October 31
- Monday, November 7

This assignment was a new experiment for Brenda. When I asked her how she conceived of the idea, she explained it had come from reading their daily quick-write journals, another example of a structure that supports learning in the methods classroom. A lot of her students were very nervous about student teaching and taking on the responsibility of running literature groups. Brenda explained to some of them, "You really have to be willing to fail first." Afterward, she began thinking that if students had a chance to try the groups in this class, that would offer a safe, structured setting in which to try their hand at running a literature circle. She suspected that many of the students would try activities that were too long or wouldn't work... but that would be part of the learning experience.

When classroom structures are in place that allow for students to take the time and have choices that allow them to make their own meaning through reading and writing, they can be faithful to their own individuality. Classroom structures are important to this process. It is difficult for students to engage in projects that contribute to personal growth when the classroom is chaotic or unpredictable. Nancie Atwell (1987) tells the story of the day Donald Graves came to visit her school. She explains that just as he was leaving, as he stood in her doorway with his coat on, he commented, "You know what makes you such a good writing teacher? You're so damned organized." When he saw Nancie's face "crumple" in response, he explained:

> Look, you can't teach writing this way if you're not organized. This isn't an open classroom approach, and you know it. It's people like you... who

make the best writing teachers. You always ran a tight ship and you still
do, but it's a different kind of ship. (pp. 53-54)

The term *natural learning* (Cambourne, 1988) is often used in
reference to new paradigms of literacy instruction. In many ways,
natural is a fitting term because that is how the learner might tend
to perceive the self-motivated process. Probably because they were
continually involved in developing their own writing ability,
students perceived writing development as a natural process. These
perceptions come to life in an excerpt from a student's final paper.
The assignment was to write a short essay on something learned
during the semester. Laura's paper is entitled, "One Thing!" and in
it she writes:

> I never thought there was anything academic about the workshops. The
> most interesting thing about [these] writing workshops is so much was left
> unsaid. You must have planned it that way. We learned so much without
> you guiding us through it... You presented your method of having us in
> writing workshops as just that, your method. So I assumed it was a way
> you preferred to teach. I didn't think I would be getting anything out of it.
> After a few weeks of slowly growing, I did see how it was affecting me. It
> was so natural that I didn't see what was happening.

This excerpt highlights the paradox of good classroom
structures—when they are firmly in place it seems as if learning is
self-guided. The organization and procedures of the literacy
workshops gave Laura the space and structure to make her own
discoveries and to chart her own learning. Her own learning helped
her understand writing at a deeper level than she had previously
done. Through the practice of writing, Laura discovered her potential
in a way that seemed natural. Though Brenda hopes her students
will feel that their personal growth in writing seems like a natural
process, she realizes the need for future teachers to understand the
importance of structure and organization. She explained this point
to her students.

Field Notes Excerpt, 9/19/94

Brenda: Natural learning—the term is offensive because it
doesn't convey all of the planning that goes into the
teaching. It takes a lot more effort and structure to do a
workshop. Holdaway's model is called natural, but in this
class what we'll be doing is unnatural... it just takes a while
to understand the underlying structure.

Brenda captures the importance of workshop structure in this passage.

> Many teachers who lecture at students mistakenly believe that a workshop format is unstructured. A closer look reveals workshop formats are often the most highly structured learning environments in schools. By the end of the semester, I won't be giving any explicit guidelines for how these students should respond to each others' work in writer's workshop. But there will be many different structures and strategies they test out, like the underlining and responding strategy of the first day's workshop, before they discover the strategies that work best for their group. Every group will have worked out their own means of responding, but they will receive a load of structural possibilities throughout the semester.
>
> (Brenda Power, 1995, p. 32)

With the daily routine in place—silent writing or reading and responding in small and large groups—students have the freedom to pursue an independent course. Though they don't realize it at the start of the semester, structures provide an important frame for students' reading and writing experiences; and experience is the most powerful teacher. In her final paper Kirsten, another student, attests to that idea.

> This class has answered many questions and calmed my nerves by giving examples and allowing me to experience for myself what a reading and writing workshop is all about. I think the biggest thing that I'll take away with me, from this class, is the confidence to run a writing workshop so that my students will benefit from it.

Workshop Routines

> A routine implements an action designed to achieve a specific outcome as efficiently as possible. Ideally, we don't think about routines. We do them, on time, as needed, without a fuss. Limited judgment is involved. Students enter their room and hang up their coats, attendance is recorded and sent off to the office, notices for parents are handed out, and candy sale money is collected and counted. If routines are effectively carried out, no one will trip over boots in the closet area, paper will be passed out efficiently, and students involved in special classes and activities, such as band, will get away on cue, all without a hitch.
>
> (Ralph Peterson, 1992, p. 63)

Predictable routines are a distinguishing feature of newer instructional practices, such as writing workshop (Graves, 1983) and reading workshop (Atwell, 1987) approaches to literacy instruction. With daily minilessons, frequent small-group and individual conferences, and daily time blocks set aside for personal reading and writing, workshop routines define the shape of the school day.

The security of a predictable schedule helps students know what is expected of them, leaving them free to follow their own interests and tend to their own projects. In elementary classrooms, while children are busy reading and writing during workshop, the teacher has the freedom to observe and interact with students. Within predictable daily schedules, children can enjoy the freedom and resources provided, engaging in activities that help them meet their potential.

Brenda believes that structures are essential to productivity. But she also acknowledges the drawbacks of too much structure or blind adherence to structures that cease to nurture creativity and productivity. She commented to one of her students, "There's a fine line between routines and ruts." She explores this fine line with students, sharing her views on the need for routines and good work habits. Her reasoning is that if you produce a little bit each day, the cumulative effect, over time, is significant. Daily writing is an essential element of her working process as a writer and scholar. She introduces these beliefs to her students early in the semester when she explains the need for structure in the form of personal routines. It's the third day of class and Brenda opens with a minilesson on routines.

Field Notes excerpt, 9/14/94

Brenda: I want to talk for a few minutes today about routines. It's really important as a teacher, and what I hope you'll work on here in this class, to establish routines. Getting under the lightening, like Donald Murray talked about, establishing a disciplined routine, is important. Writing in the morning is almost critical. If writing isn't something you're comfortable with, it's easy to let the time slip away.

Student 1: When you said write twice a week in the morning, do you mean writing for this class or just writing in general?

Brenda: Everyone has different habits. You may pick Wednesday and Saturday, but if you wait until Sunday night, it just won't work.

Student 2: I prefer working at night.

Brenda: That's fine. The point is establishing habits. And just like we talked about during the first class, it's important to lower your standards. When I was in graduate school I decided I'd do all my work on Tuesday and Wednesday night. Well, that just isn't going to work. It's much better to say I'm gonna work from 7:00 to 9:00 each night and do it religiously. Just go into your room and shut the door, and tell yourself you'll stop when Seinfeld comes on or when it's time to go out with friends.

In this excerpt Brenda offers her opinions about the importance of routines, and students offer their reactions. "That might not work for me," seems to be what one student is saying. Brenda responds by saying that work habits can be personalized to fit individual needs. But regardless of personal style, work habits and routines are still important. Without them students fall into the age-old college student trap: procrastination. Nachmanovitch (1990) writes, "procrastination is the mirror image of addiction; both are disorders of self-regulation. We are stuck in these cycles unless and until we can find the crossed signal and switch it back again" (p. 128). It is the process of finding the "crossed signal" in one's working process, and setting it back on course, that fosters productive habits and a healthy degree of self-regulation. As teachers, Brenda's students will need to help their students develop good work habits that will enable them to produce and learn. So it is important to focus on fine-tuning and becoming aware of their own work habits.

Brenda elaborates on the importance of daily practice and how the routine of writing every day contributes to writing development. Explaining about the importance of writing workshop in her methods course, she writes:

> Nancie Atwell writes of how she starts the first day of her workshop with writing, involving students in her own process. I've often started the first day of the semester with a similar routine. We begin with that brief lesson about writing, some silent writing, and some small-group discussion of what's been written. It's important for me that we don't start with a syllabus, books required, or assignment due dates. I'm looking for "mindfulness" throughout the semester in students and myself—a concentration on the task or issue at hand that shows our full attention and careful thought. You can't have that mindfulness on the first day if six of your students are worried about the price of your texts, four are wondering how they will be graded, and seven are comparing the syllabus to the one from the class they just left. So I bury the syllabus for the first hour or two of class in my stack of class materials.

(Brenda Power, 1995, p. 7)

As both an elementary and college teacher I have had a tendency to overload students with procedures and directions on the first day of class, feeling the need to do everything as it will be done for the rest of the term. But as far as first days go, a little is usually better than a lot, otherwise the students become overwhelmed or confused. And when you're building a house from the inside, you can afford to do a bit at a time. The process can be modified, little by little.

Reading Seminar: Learning Group Structures

During the last segment of each class, students participate in reading seminar groups (this segment of class is thoroughly outlined in chapter 2). In groups, students read their peers' one-page responses to assigned texts. At the beginning of the semester, Brenda gives her students explicit instructions in the form of procedures for working in these groups, just as she did for writing workshop. With time and experience, students develop independence and are able to manage the groups independently. But for the first several seminars, Brenda is there to guide and assist. Just prior to the first seminar experience, she offers this set of procedures.

Field Notes excerpt, 9/12/94

Brenda: Count off by sixes. We're going to split up into groups for our reading responses [Brenda guided students as to where they should go]. I'm gonna give you a procedure. You'll get a copy of each response. Janice and I write a response each time. So those of you who read fast will have time to read ours. But if you don't, put them at the back of the pile. I was a sophomore in college before I ever gave myself permission to skim. Research has shown that slow readers and students who fall behind always read at the same slow pace. If you're a slow reader, push yourself to read faster. Give yourself permission to skim and find one thing to respond to. You're not reading with an eye to improve writing, but rather to focus on something to talk about as a group. You'll go paper by paper, so that each person's paper is discussed. Does anyone have questions? Also, make sure you save a pile of your papers for Janice and me.

Along with providing a structure for the seminar process, Brenda used this experience-based opportunity to introduce a discussion on the issue of skimming text. This is an illustration of how principles of literacy instruction are introduced in a meaningful, active context, where multiple concepts might be addressed simultaneously. As was the case with workshop procedures, her guidelines become less specific for subsequent seminars. Before the second meeting of seminar groups, after her students had already worked through the process once during the previous class meeting, Brenda gave these directions:

Field Notes excerpt, 9/14/94

Brenda: We're going to do our group response now. You don't have to be really rigid about the process. But make sure, while you're reading, to underline a part you want to comment on. Then when you discuss the papers, make sure you get a chance to comment on all of the papers, and that no one's gets buried underneath them all.

The Power of Standards

Brenda recognizes the importance of personal passion to growth in reading and writing development. By putting in place structures and routines of the workshops, she helps students find their personal sources of passion and inspiration. And as they move through their independent courses, she incorporates additional structures of standards and expectations. These are opportunities for students to set personal goals and work to meet them. The grading criteria for the course is provided in the syllabus, given on the first day of class. Throughout the course she refers to the work that students hand in, giving verbal feedback to the group, and individual feedback on each student's paper. During the class meeting after she had read the first set of one-page written responses to the readings, she offered this feedback:

Field Notes excerpt, 9/14/94

Brenda: I enjoyed your papers, and I want to talk more about evaluation. I'll push you to do your best quality work. In many cases, and it's usually the case with our grading system, quantity is more important than quality. The more the better—and that's not quality. Research shows that grades don't help students improve... I [prefer] to think, "Where's this person at? How can I help them reach the next level?" For example, in this first assignment, some of you double spaced instead of single spaced as required. If this is the practice school of writing, then if you continue to do double spacing, at the end of the semester you'll have written half as much as your classmates, and your writing will improve half as much. Through writing, and practicing, we'll all learn to speak the same language about writing.

As assignments come up, Brenda provides specific guidelines and requirements in the form of assignment handouts. Approximately every two weeks the students are given a handout sheet that outlines assignments for future class meetings. Items on these handouts include reading assignments, activity assignments, due dates for final drafts of papers, and reminders. During the course, three short papers (two to three pages) were assigned. Many students chose to continue to work on the writing topic they chose from the first day. During workshops, and in written reminders on assignment handouts, students were made aware of evaluation expectations. On the third day of class, the meeting before the first paper was due, Brenda issued this challenge:

Field Notes excerpt, 9/14/94

Brenda: The narrative is due. It's two to three pages double spaced. If you find your piece is too long, what can you do as a writer to shorten it? If it's too short, how do you lengthen it? This may seem a bit artificial, but it's an exercise. Also, I'd like you to include your drafts stapled on the back of your final piece. Maybe you went through three or four topics. Include those, because they are drafts.

Self-awareness fuels growth and development. The more developed our sense of what is required in order to do quality work, the better we know where we stand in relation to that standard, and the more we understand the steps that we need to take in order to reach the standard. One way the ability to self-assess one's work grows is from hearing comments and questions from peers. Over time the students begin to internalize some of those voices in the form of an inner self-questioning process. The recursive nature of social learning and internalized thinking, a feature that characterizes social learning theory as discussed in chapter 3, is an underlying principle of response-based learning in the methods classroom.

The importance of self-awareness is an example of the kind of conventional wisdom that has been examined by psychologists. It is often known as *metacognitive awareness*, and is defined as the awareness one has of her thinking processes. Researchers have identified two components of the metacognitive process as it relates to reading. The first of these components is the *knowledge* necessary for reading. The following parts comprise this component: knowledge about various text structures; knowledge of reading task requirements; knowledge of strategies that need to be utilized in order to successfully read; and the learner's personal strengths and weaknesses that influence reading. The second metacognitive component is the degree of *control* a reader has over the use of the knowledge component (Brown, Armbruster, and Baker, 1986). Literacy instruction should emphasize metacognitive development in learners in order to help them acquire independence in the dual acts of reading and writing.

The construct of metacognition applies to the methods course evaluation structures that emphasize self-awareness. Brenda frequently modeled instruction that is intended to help students take a step back from their performance in order to examine it with a critical eye. For example, on the due date of the first paper, instead of moving into the next paper assignment, Brenda thought it would be more helpful to provide a structured activity that would help students reflect on their performance in the course and set goals for the future. In class she distributed a worksheet that asked students to think about their personal goals, skills they would like to work on, and group goals for subsequent classes.

Field Notes excerpt, 9/21/94

Brenda: As a teacher you'll want to cover more than you have time for—that's usually the way it is. Your papers are due today, and my first impulse was to get headlong into your next papers, but I decided it would be better to wait... What have you learned about yourself as a writer? And what have you learned about working in your group? This has to do with metacognitive awareness—a big long word, but... it has to do with thinking about thinking. You want your students to be able to monitor themselves, to understand their work in relation to others. You can fill these [goal setting worksheets] out however you want. Sentences, phrases, paragraphs. Think about how you've changed as a writer, how has your thinking changed as a teacher of writing, how has working with others in a group played a part in your process. Take 5-10 minutes and then you'll have a chance to discuss them in groups.

(Students had five minutes to fill out the worksheets.)

Brenda: Take about twenty minutes for the small group. You'll discuss as a group your goals and what you've written about. Then when you're finished I'd like you to come up and write your individual and group goals on the board.

During the small group discussions I sat with several students who were discussing their goals. This conversation took place:

Field Notes excerpt, 9/21/94

Paul: Have to be willing to read what you wrote. Everybody has to participate.

Austin: It's all about sharing—not just the teacher.

Jason: It can help... if you have a problem others might have experienced.

Gwen: I need to allow myself the luxury to freewrite and then go back and critique and revise. I have to just write.

Brian: Work on handwriting.

(After the groups had twenty minutes to discuss their goals and write them on the board, Brenda facilitated a process of categorizing the goals so she and students could identify patterns.)

Brenda: Some of the print is small. So I'll read them aloud. Then what we'll do as a group is try to categorize them. Can anyone throw out one category that you could put some of these under?

Student: Grammar. A lot of students refer to word usage, run on sentences, etc.

Brenda: Who was it? Was it Ruth? Grammar does change over time. What's not OK now could be OK tomorrow. The way you speak is different than the way you write. When you say work on grammar, there are probably a lot of things you can work on. What's another category?

Students: Vocabulary.

Brenda: Would being more creative with my language, Would you put that under vocabulary? Use a thesaurus? OK I'm gonna read you some of the ones we have left. [Spend] more time [writing/reading], freewrite, constructive criticism, polishing paper better. Any other categories?

Students: Drafts, time management.

Brenda: It seems to be a big category for a lot of you. Work habits. So I'm going to put a category "Work habits," does that sound right?

Student: Yes.

Brenda: What about more constructive criticism. Where would that be for you?

Marissa: (laughing) That was me. I think I missed the point of the questions.

Brenda: Well, you always need one that doesn't fit. If you don't it's just too neat. (Brenda totaled the responses in different categories). My goal is to work on minilessons. I think I'll address a lot of your goals in the minilessons— word choice and grammar. For our individual conferences I'll focus more on work habits. Helping you to whittle down your goals to more manageable goals.

Brenda: (read group goals) What are some categories?

Student: Constructive criticism.

Brenda: Let's read some of the others. Do you see any other categories?

Student: Organization or structure.

Brenda: OK, I'll put *S* for structure. What about, "Don't project my ideas onto what is being said"?

Student: Constructive criticism.

This activity allowed students to think about their personal and group goals, and then to discuss them. By organizing the goals, and thinking about how they can be tackled in the weeks to come, Brenda put in place a structure that was both evaluative and constructive. In my notes I remarked how the existence of the workshop in this course is an essential foundation for the discussion of content. Without the common experience of having written and responded to each other's writing, the discussion above could not have taken place in an authentic way. This discussion illustrates how the workshop model, which uses experience as a means to help students construct personal understanding, is strikingly different from the traditional lecture-oriented instructional approach where students would have been told about the importance of metacognitive awareness and self-assessment. Brenda organized this activity in order to help students chart their course of learning. Structuring goal-setting opportunities into the workshop enabled Brenda to ascertain her students' concerns, and those concerns became the content of subsequent minilessons and individual conferences. The structures of goal-setting, minilessons, and individual conferences are all interconnected, and each structure influences the content that will be covered. The next chapter will offer a more detailed discussion of content. Concluding the goal-setting discussion, Brenda offered this tip to her students:

Field Notes excerpt, 9/21/95

Brenda: As a teacher, it's important to regularly bring the class together and ask, "Where are we at? What do we do next? And what do we notice?" It will help as a teacher. I know I want to work on minilessons over the next few months, and this input from you will really help.

"What about skills?" "Where are they addressed?" These are questions often asked of whole language or workshop approaches to instruction. Many critics of whole language or workshop approaches wrongly base their criticism on the fallacy that skills are not addressed. The goal-setting activity illustrates the fallacy of this viewpoint. It is interesting to note that most of the students' responses indicated strong concern about issues of mechanics, and most students set a goal for improving that aspect of their writing. The activity provides an illustration of how student-centered instruction really does focus on the same types of concerns that form the core of traditional instructional approaches.

Two months into class, the subject of goal-setting was revisited. This time, Brenda helped her students set goals for the remainder of the semester. This activity took place after the midterm evaluation conferences when she had an opportunity to discuss specific issues with each student.

Field Notes excerpt, 11/14/94

Brenda: Take out a piece of scrap paper for a moment. We've done some goals earlier after you finished your first response group. We just finished our one-on-one midterm evaluation conferences where you talked about what works well in your group.

For this assignment, I want you to think about your goals for the remainder of the course. Try to come up with three goals. Some of you said you were interested in reading to the whole group, others said you wanted to be with a group that was more supportive, others said you wanted to work on giving more specific feedback. Think about three goals and write them down.

We'll go around the room to find out your goals. We're gonna start with you Ruth. This won't take too long.

Ruth: More constructive feedback for other groups.

Student: Not to wander off task.

Kirsten: To focus on what my peers are saying.

Nina: I'd like to share something.

Dave: To be silent and absorbing most of the time.

Nancy: I want to write in more detail... I don't think I have enough.

Student: I wanted to stop this habit I have... whenever there's a silence I tend to jump in, even if it's not related.

Student: Give more ideas to person who's reading their story.

Student: Keep group more on task so that we get through everyone's papers.

Cathy: Make my writing more concise. Simplicity is not that easy to achieve.

Eileen: Be more attentive to all that's being said.

Laura: I procrastinate too much. My goal is to do things [on time].

Brenda: The next thing is probably the most challenging thing you'll do. Get into groups of three to five. Share your goals. Decide what will be done in the next workshop. Based on your goals you might decide you need some structure for next time, or you may decide you don't.

Goal setting in the methods class was a routine aimed at helping students meet the set standards. It helped determine the course of learning for students and teacher. With the aid of a teacher-imposed structure, the students set the agenda for group and personal learning. They based their goals on what they had learned about literacy through their own reading and writing, and from interactions with others during workshop time. Initially, students' goals centered on their own writing ability, issues of writing mechanics, and craft. A survey of these goals made later in the semester reveals a shift of focus toward an emerging concern for the interpersonal skills involved in working with others.

Grading and Evaluation

The longer I teach, the less important grading becomes to me. I almost never grade anything. I try to evaluate everything. When I look at student work, and I watch them talk around texts, I try to make sense of where each student is and how I might best help them move to the next level of understanding or competence.

Grades reflect quantities, so I try to use them in contexts that are quantifiable. I set firm boundaries up in terms of expectations—students need to be in class, they need to have drafts prepared and books read for workshops, they need to have written response for reading groups photocopied. Students and I can easily quantify the number of days work came in on time, the number of days they were prepared. I require lots of preparation for my class, and it's no small feat for students to meet those requirements.

I don't grade individual assignments, but I write a response to everything, and I also often extend these responses during discussions in individual and group conferences. Students know if they're meeting expectations, or if we have to renegotiate an assignment. After the first week or two of class, students just quit asking about grades.

My grade sheets are usually loaded with A's and B's. I've worked as hard for those grades as my students have. I've expected a certain quantity of work from students, more than any class they've ever taken. The class has demanded commitment from students, and they've honored that commitment. But there is no story to be told from a panel of decontextualized letters on a page.

(Brenda Power 1995, pp. 36-37)

The evaluation process serves as an ongoing classroom structure in the methods course. Students meet informally with Brenda every two or three weeks during the semester. These informal conferences offer a chance for students to discuss personal concerns and goals, and for them to receive feedback from Brenda, providing an evaluation structure. Six weeks into the course the students are required to attend a midterm evaluation conference. Students come prepared with a self-evaluation worksheet (see Figure 4.3). The process of filling out self-evaluation forms and discussing them with Brenda serves as a mirror on their growth and learning processes, allowing an opportunity for students to be honest with themselves. The standards of evaluation for the course are spelled out in black and white on the evaluation worksheets, and class members are forced to ask themselves tough questions about their performance and participation in the course. Brenda reported that students are generally very honest in their self-analysis and rarely deviate from her evaluation of them. On October 17, Brenda offered this advice to the class.

Field Notes excerpt, 10/17/94

Brenda: [These are] guidelines for midterm evaluations. In those one-on-one conferences you'll assess your work and do some writing about it. There really aren't any surprises. If you've been meeting the expectations for class... coming prepared, etc., there aren't any surprises. You'll just come out of the conference with the sense of where you are

confirmed. In 95 percent of the cases I am in total
agreement with the student. But there are those cases where
I disagree and that's usually where a student is unrealistic
about how they are doing. If work is late or doesn't meet the
length requirement, and they still give themselves a high
grade, I will disagree. The grades are based on quantifiable
information. We don't look at essential qualities [of writing
and compare one student to another]. We don't get into that.

Figure 4.3. Midterm Evaluation Conference Worksheet

[*Page 1*]

Midterm Evaluation Conferences

Please write your responses after rereading the syllabus and the
individual assignment guidelines. Write reasons for each grade or
assessment you give yourself in the space provided.

Reading Responses

Have you come to every class session with copies of the
assignment for your group? Have you tried to respond to the
readings in different ways? Have you *consistently* met the length
requirement for these papers (full page, single space)? Have you
allowed everyone in your group an equal voice, with equal time?

Give yourself a grade:
  A Length requirement met, always prepared, good participation
  B Missed one paper or class, or missed length requirement no
  more than twice
  C Missed two or more papers, often missed length requirement
  F Numerous missing papers and missed classes

Set a goal in this category for final conferences.

[*Page 2*]

Writing Workshop

Did you come to each workshop with a draft in hand? Did you share
your paper with classmates orally each week? Did you use their
advice in your final paper?

Give yourself a grade:
  A Always prepared in workshop, always shared work
  B Unprepared or didn't share no more than two times
  C Three or more sessions unprepared, no evidence of drafting
  F Not prepared, no drafts

Set a goal for yourself in this category.

[*Page 3*]

Participation

Do you actively participate in all workshop activities? Do you question yourself and your peers as you are exposed to new materials? Do you respond to the instructor's questions (in your journal or orally)? Do you make sure you have a fair share of discussion time in the class?

Give yourself a grade:

A "Yes" response to all questions

B-C One or two problem areas

F No longer breathing

Set a goal for this category:

[Please note: You are allowed two absences all semester. After two absences, your grade is lowered one full letter per absence in this category.]

[*Page 4*]

Also consider:

What was your group goal from last month? Did you work on it or meet it?

What was your goal for improving your writing? Did you work on it or meet it?

Did you challenge yourself to read your writing to the whole class?

Did you always do your chores, and turn in your pen pal letters on time?

Questions for improving the instructor's work

What part of the class works best for you? Why?

Think of a time when you felt bored or frustrated during the class. Why did you feel this way? Could instruction be changed to avoid these moments?

What do you feel you've learned a lot about?

What do you want to learn more about?

Anything else?

Structures in the Literacy Methods Course: Bridges to Future Classrooms

"I hope to gather lots of ideas and resources over the course of the semester that I can use in student teaching and when I'm on my own."

(Nina Kirk, 10/19/94)

Toward the last half of the course, most of the discussions about teaching practices refer to the students' future classrooms. Through discussions and activities, Brenda helps them begin to identify with the role of teacher and to envision possibilities for their classrooms of the future. In the early stages of the course, students are limited in how they can personalize theories and practices that seem abstract and irrelevant to their lives. That is why most of the discussion of classroom structures early in the course have reference points based on workshop experiences. Thinking about reading and writing instruction as readers and writers helps students build their own teaching constructs. These experiences serve as the foundation for discussions later in the semester that focus on the abstractions of future classrooms.

Organizing and Assessing Structures

The challenge for teachers is always to find a structure that works, and then **not** to get so comfortable with it that you're in a rut, always doing things the same way. *Invitations* is a wonderful book to have on your shelf when you see yourself headed for that rut, or another teacher comes to you with concerns about her classroom. Routman will have something somewhere in this book to help you think through the issues. If teaching is to stay fresh for you, it is up to you to keep it fresh. No one can do that for you.

(Brenda Power, response to *Invitations*, October 17, 1994)

As Brenda suggests in the response above, sometimes teachers get into a rut. At times teaching routines can seem dull and don't help to foster the kind of learning one expects. Even worse, some structures plainly don't work or can become counterproductive. Maintaining an awareness of the functions of classroom structures is an important teaching skill. But even more important is having the ability to recognize the need to change structures that are counterproductive. Good teaching is reflective and improvisational. The capability to step back and consider why the activity or procedure isn't working or how it might be adjusted is an invaluable teaching skill. The issue of structures that don't seem to be working came up occasionally. The class had just finished watching the video *One Classroom: A Child's View* (Whitney, Hubbard, and Miller, 1988), in which a young student, Johanna, takes the viewers on a tour of her second-grade classroom. The following discussion resulted.

Field Notes excerpt, 9/21/94

Brenda: [O]ften when something doesn't work, it has to do with the task. In fact, in the video [the teacher] had a task that students had to do: Kids had to pick one journal entry to edit a week. Something that the children did over time made [the teacher] angry. Can anyone guess what it was?

Student: They were selecting the ones that needed the least work.

Brenda: Close. They would have four entries that are this long (six inches) and one that was this long (one inch). Now, you can take two approaches: 1) blame the kids 2) assess your task... When a problem happens you sit down with the student to decide what we can do to make sure this doesn't happen again.

Future teachers try to imagine what their own classrooms will eventually be like. Reading about a range of models and approaches to reading and writing instruction helps them try on the possibilities. Brenda recognizes the value of students exploring the possibilities in the methods course.

Field Notes excerpt, 10/19/94

Brenda: I know the kind of information you need is very different from one student to another. So many of you are very insecure in your perspective roles. You are reading for help and structure. Some of you are reading for the purpose of understanding whole language. Some of you are unsure of whether or not you want to be a teacher. You're reading and thinking, "Is there anyone in here who I could be like?"— "deciding whether or not you'd like to be a teacher."

Students are eager to see how other teachers structure their school day. Classroom schedules are an important consideration for new teachers. Seeing a range of schedules from other teachers' classrooms helps them to define their own priorities while they are surveying a range of possibilities. Deciding how to carve and fill the classroom day is the first place many teachers start when planning for the year to come. And as the discussion on classroom structures reveals, the manner in which it is shaped bears a direct relationship on what will be learned.

Practicing the Art of Planning

> Planning is my favorite part of teaching. I'm almost in a dream-like state for many days over the summer or breaks, when I consider all the possibilities for what students and I might do during the semester, weighing that against what I feel we must do. I talk about the options with colleagues and former students, I argue with myself about what might work. Nothing could be more energizing or exciting. Playing with the structure of class is part of planning. Figuring out how I'll respond to students is part of planning. But I also accept that most of the planning must take place in the midst, as I work with students, and see what it is they need.
>
> (Power, 1995, p. 32)

From the beginning of the semester, the methods students have the opportunity to live the structures of literacy workshops and the generative power of wide open spaces of time. But they still have lingering questions about issues of classroom planning. Brenda helps her students explore and understand the issue of planning in several ways. One way she does this is by having them interview classroom teachers about their planning processes, and then assigning them to plan instruction based on that approach. These are Brenda's instructions.

Field Notes excerpt, 9/28/94

Brenda: Interview the teacher [you were placed with] about how she plans, and we'll have time to discuss when you come back as group. Then I'd like you to talk to the teacher and find out something you can teach to those students. I want you to plan the way the teacher plans, instead of me giving you a format. Planning is the most fun thing that you can do as a teacher. There are so many things to do and so much to choose from.

Students returned to the methods course after interviewing teachers reporting that many of them had explained a lot of what they do in the classroom is a result of "winging it." To an experienced teacher, flexibility for spontaneous learning opportunities require open-ended plans. But to the novice, "winging it" might seem a dubious planning approach. Without experience they have not yet acquired a teacher's intuition, an element that is vital to sophisticated instructional planning. The class discussion of the teacher interview process brought up other interesting issues concerning curriculum and top-down administrative mandates.

Field Notes excerpt, 10/31/94

Student: [To the question] What are your plans? The teacher said "I just wing it" (other students comment that they had similar responses).

Student: It was interesting that she asked the kids what they already know and what they want to learn.

Brenda: And just the idea of winging it... I know those teachers and I know what they mean when they wing it. You really lose any kind of spontaneity when you aren't flexible.

Janice: But they have a lot of background of experience they can draw on... so your idea of winging it might be a lot different than theirs. When you start out you might have a lot more written than you do later.

Brenda: Yeah, I think the first two or three years there is so much front-loading until you get to know the curriculum. But after a while it's more a question of orchestrating.

Janice: I wonder if some administrators require [lesson plans].

Brenda: Oh, yeah. I think they do funny things with them too. My aunt who's a reading specialist in Michigan was required to write these elaborate lesson plans. She would stick in the middle "If you're actually reading this, I'll buy you a milk shake." And each week she'd up the ante until she got to: "I'll buy you a Cadillac." She never got a request from the coordinator, "Where's my milkshake?" So she knew no one was reading them.

I think unless there's a purpose for these plans, there is no point in doing them. And some of the teachers' responses that they don't have a plan is a reaction to the traditional kinds of plans required in curriculum guides. It's their way of saying how different their kind of planning is. One of my friends always says "curriculum is what happened." If you don't have some sort of assessment that is individualized to meet the needs of each student, you really won't know what was done.

Brenda recognizes the importance of limits—the least is often best. Minimal plans enable the needs of members in a community to determine the next course of action. This is not an easy thing for inexperienced teachers to understand. Perhaps the experience of interviewing teachers in order to begin to understand the improvisational side of instructional planning helps them understand the subtle structures that are present even in the act of "winging it."

Methods students have a chance to try their hand at planning, implementing, and critiquing their literature circle lesson (previously described in this chapter). When the literature circle assignment was discussed, one student had questions about Brenda's expectations for plans, "What do you expect for a lesson plan?" This question was a lead into a vitally important issue for new teachers—daily lesson plans.

Field Notes excerpt, 10/17/94

Brenda: You don't have to do a long plan. But you should have a half page or page description...whatever will help you lead the group. Just a plan of what you're reading, what you plan to do, materials you'll need, etc.

When I plan activities for this class I need to list what we're doing and what I'll need...that's all. Keep it simple.

What I'll do in response for that, if you turn in a plan that doesn't reveal all the materials you used, I'll respond that you should think about that next time.

After trying their hand at leading literature circles, some of the students discovered a common teaching dilemma—there is never enough time in the day to get to all that you had planned. And it provided an ideal opportunity for Brenda to discuss a helpful solution.

Field Notes excerpt, 10/19/94

Brian: I had a whole list of activities, but [didn't have time so I] just went through and told them what we didn't get to.

Brenda: That's something to think about with all your groups. How much was spent within the group in the text and writing about the text and talking about text? Sometimes you feel you aren't doing your job because you're trained to think that you're supposed to have so many activities beyond reading and writing.

(Later in the morning Brenda made this related comment.)

Brenda: I think in your reading groups, you'll come up with a lot of neat activities. If you think of it in terms of a carpenter, you want to have a lot of tools, but you'll probably use the hammer the most. And in terms of instruction, you'll use that routine of reading and writing, over and over, so you can see patterns. You don't want your role to become thinking up activities, haphazard, rather than relying on the same structure day after day in order to observe patterns.

The discussion over lesson plans conjured up a series of images for me. Mostly I thought about the spiral-bound plan book from my days of elementary-school teaching. During my first year those little boxes were filled with textbook titles and page numbers. As a new teacher I was uncertain about what my plans should cover. At the time I vaguely recollected instructions from a foundations course in which we had identified behavioral objectives and criteria for evaluating each student's progress. But those recollections left only a residue of understanding that caused me to feel more confused and perplexed. As an observer in this class, where planning issues were addressed through a context of practical, authentic experience, I was able to see how methods students might begin to think about planning in their distant classrooms as being largely flexible and improvisational.

Workshop Structures in Distant Classrooms

The workshop experience provides a rich experience base so that as issues of literacy instruction come up they have personal relevance to the methods students. After having a number of weeks to think and act as readers and writers, information relating to future classrooms is more meaningful since it is offered in the context of concrete experience. The relationship between experience and understanding is especially striking where writing conferences are concerned. Conferences are an important feature of writing workshop, and facilitating successful conferences with students requires skill and knowledge. A month into the course, after her students had participated in eight writing workshops, Brenda offered advice about writing conferences, some models of conference procedures, and a chance to discuss related issues. This excerpt nicely illustrates how Brenda helps students think about issues they will face as classroom teachers by providing concrete examples and relating them to the common community experience.

Field Notes excerpt, 10/12/94

Brenda: There are a few stock questions, those three or four, that you'll have in your repertoire to open up conferences.

Student: I remember reading how sacred that conference time is.

Brenda: Recently I was observing a fine young teacher and noticed how many interruptions she had. And a lot of teachers schedule in those interruptions by saying, "Come to me when you get done with your work." No matter what age group you work with, there will be those few children who interrupt. Conferences with children are so intense. You're pretty exhausted after twenty minutes in conferences. (Brenda puts up overhead: Pat McLure's Conference Principles. See Figure 4.4)

Figure 4.4. McLure's Conference Principles

Pat McLure's Conference Principles:
1. Let the writer lead.
2. Know the history of the child, and the piece of writing.
3. Always include follow-up.

Brenda introduces a real teacher's conference structure as a possible model for students to use in their own classrooms. Then she discussed the importance of each principle and how it influences the development of writing. The first two principles in this example are closely linked to the constructivist and social learning perspectives. Letting the writer lead will help the teacher provide next-step instruction that is in tune with the needs of the learner. Class discussions around simple principles such as these help methods students expand their own understanding of workshop structures. This is the discussion that surrounded the issue of conference principles.

Field Notes excerpt, 10/12/94

Brenda: When you know who children are as writers, that Jake is very independent and Jane is very dependent, you'll know the writing better and the writers better. Unless you know kids you won't be able to individualize your responses.

The third principle is "Always include a follow-up." So if the last thing isn't concrete and reinforced you don't know what it is they will do next, and they'll have a hard time following through.

Nancie Atwell adds two more:

- Keep conferences short. Frequently check writers, and get a global sense of who your class is.
- Avoid yes/no questions.

When I first began working with children as a researcher I used these principles. I found the hardest one to work through was this last one—avoiding asking yes and no questions.

Any questions?

Nancie Atwell, in her book, talks about the status-of-the-class. It's helpful, especially if you have fifty or sixty students a day. You ask quickly what the students are working on. Go right through the whole class and find out what children are working on each day. You see patterns over time. Melody is working on her first draft and never seems to move past that. Ruth seems to work on the same theme time after time. Status of the class gets them thinking about writing workshop and what they might work on that day.

What I'm going to show you next is a third grade teacher, Jan Roberts, and what ends up being about ten or twelve conferences in a few minutes. What she does twice a week is a status-of-the-class. With a few she stops and has longer conferences 'cause she knows that's what they need. With some they are really brief.

(Shows video tape segment from *The Writing and Reading Process: A Closer Look*, Whitney, Hubbard, 1988)

Brenda: Think about those conferences; What struck you? Then look at these [principles] and think about Nancie Atwell's "keep it short" and "avoid yes/no questions."

Student: I had an image of you calling children up, one at a time and spending more time with them.

Brenda: I would advise you not to call them up to your desk. Nancie Atwell recommends taking a little seat around and bringing it to them as they work. If you go through the class alphabetically, you might miss one who needs help right away. Other things you notice?

Student: She left it up to the writer which method she'd use to get the message across.

Brenda: You might want the writer to lead more than she did. Think about, if you're walking around the room with a clipboard, think about that. You're conveying to children your status and authority.

Another principle, focus on the meaning that is conveyed, rather than mechanics.

The conference principles presented here are streamlined and open-ended. They provide enough structure to prompt reflection and discussion, yet leave freedom for creativity and imagination to flourish. They are a good example of the kind of classroom structures that support self-motivated learning in students. Hearing examples of practicing teachers' conference principles and seeing actual teacher-student conferences on video exposed the methods students to a wide range of options for developing conference structures of their own. But also important was Brenda's question, "Think about those conferences; what struck you?" It prompted students to react to the theoretical on a personal level.

What's Going on Here?

> I really believe in a minimalist approach. I think the barebones is best because you really see what people do when left to their own devices. I would really rather see where you go on your own. What really needs to happen is me asking myself, *What's going on here?*
>
> Brenda Power (Field Notes excerpt, 12/7/94)

Once internalized and made a part of the professional consciousness of a teacher, "What's going on here?" is a question that can structure thought and action. It is at the heart of the reflective teaching cycle in which a teacher observes a given student or situation, questions and reflects about what it reveals, and plans and acts accordingly. It is a distinctive feature of the reconceptualized image of teacher. Experience in the classroom has helped me come to know that there is no such comfort as a set of predetermined procedures for teaching. The course of instruction is not predictable or linear, but instead winds its own path as a result of interaction between teacher and student. This ambiguity often frustrates undergraduate students who naturally want answers to their questions. They are accustomed to being given an essential body of information to remember. In many ways a curriculum that *asks* rather than one that *tells* is unsettling. But once they become familiar with those expectations, learning can be personally fulfilling and engaging—a welcome change for many.

Chapter 5

Living in the House: Understanding Curriculum and Course Content

As a beginning college teacher I vowed to help prepare my students to avoid the kinds of pitfalls I experienced my first year as a teacher. I wanted to be certain they understood the tenets of newer theories and practices in the teaching of literacy in their classrooms. I wanted them to be prepared. So, during the weeks prior to the start of class, I made elaborate plans for the semester's curriculum, charting dates and listing specifically what issues, theories, and practices I would cover during each class meeting. I spent hours combing through texts, familiarizing myself with important theories and pedagogy, and planning almost every word of my presentations, which focused on procedures, information, and steps. But my elaborate and time-consuming planning schemes never delivered the results I hoped for. Though I was critical of the lecture as a method of instruction, I could think of few alternatives. So as a researcher in Brenda's literacy methods course I was keenly interested in the method of curriculum and how content was addressed. Specifically I wanted to learn by what means topics, theories, and practices were covered.

Earlier, I compared classroom structures to the structures of a house—they are the fixed, permanent constituents of the classroom routine. They function to provide shape, support, and security. If classroom structures are the physical structure of the house itself, then classroom content is that which exists within its walls. Someone once said, "curriculum is what happens." In this chapter I will describe *what happened* in the methods classroom. I'll describe the method of curriculum used to cover some of the ideas and principles about literacy teaching and learning that served as alternatives to the traditionalist methods, such as the lecture format.

Experience and Course Content

In the previous chapter I looked for different levels of experience in the *classroom structures* data category, identifying what learning occasions were embedded in a context of experience compared to those that were decontextualized, referring to a *distant classroom*. I used the same approach with the data in the "classroom structures" category. As I scanned my notes, I recognized that similar patterns existed. I labeled learning situations having reference points in the context of immediate experience *here and now* (H). I labeled learning situations that bridged an immediate, contextualized experience with a decontextualized, abstract time or place *bridge* (B). I labeled learning events that referred to abstract, decontext-ualized situations *distant classrooms* (C). A look at Figure 5.1 reveals the pattern of content-oriented learning experiences as they occur throughout the methods course. Just as issues of classroom structure had initially been addressed within the context of immediate experience, so had issues of course content. For example, students initially learned about theories of writing development as writers and readers. Content discussions that referred to theoretical issues in composition were initially embedded in the here and now of practicing the craft of writing. Notes which I labeled as "B" or "C" came predominantly toward the latter weeks of the semester. As the semester progressed, instances of decontextualized references to theory and practices occurred more frequently. When theoretical ideas were discussed, they initially referred to immediate experiences, and then gradually to more abstract situations.

Figure 5.1. *Course Content Domain* **(coded by reference to learning context and subcategory)**

B:TH	Content: p. 8.	Bringing classrooms to you
B:TH	Content: p. 8.	Principles of literacy instruction, class discussion, video *Time and Choice*
H:TH	Content: p. 10.	Students' discussions of texts in seminar groups
C:TH	Content: p. 14.	Language parallels
B:TR	Content: pp.15-16.	Emergent literacy: "What does this child know?"
B:TR	Content: p. 16.	Teacher research; Reading Interview
C:M	Content: p 19.	Titles. "Ms." versus "Miss"
H:CR	Content: p. 20.	Flowery writing versus effective writing—good verbs
H:CR	Content: p. 22.	The importance of writing yourself and sharing
H:TR	Content: p. 23.	Reading interview discussions, TR, reasoning out results
B:TR	Content: p. 24.	Harste, Woodward, and Burke (1984) overheads. What does this child know?
C:TH	Content: p. 24.	Invented spelling; content versus spelling (vowel emphasis)

C:TH	Content: p. 25.	Real reading and writing, issue of direct instruction.
H:TR	Content: pp.28-29.	Brenda's model of classifying goals and use for mini-lessons
H:CR	Content: p. 33.	Mechanics problems in papers (minilesson handout)
H:TR	Content: p. 33.	Minilesson based on goals (verbs)
C:TH	Content: p. 35.	Phonics and writing workshop, writing development
B:TR	Content: p. 36.	Phonics (list all sounds you hear child trying)
H:CR	Content: p. 39.	Writing tips; shape of text
H:CR	Content: p. 39.	Topic choice; knowing yourself as writer
H:CR	Content: p. 41.	Judging your audience
C:M	Content: p. 45.	Professional expectations
B:TR	Content: pp. 47-48.	Interviewing pen pals; discussing findings
H:CR	Content: p. 49.	Vocabulary development
H:CR	Content p. 51.	Titles; underlining phrases and group conference
B:TR	Content: p. 54.	What do children know and how would you respond?
H:CR	Content: p. 58.	Pleasure reading; knowing yourself as reader
H:TR	Content: p. 61.	Literature circles activity came from journals; sharing activities
C:CR	Content: p. 59,	Real reading, versus activities
B:TR	Content: pp. 61-62,	Teacher research—home surveys, classroom connections
C:TH	Content: p. 65,	Theories of reading
C:TH	Content: p. 67,	Frustration level of students
C:TH	Content: p. 74,	Curriculum is what happened
C:TH	Content: p. 77,	Ability group discussion
C:TH	Content: p. 77,	Goals for reading
C:TH	Content: pp. 83-4,	Basal discussion, worksheets
B:M	Content: p. 84,	Role plays
C:M	Content: p. 96,	Professional knowledge, tips on inviting speakers
H:M	Content: p. 97,	Comparing their experience (medical school tape)
B:TH	Content: p. 101,	Continuum, identifying beliefs and naming them

It seemed apparent that Brenda was deliberately structuring learning experiences that moved from the concrete to the abstract. When I asked her about the patterns I was seeing, she explained:

> I wasn't really conscious of the move from the concrete to visions of future classrooms, but it makes sense. At the start of the semester, I want students to get involved as quickly as possible with what's happening in the moment in the class. But by the end of the semester, I want them to be thinking about their own classrooms, and developing confidence in their teaching abilities. (personal communication, 4/10/95)

I looked for other themes that would help me understand how Brenda addressed content in the methods course. A second analysis of the data helped me see other patterns. Initially, I looked for ways to categorize content around topical issues in the field of literacy instruction. I had just completed three years of doctoral-level course work. I seemed to see everything in terms of theoretical camps or schools of thought, and I was looking for a pattern in the sequence of topics in this classroom that made sense to me from that perspective. I noticed that different topics came up which could easily be assigned to a range of schools of thought. But they were scattered. For example, situations that could be labeled *reader-response theory* came up frequently, but not in a predictable or linear order. *Teacher as reader/writer* and *writing development* appeared consistently throughout the notes, but again not in a linear or predictable order. There didn't appear to be a thematic structure to the ordering of topical content. So I looked for other explanations that would help explain topic organization.

I scanned the notes I had written in the margins of my data list (see Figure 5.1), and noticed that two subcategories came up frequently—*craft* (CR) and *teacher research* (TR). The first category concerned the presentation of reading or writing theory presented in a context of involvement in the reading or writing process. The second category, *teacher research*, represented situations in which content was addressed in a research-oriented or inquiry-based way. These situations functioned to help students understand theoretical and practical issues of literacy development and instruction. Both categories contained highly contextualized learning experiences in which content was in some way linked to personal experience. These new subcategories could account for most of the "course content" samples. But there were still others that didn't fit my categories. I finally labeled these samples either *theory* (TH), references to theory that were neither craft nor teacher research oriented; or *miscellaneous* (M), examples that didn't fit either category. Finally, after I had analyzed and interpreted all of the data for references to the content categories just described, I discovered another set of situations that were important components of the course curriculum. Students were assigned to write personal narratives of past learning experiences. As well as serving as an opportunity to become self-reflective, this assignment provided an opportunity for every student to hear and respond to the learning stories of their classmates. It helped students better understand their personal biases and challenge mistaken assumptions about teaching and learning. Thus, the process of writing, sharing, and critiquing these stories served as another component of the curriculum.

In this chapter I will explore the theme of curriculum and course content using the categories of *craft*, *teacher research*, and *autobiography*. These pedagogical approaches can be understood as representative of a reconceptualized literacy methods curriculum.

They involve students in a continual process of construction and reconstruction of ideas and concepts that help constitute the curriculum. The methods course curriculum is not technical or linear, established by outside authority such as the instructor, the college of education, or a textbook publisher. It is unique and individual, emerging and evolving as the instructor responds to the immediate needs and concerns of students. Thus, like other examples of reconceptualized curriculum, it emphasizes the experience of the individual—the student—over a more formal, predetermined curriculum. As Graham (1992) writes, "it acknowledges the student's search for meaning as an interactive and reflective process undertaken in a social milieu" (p. 27). I will describe how the process of engaging in the craft of writing or the experience of reading provided a context of involvement for the methods students that helps them explore the content of literacy instruction. Next, I'll describe the teacher research activities that involved students in a process of active construction of concepts and ideas. In the final section of this chapter I will explore how self study and autobiographical inquiry helped students reconstruct existing notions about teaching.

The Importance of Practicing
What You Will Eventually Teach: Exploring Craft

> Anyone who studies an instrument, sport, or other art form must deal with practice, experiment, and training. We learn only by doing. There is a gigantic difference between the projects we imagine doing or plan to do and the ones we actually do... [W]e are inevitably taken aback by the effort and patience needed in the realization. A person may have great creative proclivities, glorious inspirations, and exalted feelings, but there is no creativity unless creations actually come into existence.
>
> (Stephen Nachmanovitch 1990, p. 66)

I thought I must have misunderstood when after I attended my first doctoral-level graduate course I was told I would be required to write a one-page, single-spaced paper and bring enough copies to distribute to my classmates each week. Surely, I thought, I must have misunderstood. I called the professor, "...and the one-page paper...is that just for this next class?" Brenda responded, "No, you need to do one of those for each class." I was stricken with fear. Writing a full page that all of my classmates would read?!? Dropping the course had entered my mind, but in spite of the weekly assignment, I decided to tough it out. Initially, I found the weekly writing extremely difficult. Each week I rushed to finished the assigned reading days before class so I would have enough time to compose a meaningful and articulate response, or at least one I wouldn't be ashamed to share. But, as time went by, I gained confidence and skill as a writer. After a year of practice I could whip off a pithy response in a matter of minutes. As a direct result of writing practice, my writing skills have greatly improved. I can now capture my thoughts more efficiently and forcefully on paper. Not only have my writing skills improved, but my ability to communicate with other writers about the writing process has improved as well. Consequently, I feel more competent and confident as a teacher of writing composition and instruction. This principle, the importance of teachers being writers, is described by Ruth Nathan.

> Authors understand that advice, while necessary, must be given at the right time and by a trusted individual. Because this is so, it is essential that you write if you are going to be a good writing teacher. It doesn't really matter that you write well; that's almost (but not totally) irrelevant. What does matter is that you attempt to write something well, and then that you read your draft to someone else. In other words, practice putting yourself on the line. It is knowing how a writer feels when a piece is shared, the chemical twang, the wildly beating heart, the mental involvement, the "I'm out there and feeling vulnerable" sensations that you must comprehend if you want to do a decent teaching job. (1991, p. 19)

Brenda shares this excerpt with her students on the first day of class, explaining that it is sometimes hard to share writing with others, and that kids experience insecurity too. Then she explains how students should discuss their work, underlining the part they liked and discussing that part with the group.

Teachers who write regularly know the writing craft well enough to give good feedback, and students need good feedback about their writing in order to improve. They need to have the weaknesses and strengths in their writing specifically pointed out so that they can make necessary modifications. This is a little piece of conventional wisdom that has been backed by empirical research findings in educational psychology. When teachers provide explicit and specific feedback about student performance, learners experience stronger motivation, and consequently greater success (Wiener, 1986). In these cases, students are better able to identify the things that they are doing well in order to continue them, and to understand their weaknesses in order to change them. Writing teachers who are one with the pen are naturally going to understand more intuitively the demands inherent in teaching writing to their students.

When a writing teacher is herself a writer, she will be less inclined to trivialize the writing process by imposing a series of artificial steps on her students. I'll illustrate my point with a story. The summer before I began my first teaching job, I read Lucy Calkins's book, *The Art of Teaching Writing*. That fall, just before school began, I hung a chart on the bulletin board in back of the room that described the writing process I had read about the previous summer. My chart was impressive—colorful, well illustrated, explicit, and laminated. In bold letters on the top of the chart I wrote "The Writing Process." Below that heading I listed the steps in composing a piece of writing: (a) brainstorm, (b) draft, (c)revise, (d) edit, and (e) publish.

I didn't know it then, but I was starting backwards. I didn't realize that I needed to allow my students to inform me of their writing processes, and by taking their lead, help them develop more efficient writing strategies. I couldn't have known that at the time. For one thing, I didn't know enough about how children learn. But also, I didn't write enough myself to know there was a problem with my approach. I had only a superficial understanding of workshop structure and someone else's advice on how to teach writing. Consequently, I imposed artificial structure onto the writing process, and I expected my students to follow the "writing process steps." Donald Graves recalls overhearing two teachers who resemble me in my first year of teaching.

> Set steps are the bane of my existence. I once overheard two teachers speaking, "Do you use the six step or seven step Graves?" I about croaked. Unfortunately, I am sympathetic to their predicament. This is what happens when something like process work gets mandated and teachers have no chance to be prepared...by actually doing the writing. Writing is an art form and if there is no chance to work in a studio then paint-by-the-numbers is the end product. (Personal communication, 1/29/95).

Brenda recognizes the need her students have to work in a literacy studio so they won't fall into teaching patterns that resemble a "paint-by-the-numbers" approach. Brenda trusts that her students will become more sophisticated readers, writers, and response givers as the course proceeds. It is the sophisticated, self-aware knowledge of the writing process that is an invaluable asset to the successful writing teacher. A familiarity with the writing process is essential in order to be able to provide students with the kind of instruction and feedback necessary for growth. Once students became accustomed to the routine of writing and responding, they were free to make their own decisions. While some structures remained, such as minilessons, response groups, and large group sharing, sequences and patterns of writing and responding developed according to the needs of individual writers. The freedom to write and respond as one pleased was intentional. Brenda wanted her students to learn to know themselves as readers and writers. After the methods students became comfortable with the regular routines, their individual and group working processes shaped and defined the workshop.

For most people, the actual writing process can be frustrating, difficult, hard work. As Brenda explained, "I don't necessarily *like* writing; but I love to have written something." But if a writer knows her personal process of composition well enough, she will be more confident that some reward will come as a result of the hard work and frustration of wrestling words to the page. In developing this kind of powerful self-awareness, there is no substitute for plenty of practice. Trust in the writing process only comes through the experience of writing. I discovered this when I examined the results of a teacher-research survey of my kindergarten and first-grade students several years ago that confirmed writing time to be the overwhelming favorite, outranking recess and gym class! Even college students, many of whom have been conditioned to dread the act of writing, can develop confidence, skill, and a positive attitude toward writing. Through the routines that support writing in the methods class, students have an opportunity to play with the pen while they develop self-awareness of their writing process, and with ample practice most students eventually learn to love the pen. No one says it better than Louise.

[I] would have to say that the most important thing that I have learned in this class, is how to write.

Before I took this class I knew how to write, but I never liked it because I didn't think I was very good at it. Writing was nothing but a dreaded assignment to me. I could never think of anything clever to write, I didn't think I was creative.

On the first day of class we got to write without censoring ourselves! I had never been told to write like that before. It was really easy for me to sit down and write exactly what was on my mind, and within a short fifteen minutes I had written almost a whole page! Usually it takes me more like an hour to write that much. I have learned to write what you feel and think and not worry about it until after you are done with the piece...

Now I look forward to writing. Never did I think that while taking a class to teach children how to write or write better, would I learn how to write better myself. This class has made me open my mind to the writing process, and see that it is not something to be feared, but something to be enjoyed. Everyone can write something wonderful if they try, even me. You don't have to be Shakespeare.

(Final Paper, Louise Wilkins)

Exploring Craft

The glibness with which I go into a classroom with students to respond to complicated papers disappears when I have my own experience of struggling with my own text.

(Dixie Goswami in Gillespie, 1994, p. 96).

For students of all ages, writing is often seen as an elusive activity that's shrouded in an impenetrable mystique. With this perception, it is understandable that a resistance toward the writing process develops. "I'm a terrible writer," is a statement I've heard countless times from elementary and college students alike. The literacy workshops were nonthreatening, low-stress opportunities for students to explore the craft of writing. Issue by issue, students were helped to penetrate the writing mystique. Each day practical strategies and pieces of conventional wisdom about writing made their way into the collective conversation. For example, on the first day of class, after the freewrite which took place after the small groups finished discussing their writing, Brenda facilitated this discussion.

Field Notes excerpt, 9/7/95

Brenda: What was that like for you, first as a writer?

Student: I kept drifting

Student: Trying to remember the experience right was difficult.

Brenda: A tip from journalism. If you can't remember a word or a date, just put "TK" into the text. That's your signal to come back later.

Student: I couldn't think of much when I was drawing the map. But when I started writing I had a lot to say about the outside of my house, rather than the inside.

Brenda: Getting started writing causes you to be surprised by what you write.

Student: [The] more I got started, it just came.

Brenda: What about the experience of reading to the others in your group?

Student: My piece sounded really repetitive at the beginning.

Brenda: A lot of time the first section is the weakest. In terms of physics, it takes lots of energy to get started—to break the inertia. It takes much more energy to get a system in motion than it does to keep it going. Revising the beginning is hardest because it's hardest to start. And it's usually the worst writing. Sometimes it's best to throw it out.

Student: I didn't think I said anything. The response I got helped me see the good in it.

Brenda: Gertrude Stein said writers don't need any more critics. They need support. What was it like giving response?

Student: One image evokes my own memories. [It was] hard to focus on the rest of the piece of writing being read to me after that.

Brenda: To help if you space out on a conference [you can say] "tell me more about that."

[Every day there will be an] optional whole-class share. Would anyone like to read to the class?

Student: I will if you let me into the class (a student who wasn't enrolled and wanted permission to join).

Brenda: OK, Nothing like a bribe!

(Student read her piece about her memory of having her hair washed by her mother)

Brenda: [It's] always optional to read to the whole class. But I challenge you to do this. As a teacher you need to take risks.

We'll start Monday with writing workshop. 'Till then, work on this piece or another topic by adding to it, deleting parts or starting from scratch. A few papers are due in this class. Unlike other writing, these papers are short, two- to three-page papers. The point isn't to write two to three pages and stop. You could do that in an evening. But the point is to work your way through revisions.

During that brief writing share, Brenda covered substantial content. Writing tips, teaching strategies, and theories about teaching and learning were offered within the active context of the writing response groups. Brenda used the large-group writing share time to introduce theory as well as practical applications of composition theory. The principles covered in the writing share segment of the first class are listed in Figure 5.2. Mistakenly holistic approaches are criticized because they fail to cover skills as efficiently as more traditional approaches. But as this table illustrates, experience-based learning, in this case the experience of practicing the craft of writing, skills, and other content are addressed.

Figure 5.2. Content Covered During "Writing Share"

- A tip from journalism, inserting TK when you can't think of a word helps the writer maintain the flow of ideas.
- Just getting started, even if you don't have a clear idea of what you want to say, is a strategy to arrive at a focus for writing (Murray, 1991).
- Initial writing is often weak and needs to be sacrificed. But it was important nonetheless, for its function in contributing to what you eventually do end up saying (Dillard, 1989).
- Use the "tell me" strategy to initiate a discussion over a text you are having difficulty finding a connection with (Chambers, 1985).
- Taking the lead from the writer is important (Graves, 1983).
- The importance of risk taking as a teacher (Nathan, 1991).

Brenda used minilessons as a means to offer her students tips and strategies to help them improve the essential qualities of their writing. The minilesson was briefly discussed in chapter 2, and a list of minilesson topics appears in Figure 2.4. In this section I will explain in greater detail how issues of the writing craft were addressed in the methods course through minilessons and large-group discussions.

The Lead

> It is the beginning of a work that the writer throws away... A painting covers its tracks. Painters work from the ground up. The latest version of a painting overlays earlier versions, and obliterates them. Writers, on the other hand, work from left to right. The discardable chapters are on the left. The latest version of a literary work begins somewhere in the work's middle, and hardens toward the end. The earlier version remains lumpishly on the left; the work's beginning greets the reader with the wrong hand.
>
> (Annie Dillard, 1989, p. 5)

Writing a good lead can be a challenge. The writer often has a strong sense of what she wants to say, but first drafts are usually the worst. And, inevitably, the first try fails to meet expectations. Writing good leads requires experience and wherewithal. On the second day of class, Brenda began writer's workshop with a minilesson (Calkins, 1986) on leads. She explained:

Field Notes excerpt, 9/12/95

Brenda: I want to talk for five to ten minutes about your lead. Think about different ways to start out your piece. I want to talk about different models. Ways to start a piece in order to give it punch. (Brenda read a lead from a former student's piece which had a lead with dialogue.) One of the most powerful ways to start a piece is with dialog.

[In] the circular lead [the] beginning connects to the end. "Two cars collide at a rapid speed" (the beginning of the lead from the piece she had just read) repeated at the end. Take [the] climax and put [it] right at the start—rework from there. I suggest that you look at the lead and see what you can cut out.

Brenda read the lead of "A Paper on a Paper," by Jane Campbell (1993), which appears below. Then she explained how the author had rewritten the lead based on feedback she had gotten from the teacher and her writing response group.

> And the professor said, "Write about what you notice in the literature, what surprises you, intrigues you, puzzles or frustrates you, what you like or dislike, what is good or bad. Write about what engages you. Relax and enjoy it. Your four-page essay will be due on Friday. Have fun. On Monday I eagerly read the assigned novel. "

Using Good Verbs On Monday, September 19, 1994, Brenda began writer's workshop with a minilesson on the importance of strong verbs in good writing. Her presentation follows.

Field Notes excerpt, 9/19/94, p. 20

> Brenda: I want to talk for a few minutes about what makes writing good... Lots of times students who have been "good" writers have lots of *flowery* language. [We are] taught to improve writing by adding words, adjectives and adverbs. What does [good writing] have? [The] difference is verbs. Good writing has good verbs. Ask yourself, are there any adjectives you could eliminate? Then circle your verbs and find out if you could change them. If there are lots of *was*, *were*, [or] *is*, see if you can find some more grabbing. If you can use a distinctive word for a verb, that's what will catch your reader.

Challenges are embedded into the stream of activities and involvement of writing workshop. One such challenge occurred during the sixth class meeting as Brenda gave a minilesson that centered on a writing strategy intended to help develop strong language. It began with a few minutes of drama. Brenda stood at the front of the class, writing something on the board. Abruptly, she turned to the class and complained angrily, "You guys just never listen!" She threw the eraser on the floor and stormed out of the room, slamming the door behind her. The class was astonished and bewildered. After several seconds one of the students got up to answer a knock at the door. Brenda reappeared, smiling. "Can I come back in?," she asked. After the contrived outburst Brenda asked the class to describe what they had just witnessed as she wrote their observations on the board. She instructed the class to read their observations, paying close attention to the verbs that carry sentences. Within that context she challenged her students to focus on using strong verbs in their own writing.

Field Notes excerpt, 9/26/94

> Brenda: A week ago I talked about verbs. Look at how the verbs carry these sentences (Brenda circled the verbs). Spend a few minutes freewriting. [Here is a] challenge: Can you capture the images using strong verbs? If you pick something that peters out after a few minutes, go on to something else. Take about ten minutes.

Mechanics During the class after the first set of papers were due, Brenda presented the class with a "Mechanics Minilessons" handout, featured in Figure 5.3 below. She compiled the contents based on the problems she had seen in the papers her students had submitted. Before she distributed the handout, Brenda explained that too often teachers spend too much time commenting on and addressing mechanics issues in papers, and that takes attention from the more worthwhile response on the content of papers. She explained that she found it was better to look globally at mechanics issues and address them in the whole-class context. This process of observing and assessing the work of students and using that information to inform instruction is an example of teacher-research oriented, or inquiry-based instruction, which will be discussed in the next section of this chapter.

Figure 5.3. Mechanics MiniLessons Handout

Mechanics Minilessons

These are grammatical, spelling, or mechanical problems that were in many of the papers I looked at this week. Most of you had at least one of them in your paper. I expect you to master them all by the time you write your next paper, so read carefully and save this sheet for reference when the next paper is due.

1. It's/Its

This is a tricky convention that students have trouble understanding. *It's* isn't the possessive form of the word. *Its* is. Correct use—"The dog wagged its tail." An easy way to remember this one—you should always be able to substitute the contraction "It's" for "It is." If you can't substitute "it is" when you use "it's," you've used the wrong form. For example, "The dog wagged it's tail" couldn't be read "The dog wagged it is tail." So...the correct form must be "its."

2. Quotes at the End of Sentences

Quotation marks go outside of the periods at the end of a sentence, or commas in a sentence, no matter how bad it looks to the naked eye. See the end of the sentence above that ends with "its." This isn't true for sentences that end with question marks or exclamation points. Examples: The correct form must be "its." The correct form must be "its"? The correct form must be "its"!

3. Definitely/Definately/Defanitely

The all-time favorite misspelled word of college students. There is no "a" in definitely.

4. Hyphens for Modifiers

Two words together modifying another noun should be hyphenated. But when they appear alone, you don't hyphenate them. Example: A first-grade classroom. But if you're talking about teaching first grade, no hyphen.

5. Split Infinitives

Have you ever wondered what one is? An infinitive is a verb with "to" before it—"to love," "to teach" are infinitives. There is a rule in many grammar books that says you can't "split" these, which means to put a word between "to" and the verb. "To truly love" is an example of the dreaded split infinitives. This is a silly rule—it dates back centuries ago to the time when rules of Latin were applied to English to gussy the language up. You can't split an infinitive in Latin (they are one word), but to not split them in English leads to some awkward writing. "To split them not" is what the grammar police would want. Split infinitives are fine with me, but you might want to be aware of the rule if you're challenged someday about it by a parent or administrator. Dazzle them with your knowledge of the Latin roots of the rules imposed on our Germanic language, and they should be impressed. (Power 9/94)

The Structure of Text. Every piece of text has a shape. The more a writer is aware of the shape her text is taking, or the shape she wants her text to take, the more effective the piece. Brenda discussed the issues of text shapes in the following writing workshop minilesson.

Field Notes excerpt, 9/28/95, p. 39

Brenda: I'm going to talk to you about what you can do when you get stuck in your writing. The book I have is *The Literary Journalist*, by Norman Sims. [It explains] about how many journalists are using literary devices. News writing is now just as creative as other kinds of writing. [This particular part is] about how [writer] John McPhee finds a shape in his writing. The passage is about the structure of text...how the text's shape influences the text.

Brenda read an excerpt from Sims's (1984) *The Literary Journalist*, a part of which is excerpted in the following quote. Sims narrates a conversation he had with writer John McPhee:

> "The piece of writing has a structure inside it," he said. "It begins, goes along somewhere, and ends in a manner that is thought out beforehand. I always know the last line of a story before I've written the first one. Going through all that creates the form and the shape of the thing. It also relieves the writer, once you know the structure, to concentrate each day on one thing. You know right where it fits...."
>
> McPhee rummaged around in a file cabinet for a moment and came up with a diagram of the structure in "Travels in Georgia." It looked like a lowercase "e."
>
> "It's a simple structure, a reassembled chronology. . . I went [to Georgia] to write about a woman who, among other things, picks up dead animals off the road and eats them. There's an immediate problem when you begin to consider such material. The editor of *The New Yorker* is practically a vegetarian... That served a purpose, pondering what a general reader's reaction would be. When people think of animals killed on the road, there's an immediate putrid whiff that goes by them. The image is pretty automatic—smelly and repulsive. These animals we were picking up off the road were not repulsive. They had not been mangled up. They were not bloody. They'd been freshly killed. So I had to get this story off the ground without offending the sensibilities of the reader and the editor."
>
> McPhee and his friends ate several animals during the journey, such as a weasel, a muskrat, and, somewhere well along in the trip, a snapping turtle. But the piece *begins* with the snapping turtle. Turtle soup offends less than roasted weasel (p. 13–14).

Then Brenda continues the discussion of text structure.

> Brenda: One of the things I do when I don't know where a piece of text goes is [to consider] the shape of the piece. We've already talked about how the circular ending ...[it] gives the reader the illusion that things are all neatly tied up. The chapter I'm writing...the first line is "Teaching begins with love..." but it's an academic piece and I run the risk of turning people off. So I add, in the first paragraph, "a love of structure, a love of response, a love of surprise..." A lot of writers go for straight line chronology. If you're stuck and don't know where to go, think about whether there's a geometric shape you could work your piece around.

Vocabulary Development One of my all-time favorite high-school classes was a course on word etymology. I love learning new words and having at the tip of my tongue or pen exactly the right word to express my precise meaning. Part of being a good writer is being able retrieve just the right word at the time you need it. This is a minilesson activity that focused on vocabulary development. Notice how the students contributed to the content of the lesson, rather than it following one that stems from a formal or official curriculum such as an English textbook or handbook.

Field Notes excerpt, 10/5/95

Brenda: I wanted to talk a little bit about developing vocabulary and what you need to do. That was a big point in many of your papers. It would be great if we as writers [could] take this little portion of time in writer's workshop and open up your thesaurus and make you language richer. Writers love words—love using them, thinking about them, and learning more of them. What I'd like to do is share how I learned one new word ten years ago. Then we'll hear from you.

The first article I sent out for publication came back rejected. I was crying as I read the rejection. And to make it worse, there were many words I didn't know in the rejection letter—one was "smarmy." I looked it up and it meant *sickeningly sweet in an artificial way.* Think of a word you like. Think about why you like it, where you learned it, where you heard it first. Anybody? (Brenda wrote the words and definitions on chart paper as they were offered.)

Student: lackadaisical—[At] the football game against BU (Boston University). The BU coaches were saying, "Don't be so lackadaisical." I thought those Boston players must be smart!

Dave: Loquacious—Very, very talkative.

Brenda: How'd you pick up that one?

Dave: I was reading the dictionary. I used to look for big words.

Student: Bold/boldness.

Cathy: Paradigm. I remember the first time I heard it, I had trouble pronouncing it. It's used a lot. More or less, philosophies, shifting of perspectives.

Brenda: Shift in belief systems. Shows up a lot in education.

Student: Vagabond. My parents would read it to me in fairy tales. It means bum.

Student: Altruism.

Brenda: Who knows what it means?

Janice: Selflessness, caring for others.

Brian: Obsequiously.

Kirsten: I think of obsequious—kissing up. Subtle, manipulative.

Gwen: Veneration

Brenda: What does that mean?

Gwen: To worship—more than just follow. To take what that person does as the final word.

Student: A teacher said my paper was "pithy."

Brenda: I like that.

Student: It means to the point or focused.

Brenda: What I'd like you to do is listen, and learn a new word in context. See if you can't learn one new word. If that doesn't work for you, see if you can't learn some of these words (pointing to words on the chart paper) and learn it in context. Bring those new words in next Monday.

Being writers and taking part in the writing workshop helped the methods students understand the relationship between writing mechanics and writing development. Kirsten explains how she sees her role in addressing grammar in the teaching process.

> I understand that grammar will fit into this process, and it's just that, a process. I am free to teach a minilesson on what I feel is important and what I think is essential for the majority of my students at that particular time in their writing. Worksheets don't need to be distributed and the students don't have to practice their grammar through repetition. They will be able to use their new-found rule of grammar in their writing. Experiment—that's what we want them to do; we learn through our own mistakes better than someone else's. (Final paper, Kirsten Peters)

The Experience of Reading

As a fifth-grade teacher, I used to take my students to the library each week. Our school cafeteria doubled as the library, and one of the office assistants had long ago assumed the role of librarian. In the library, children's literature was housed in shelves along one wall, and adolescent literature along another wall. During one of our class visits, a struggling fifth-grade reader found a picture book he wanted to take out. When he lined up to have it checked out, the librarian sternly told him, "What are you doing with that? That's a baby book. Put it back and get another." I was speechless and didn't know how to react to her comment. I knew that this particular boy needed high-interest, low difficulty books in order to motivate him and boost his confidence as a reader. He had made a good selection. The librarian's comment revealed her understanding that reading materials that are too easy for pleasure do not serve an educational purpose. Like many people who belong to the *no pain, no gain* school of conventional wisdom, she seemed to believe that a task must be difficult in order to promote learning. Most methods students have come up through an educational system in which most teachers hold similar beliefs. This is one example of an assumption Brenda encourages her students to challenge. Learning about oneself as a reader and writer often means challenging long-held assumptions about what is good or bad in terms of learning. Brenda touched on this issue with her students during an integrated literacy workshop.

Field Notes excerpt, 10/17/95

Brenda: For our morning workshop I'd like you to take time to either write—work on a draft, a letter to a friend, or [work on a] to-do list. Or, you can do some reading. You can really read anything you'd like...magazine, novel...but there's one kind of reading I'd like you not to do and that's textbook reading. Really try to use this time to read the kind of material you don't normally get to...like a novel you were reading over the summer.

The argument shouldn't be simplified to the point where preservice teachers begin to think that difficulty is necessarily bad. In one respect there are elements of the no pain, no gain perspective that are valid and need to be explored with students. For example, according to instructional methods of the Reading Recovery program, the difficulty level of a text is of central importance in relation to reading development. For example, if a child is reading at an accuracy rate between 90 and 95 percent, the material is within her instructional range (meaning that there are sufficient challenges to promote learning without interfering with comprehension). If the accuracy level is lower, the material is too difficult; if the accuracy level is higher than 95 percent, it is an appropriate book for independent reading (Smith and Elley, 1994). The point is that children need plenty of opportunities during the school day to do a range of types of reading, from instructional to independent.

This point was discussed in the course during the analysis of a home reading survey (an activity that will be explored in greater detail in the next section of this chapter within the discussion of teacher research). Comments from this discussion are particularly relevant here because they address the importance of expanding the quantity of time during school when children are reading.

Field Notes excerpt, 10/17/95

Brenda: [T]he literature tells us that reading is reading. The more you read the better you'll read. It really doesn't matter if you're reading *Time Magazine* or Shakespeare, as long as you are engaged with the text. What matters is the quality of the experience, not whether it's on the top of the classic literature list. You should see some of the junk I read . . .and I do it with pleasure!

We'll look at the difference between reading for information versus reading for pleasure. Sometimes those activities can take the pleasure out of the experience. It doesn't matter how good the activity is, if you always expect an assignment will follow the reading, you take the enjoyment out of it. It's important to include opportunities to read for pleasure, without assignments, in your school day.

[O]ne of the issues I mentioned already [is that] in traditional basal programs research shows that reading [takes place for] two to seven minutes [a day]. One of the ideas behind the use of real books is that real reading does go on. But when you go into some of the classes that are whole language or literature-based, there is still so much emphasis on activities. Think about keeping reading a priority. [Ask yourself] Are you still keeping in mind your top priority...lots of reading and writing by your students?

Teacher Research:
Learning the Art of Classroom Inquiry

The reality of the classroom world out there—how my students perceive it—is different from my mental construction of classroom reality. Acting solely on my understanding of classroom issues and concerns—the reality in here—may eliminate the possibility of finding the best course of action. Learning doesn't necessarily occur because I have presented a concept to a group of students. Rather, learning consists in what meaning each individual student made of the presentation or activity. The better I can understand my students' meaning constructions, and the degree to which I can build subsequent action upon that understanding, the better I reach students. In teaching I need to take deliberate steps to read the classroom world from the multiple perspectives of my students in the most accurate terms possible. Brenda shares this perspective, and sees the value of teacher research in helping teachers to develop self-reflective, inquiry-based instructional practices. She shares her thoughts with students.

> One of the things I believe in is teachers being researchers in their own classrooms. The model has been university researchers going into classes and collecting information and then telling teachers what's going on. The new model is that teachers are in the best place to explain what goes on in their classrooms. Part of my job at the university is to help you become better at researching your classrooms as teachers.
>
> (Brenda Power, Field Notes excerpt, 9/14/94)

Brenda's statement reflects her belief that teachers are in the best position to explain and understand their students' learning.

She sees one aspect of her role as a teacher educator as that of helping future teachers acquire the skill and competence necessary to become researchers of their own classrooms.

Teacher research is quickly becoming a widespread, grassroots movement. It is gaining credibility and respect among the traditional educational research foundations and organizations. The names of teachers are beginning to appear alongside university researchers in professional convention programs from organizations such as the National Council of Teachers of English (NCTE), the International Reading Association (IRA), and the American Educational Research Association (AERA). And teachers are asserting their voices and being heard in all manner of professional journals. Teacher research can be understood as both research methodology and progressive pedagogy, which offers a solution to the dichotomy to which Hullfish and Smith (1961) refer.

> On the one hand, the teacher is encouraged to study the psychology of learning and thus become more scientific in his [sic] teaching. On the other hand, it appears that the more scientific the psychological study of learning becomes, the more tenuous become its connections with the problems the teacher actually confronts. What is the teacher to do? What is needed, of course, is a theory of education (including a theory of learning) that will enable the teacher to continue to engage in the art of teaching, using the lore of the profession in a more consciously reflective manner. (p. 171)

Though written over three decades ago, their appeal is particularly relevant today. It's a compelling justification for teacher research as an answer to the theory/practice dichotomy that many teachers face. Teacher researchers pose their own questions concerning classroom issues, seek answers, and base their instructional processes on that cycle of inquiry. Curriculum arises from teachers' personal insights and those are based on observations and subsequent consideration of individual students in the classroom. Given her belief that teachers should be making decisions about what is taught in the classroom, Brenda is committed to helping future teachers acquire research tools and the ability to use them. Much of the content of the methods course is covered through involvement in data collection and analysis activities.

Brenda uses research techniques in the methods class as a vehicle to access course content. By asking her students to become inquirers, seeking out answers to their own questions, they are engaged in the dual acts of learning teacher research as both a pedagogy and as a means to explore literacy instructional theory.

Theoretical Tenets of Teacher Research Teacher research is built on a long tradition of educational philosophy. Dewey (1933) illuminated some of the principles of thoughtful teaching. He believed teachers needed to be reflective, basing their actions not on habits, routines, and educational traditions, but on their own more flexible, responsive approach to teaching, which is based on personal observations and conclusions. He wrote:

> [R]eflection implies that something is believed in (or disbelieved in), not on its own direct account, but through something else which stands as witness, evidence, proof, voucher, warrant; that is, as ground of belief. (p. 11)

> [A]long with noting the conditions that constitute the facts to be dealt with, suggestions arise of possible courses of action. (p. 103)

Dewey (1933) emphasized the need for a teacher to base her actions on a "ground" of belief. These beliefs should consist of ideas that are formed through classroom observations. Dewey (1933) explains:

> A technical term for the observed facts is data. The data form the material that has to be interpreted, accounted for, explained; or, in the case of deliberation as to what to do or how to do it, to be managed and utilized. The suggested solutions for the difficulties disclosed by observation form ideas. Data (facts) and ideas (suggestions, possible solutions) thus form the two indispensable and correlative factors of all reflective activity. The two factors are carried on by means respectively of observation (in which for convenience is included memory of prior observations of similar cases) and inference. (p. 104)

For Dewey, the collection and analysis of data help a teacher form ideas that help solve specific instructional problems.

Closely linked to Dewey's notion of reflective practice is the classroom-based, action-research movement. A leader in this movement, Lawrence Stenhouse, argued that teachers should be researchers of their own practice and should develop the curriculum through methods of their own inquiry (Pollard and Tann, 1987). He emphasized the potential for classroom-based teacher research to keep schools dynamic and viable institutions. Stenhouse (1985) wrote, "The improvement of schooling is bound to be experimental: it cannot be dogmatic. The experiment depends on the exercise of the art of teaching and improves the art" (p. 69). Viewed through the framework of reflective teaching or classroom-based action research, teaching is an act of artistic experimentation—it involves thinking, risk taking, improvising, hypothesizing, and exercising intuition.

Teacher research borrows many of its practices from the field of qualitative research. In fact, in their book *The Art of Classroom Inquiry*, Brenda Power and Ruth Hubbard (1993) include many strategies for data collection, research design, and data analysis that are borrowed from the body of literature on qualitative research. In the field of qualitative research, the researcher develops theories that are grounded in relation to observations of the culture under study. Teacher research methods parallel ethnographic research but are characterized by one important distinction: Teacher research builds grounded theory and puts it to immediate use. A teacher researcher uses emerging theory to change or modify instructional practice and practical classroom activity.

Brenda included a range of activities in the curriculum that enabled students to participate in the reflective cycle that are similar to the one illustrated above. She believes and future teachers must experience the inquiry process before they will be successful teacher researchers in their own classrooms. Below are some approaches she used in the methods course that involved research steps, including collecting and analyzing data, and making instructional decisions.

Learning to "Play" with Data Like great scientists, competent teacher researchers have a talent for analyzing data. Biologist Gary Lynch explains, "[I] love to pore over the data...I just sit there and analyze it this way and that. Graph it this way, graph it that way. I can sit with data for hours, just as happy as can be" (in Johnson, 1991, p. 28).

Louis Pasteur's skill in drawing and his keen observation skills were factors that contributed to his ability to do scientific work (John-Steiner, 1985). As it is in science, so it is in the field of teacher research. The first step in being able to implement assessment-based instruction in the classroom is being comfortable analyzing data. When I enrolled in my first research course and was told I would have to collect and analyze data, *tedious* was the word that came to mind. But it was a required course, and I persevered. As it turned out, the data I ended up collecting were the writing topic lists from my kindergarten writing workshop and notes about topic choice from interviews with my students. The analysis involved looking for patterns and relationships among my kindergarten students' writing topics. Data collection and analysis had turned out to be fascinating. By the end of the course, the data collection and analysis processes that I had so dreaded invigorated my teaching.

Gathering, organizing, and making meaning from classroom data is a process Brenda wants her students to feel comfortable with. She hopes they will see the research process as a way to develop their teaching. In the methods course, students began analyzing data on the fourth class meeting. Previously they had been given a handout, "Burke Interview Questions" (Weaver, 1988), and were asked to interview three people. The Burke interview is used by classroom teachers to provide baseline information about their students. It is a helpful tool for teachers to use because it helps get at students' beliefs about the reading process. In class, students cut their completed interviews and divided them into categories according to question number. After each group was assigned a different interview question, Brenda gave the students some initial guidance in the data analysis process.

Field Notes excerpt, 9/14/95

Brenda: Look at all of this data and see if you can organize it into different categories. For example, can someone read me a question?

Student: "Who is a good reader you know?"

Brenda: OK. You might find that some say their mother, so that might be a category. But you might find that people also name other family members, and that might become a category.

What I want you to do is put them into categories. See if you can take all this information and see if you can come up with at least four categories. If you just have two, then the categories are probably too broad. You might have a few that don't fit anywhere. Those can be a miscellaneous category. Then see if you can sketch out the categories graphically. This might be a bar chart or a pie chart. How can you take these responses and represent what our culture says about reading. It's a real messy exercise. And that's the way classrooms are. It's never really neat.

Are there any questions about what I just said? I'll be going around anyway.

(The groups worked for about twenty minutes organizing and charting their data.)

Brenda: If your group finishes, we're going to meet as a whole group at five after 11:00, so you can take a break.

We're gonna talk about this on Monday—what you learned about reading, but also what you learned about your own group process.

On Monday, September 19, during the next class, the students discussed their findings from the Burke data analysis project. This discussion took place.

Field Notes excerpt, 9/19/95

Brenda: Was it hard to come up with categories?

Student: No.

Brenda: What about the responses themselves? Were there things that surprised you?

Student: Yes, "Is there anything you'd like to do better?" Most said "no."

Brenda: Yea, I was in your group when you discussed that. It's sort of like when you ask someone, "What would you like to do better in your waterskiing?" Unless they value the activity, they will probably not be able to think of ways they would improve—they may not want to improve. Any other responses that surprised you?

Student: Yes, number of males who were good readers was significantly lower than the number of women.

Brenda: Why?

Student: Number of mothers that read to children and the fact that most teachers are women.

Brenda: Yeah, I'd say so. More boys are referred for special services in early grades. Also, whenever there is such a clear difference in terms of gender it's important to look deeper. Other responses?

Student: What would you do to help reader. What I thought was strange was there were only two who said "Make the reading fun."

Brenda: But if it's true that only 15 percent of our culture enjoys reading, then it would make sense that so few would believe it's fun.

Student: For ours the question was "how did you learn to read?" Some of us still feel that until we can read a complete sentence."

Brenda: The definition of reading for most folks is that you can pick up a book and read it. At the end of this semester you'll have a much richer idea about the definition of teaching. You can do an activity like this with your students. Like with spelling, have them go back to the home and interview parents and others in order to find out what some of the beliefs are about spelling.

The Burke interview helped students explore the cultural significance of reading and why it is or isn't valued in our culture. The students had an opportunity to explore the potential meaning of interview responses and were guided to think about what implications those meanings have on reading instruction in the classroom. The importance of this exercise in helping students define their beliefs about the reading process came up as a personal issue for me in my notes.

Field Notes excerpt, 9/14/95

PN: The Burke analysis project itself is one that prompts students to examine cultural assumptions about reading and the reading process. It helps these students become more critical about the beliefs that drive their practices.

Throughout the course, students had opportunities to make sense of many sources of information. Brenda took the role of guide during those processes, helping her students find a starting place for the analysis process, offering strategies for sorting and organizing, and insights for meaning making.

During the fifth class meeting, Brenda prompted her students to consider goals they had for themselves and their groups during the course of the semester. This process was discussed in chapter 4 as an element of classroom structures. Once students had listed their individual and group goals on the board, Brenda enlisted their feedback in identifying categories. The goals that the methods students listed became the curriculum. Topics for subsequent minilessons were identified through this process. Brenda makes the connection between curriculum and assessment clear when she says, "[This exercise] will help me as a teacher. I know I wanted to work on minilessons over the next few months, and this will really help" (Field Notes excerpt, 9/21).

The methods students had another chance to collect and analyze data. They were assigned to interview their pen pals (pen pals were kindergarten through second grade students at a nearby multiage elementary classroom who they corresponded with and met throughout the semester). Each year students in Jane Doan and Penny Chase's multiage classroom do a "Pumpkin Project." It is an integrated project for which students plant, harvest, and sell pumpkins. Methods students visited their pen pals at their school, interviewing them about the project. The questions asked included:

1. What didn't you like about the project?
2. What things are you interested in?
3. Why do you do this project every year?
4. Tell me about the pumpkin project.
5. What do you like best about Jane and Penny's class?

When the methods students returned to class, they shared their data in groups, cutting, categorizing, and graphing their results in order to share their findings with classmates. This activity gave the methods students an opportunity to discuss integrated learning projects, elementary students' perceptions of the purpose of the project, what aspects of the project they most enjoy, and what these elementary students like/dislike about their class.

Learning to Make Meaning of Research Data Research tools used, such as the Burke Reading Interview and pen pal interview questions, provide opportunities to explore larger issues in literacy education.

The purpose that collecting and analyzing data of any kind serves is to help the researcher identify and understand patterns. These patterns serve to explain dimensions of reality in the classroom world. Simply collecting the answers to interview questions doesn't, by itself, reveal anything. It is up to the researcher to make meaning.

Methods students were guided through the process of making meaning as they engaged in frequent data collection and analysis activities, such as those described above. In mid-October the methods students had another opportunity to explore literacy issues through a home literacy survey. Brenda asked each student to survey several people. The survey questions had to do with the quantity and quality of reading and writing done at home. Methods students brought the results into the classroom for an analysis activity. Brenda divided the class into groups and asked them to categorize and graphically display the results on chart paper. The class discussed the findings. Students were surprised to learn that so many people surveyed did a lot of pleasure reading. One student suggested that timing was important. She did her surveys over the weekend when people had more time for pleasure reading. Several students were surprised that their survey results indicated that one-third of writing time was spent organizing our lives. Brenda suggested that this might be how many people see writing, as a management tool.

Through the home reading survey/analysis activity and the group discussion that followed, the methods students explored the kind of literacy issues that influence instructional practices, such as the importance of making certain that elementary students get plenty of opportunities to write and read for pleasure. Through this experience-based activity, and others like it, future teachers had an opportunity to construct their beliefs about why and how people read and write. These beliefs will influence how they structure learning situations in their classrooms.

Teacher Research as Professional Development Brenda employed teacher research as a pedagogy—as a method of covering literacy education curriculum. But toward the end of the course, in mid-November, teacher research was presented as a topic of professional development. Brenda described the philosophy of teacher research and then showed the videotape, *Taking Back the Classroom: The Alaska Teacher Research Network*. Brenda explains how teachers need to focus on research, but also need to focus on the students who are in the classroom. And as a teacher, you can't know what to focus on until you know the students. She explains the importance of reflective practice—an approach to teaching that involves inquiry and assessment in order to determine instruction—referring to her own practices in the methods course in order to illustrate the reflective teaching process.

Field Notes excerpt, 11/16/95

Brenda: The quick write responses (daily journal entries students make to which Brenda responds after each class). Within twenty-four hours I read those responses. They help [make] immediate changes in instruction...the place it's happened the most is with the group work. I wouldn't be able to think of specific things to help you without that immediate feedback.

One thing I saw was that you feel insecure with your teaching...the literature circles evolved from quick write journals. I found that some peoples' groups really weren't working. When I had that response, I tried to find out how I could change groups to meet student's needs.

If you don't have a regular way to reflect on what's going on, then it's hard to adjust instruction. The goal should be to meet everyone's needs in the classroom. The method of doing that is reflective practice where teachers collect data and analyze it in their own classrooms—teacher research. It's a huge change. [According to] the former model of research, an outside expert goes into a school...sets up a control group, an experimental group, and then states if it worked or didn't and the curriculum is changed based on these findings. But people are saying you can't know what the students need if you don't know the students.

For example, with this class, many of you don't often enjoy the large group share. Most of you are more comfortable writing in your journals or response groups. If some outside expert said you should have large group share, it might not be appropriate for this particular class.

The old model is based on agriculture. All the work or research was done with the idea that you want the largest yield possible. You don't really care if a bunch of crops get lost along the way, as long as over time the gain is positive. The same is true in schools. The yield is the test score. But teachers don't feel that way. They are careful gardeners. They want every plant to thrive. There has been constant conflict between those who want the overall yield to show improvement versus the teachers who want individuals to thrive.

It's catching on. All the new studies that are winning awards are either done collaboratively with professors and teachers, or by teachers. For the first 60 years in our profession it was just the professors that won the awards. Maine is a real center for teacher research.

Student: How do you represent it?

(Brenda described how there were many ways. She discussed the traditional way of writing research is written in a voice that speaks to an audience of other researchers. The new trend is to write jargon-free in a voice that teachers can understand.)

Student: I agree. The jargon is not what I understand and gain from.

Brenda: The standard is first-person narratives. What are your opinions about research?

Student: I like reading research when they give specific examples.

Brenda: Even examples in research have changed.

(Another student talked about the voice of the authors in the books she read in one of the course texts, *Invitations*, versus other texts from social studies that were boring.)

Brenda: The shift to first person is very important. Third person reads as if the information came down from God on tablets. When someone says that "research says" or "it is known," there is no room for discussion.

Brenda: Is [teacher research] something you could do?

Student: Not the first couple of years (laughing). But I think it's something you *have* to do. We talk about reflective teaching, I can see how you could get in a rut if you don't.

A discussion of Brenda's reflective teaching practices in the methods course, and new trends in professional development efforts among teacher researchers, reinforces the importance of inquiry in the teaching process. Inquiring teachers rely on good theories to guide their actions. But they also trust their intuition. They balance their knowledge about teaching and learning with their knowledge of children in order to make instructional decisions. In this way, teachers take risks, and make occasional mistakes, and take more risks. They think and act in the midst of practicing their art.

"Kidwatching": Answering the Question, "What Do They Know?" Based on constructivist perspectives of learning, all children build their own, unique understanding about a given idea. It is important for the teacher to discover what the child knows in order to help her progress to higher levels of understanding. For future teachers, some of them unfamiliar with the thinking and reasoning processes of young children, tracking a child's logic is a new experience. But teachers need to continually ask themselves, "What does this child know?" Methods students discussed the importance of assessment-based instruction. When the teacher has the responsibility of being record keeper, sharing the records and using them to shape the curriculum, it really does send a message to students that whatever they do is valued, and that their improvement is noticed and expected.

Throughout the course, methods students had an opportunity to look at real data from classrooms, including language and writing excerpts, in order to develop their skill at posing and answering the question, "What does this child know?" During one of the presentations the class explored theories of emergent literacy and language development. Brenda showed overheads of children's writing samples and prompted her students to consider the young children's perspectives. This exercise stresses the importance of "kidwatching" (Goodman, 1978) in the classroom.

Early in the semester, Brenda introduces an important topic that is at the core of developing perspectives in literacy education—the parallel between oral and written language development. After she explains how educational paradigms concerning language learning have changed, the students have an opportunity to engage in the kind of thinking that the newer paradigm asks of teachers, analyzing young children's responses to print.

Field Notes excerpt, 9/14/95

Brenda: I want to focus now on parallels between oral and written language development.

For a long time writing was taught a certain way—through the five-paragraph theme. Twenty years ago good writers began discussing their own writing habits. Those who read and wrote all the time said "What you teach in school isn't my process at all." That has informed school instruction.

Another factor is learning and understanding how children learn oral language. They asked: "Do the ways we teach reading and writing parallel the way children learn oral language development?" And in most cases they didn't. So these two elements, the ways people read and write in real life, and the principles of oral language development, have dramatically changed reading and writing instruction *(Brenda showed Figure 5.4, which appears below).*

Brenda: As long as children are moving through the phases, it doesn't matter what the pace is. Development is different in each case... We don't really worry about it. We look and compare. But we do in school, especially in a basal program, we expect all children to move at the same, predictable rate.

Figure 5.4. Parallels Between Oral and Written Language

Parallels Between Oral and Written Language
1. We expect success.
2. Adults do not, indeed cannot, teach the rules of language structure directly.
3. Children's focus of attention moves from the whole (the idea they are trying to communicate) to the parts; gradually they are able to articulate more and more parts to convey the whole.

4. Errors simply reflect the stage of a learner's development.
From: Weaver, 1988

Brenda also showed overheads of young children's responses to environmental print, including packaging labels for gelatin, toothpaste, and candy (Harste, Woodward and Burke, 1984). With each overhead, Brenda prompted the class to attempt to follow the child's logic, asking, "What does the child know?" Brenda also showed overheads of children's scribble writing from several different cultures (Harste, Woodward, and Burke, 1984). By showing these overheads, Brenda helps her students understand the importance of "kidwatching" and assessing a child's existing knowledge. Brenda wants her students to understand the importance of observing students in the classroom. One student, Cathy, demonstrates a critical awareness of the importance of observation and how it relates to the way she eventually hopes to teach.

> One of my hobbies has always been people-watching. I've done it for as long as I can remember, especially during classes when I should have been listening to the teacher. So, as an astute observer, I've noticed that while many people may be terribly proficient in one area, they haven't got a clue in other [subjects]. For years I excelled in reading, language, and writing, but when it came to subjects such as spatial manipulations in geometry, I was lost. Now, as a prospective teacher, I realize the impact of these observations. I visualize my role as a teacher as one who decodes the ways in which individual and groups of students learn best. My task is to provide an environment that allows for students to discover their strengths. This theory is like a ring of keys that unlock the many doors to student learning and understanding. Perhaps my feelings regarding multiple intelligences is why I've so vehemently opposed standardized tests and other forms of assessment that fail to consider the knowledge of the whole child. (Cathy's reading response, 10/17/95)

Working from Within—Writing Personal Narratives

> Like some modern painters, my students and I have come to feel that we rarely need to refer to subject matter outside ourselves. We work from a different source. We work from within.
>
> (William Pinar, 1994, p. 10)

Under the domination of empirical-analytical and traditionalist perspectives, the methods course curriculum has typically emphasized the importance of covering a set body of knowledge, the appropriate sequencing of activities and concepts, and the effective evaluation of student progress based on a predetermined standard. In such situations, regardless of the particular strengths and needs of the individuals who compose a class, the curriculum materials determine the official curriculum, and the official curriculum reigns supreme. As a result, the individual's experience of those materials is ignored (Pinar, Reynolds, Slattery, and Taubman, 1995, p. 519).

According to reconceptualist models of curriculum, the individual's experience precedes the official curriculum. The learner becomes the focus of attention rather than the predetermined goals stated in the official curriculum, syllabus, or textbook. This is not to say that curriculum is based on the theory of solipsism (the notion that only the self exists)—a primary criticism of self-study, in curriculum theory and educational research. When we work from a framework of autobiography or self study we are not disregarding other things and people outside our immediate realm of existence; rather, we understand that knowledge is a personal construction and that any new stimulus must necessarily filter through a lens of individual perspective. As Pinar (1994) suggests when he refers to reconceptualism, the more official and public world of objectives, instruction, and curriculum don't necessarily cease to be important. Rather, in order to understand the complete influence those public worlds have upon us, we must first systematically search our inner experience. Within the framework of a reconceptualist methods curriculum, the private is emphasized over the public. The sequence and manner in which content is covered arises as a result of the many encounters between student and student, student and text, and student and the teacher.

Brenda employed the autobiographical method when, early in the semester, she assigned her students to write a short personal narrative on the topic of learning to read or write. This assignment is derivative of writing process methods (Graves, 1983; Calkins, 1986; Atwell, 1987), but resembles *currere* in several ways. After selecting a past educational experience, students spent time in class freewriting, reading their pieces aloud to peers and receiving feedback, and responding to their peers' writing. Over time, each student composed a piece of writing that either analyzed, interpreted, or made sense of past experience. The method of *currere*, or the autobiographical approach to the study of curriculum, described in chapter 3, is particularly relevant to the personal narrative assignment discussed here. Elements of each stage of *currere*—regressive, progressive, analytical, and synthetical—can be seen in the assignment. The assignment was part of the writing workshop described in chapter 4, but deserves special attention here because of its potential to help students examine educational experience and, as a result, general principles relating to curriculum, teaching, and learning. This assignment allowed students to explore a theme that was meaningful in the context of their personal schema of teaching and learning in order to arrive at a heightened sense of personal awareness.

For many students, pleasant memories formed a foundation of positive attitudes toward school. These strong foundations of experience provide many with a source of motivation for becoming a teacher. For example, in Gwen's piece, "Journeying Down the Yellow Brick Road," she recalled her early love of books and how that joy influenced her development as a teacher.

> I remember the first teacher I ever had… It was in her class that I began my "career" as a student. Before entering school, I had been widely exposed to books, letters, pictures, and their correspondence to each other. My parents were readers as well as my brother and sister… I would imitate their reading habits by propping up my favorite teddy bear and group of dolls in a row on the worn, tattered, toy-room couch. I would be the teacher and would sit on a small stool, facing them. As I went through the picture books, I wove fantastic tales, being sure to show each picture to them and point out every detail, before going on to the next page.

Gwen went on to explain how those fond early memories fostered an enthusiasm for school, and how she grew to be an interested and motivated student. It is interesting that, even as a child who had not yet begun school, Gwen already had a teaching construct that helped inform her behavior. Her idea of teaching was demonstrated when she lined up her dolls on the playroom couch and faced them in her role as their teacher, and again when she showed her dolls each picture and pointed out every detail before turning the page of the book.

Among the personal narratives were many fond memories of early encounters with books. But for every fond memory, there were one or two bad ones. One of Gwen's classmates, Elisha, recalled a compelling incident that illustrates the damaging potential of teacher bias. Elisha tells how she was an avid reader as an elementary student. She was a good student and easily managed to complete the frequently assigned oral book reports. This earned her the favor of her English teacher. One day, feeling confident and a bit conceited, she strolled to the front of the room to share her report on the latest nonfiction book she was supposed to have read. In the paper entitled "The Day My English Teacher Went Insane," Elisha writes:

> [I] stood and walked grandly to the front of the room. I cleared my throat, and began to speak. Confidently, I extolled the fine merits of my incredible book. I completed my fine performance with a smug smile. Now I just had to sit back and wait for everyone to praise my rare talent for delivering book reports.
>
> A hand shoots up in the front row. It's that stupid pest! You know all seventh grade boys are stupid, but this kid is the worst! Undaunted, I call on him.
>
> He whines, "I thought our reports were supposed to be on a nonfiction book. That story really can't be true."
>
> My world falls apart. My life flashes in front of my face. My mind whirs.
>
> Could he be right? What books did the other kids do? My mind vaguely recalls Jill's report on a whale book. What did Joe do? Didn't he do some stupid story about baseball? Is that stupid boy really right?
>
> I'm frantic. I DID THE WRONG KIND OF BOOK!
>
> [D]istantly I realize I hear voices. No, it's one voice, my teacher's voice. What is she saying? Will I get detention? Or maybe...GASP...expelled?
>
> "Now I'm surprised at you," she says to the boy in the front row. "You know Elisha would never do anything that silly. If she says it's nonfiction, then it is."

This incident had the effect of altering Elisha's prior images of her teacher as one who was both knowledgeable and fair. By way of her action in this instance the teacher demonstrated to Elisha that her teacher did not consider the distinction between fiction and nonfiction worthy of elaboration, or, her teacher did not value her classmate's comment enough to warrant an honest response. The curriculum of the methods course was influenced by Elisha the day she read her story to the class. On that day, as on others, the importance of honesty and respect for students were issues that permeated class discussion.

Another methods student, Louise, wrote about the issue of teacher power and the importance of student choice. She was once assigned a book report for which she had to read a biography of an important figure in history. The book had to be at least eighty pages in length. After a long visit to the library, Louise returned to class empty-handed. She hadn't managed to find a book that captivated her interest. She began to wonder why she shouldn't be allowed to choose her own book, and finally decided to approach the teacher with her request. This is an extended excerpt from Louise's paper entitled "Free Write Number Two."

> It seemed like every book we read for these book reports was BORING! I wanted something exciting, something adventurous, the kind of thing you read that somehow reaches deep inside of you. Maybe I just wanted to read something where the characters are my age and going through the same things I am. Sixth grade is a time of big change in a girl's life, I wanted to know that I wasn't the only one going through these changes. I hear that new book by Judy Blume, *Are You There God, It's Me Margaret*, is pretty good. I haven't had a chance to read it yet, but I bet if I did I would get an excellent grade on the book report, something that my parents could put up on the fridge...
>
> [F]or the next day or so I couldn't stop thinking about how much better it would be if we could select our own books. I was in English class reading the sleep-provoking book I had picked, when I decided to do it. I slowly got up from my chair and cautiously walked up to the teacher's desk. I felt like Dorothy going to ask the Wizard to help her get home to Kansas.
>
> I stood next to him, and I felt about an inch tall, finally he acknowledged my presence. "Yes Stephanie, is there something you want?" I suddenly felt a lump in my throat as big as a tennis ball.
>
> "Um, yeah. I was wondering if I could ask you something," I stated in a shaky voice, trying hard to swallow the tennis ball.
>
> "What is it?" His attitude was not helping any.
>
> "Well I was just wondering if sometime we might be able to pick our own books to read."
>
> "Why would I want to let you do that?" was his reply in a very deep, lion-like voice.
>
> "Because it would be fun, no offense, but these books we have to read are pretty boring."
>
> He looked at me with his black eyes piercing right through me, "Excuse me."

"Well I just think that a lot of kids would do better on their book reports if they could decide what to read, I know I would. We would probably enjoy them more too, after all isn't that what school is for, to learn and have fun doing it?"

He kept staring at me like I was stupid or something. "No" was his reply to my plead. "Now please go back to your seat and finish your work."

I walked back to my desk as quickly as I could so that no one would notice how red my face was. It was painfully obvious how disappointed I was about the whole confrontation. I finished my book and wrote my silly book report, and turned it in and got a C on it.

(For the next assignment the teacher left room for the freedom to choose that Louise had previously requested.)

"The book you choose can be anything you want for this next book report." That was two days ago, I am done the book and I have already written the report. I got an A.

Louise's recollection conveys the poignancy of early school memories. In her story, school represents a place where she is powerless and the teacher dictatorial. Even when she attempts to appeal to her teacher's sense of reason, explaining the benefits of reading books that are enjoyable and interesting, she is ignored. Rather than taking her request seriously, explaining the rationale behind the assignment and helping her find a suitable book, Louise was sent back to her seat, embarrassed and humiliated. Her story helps remind the reader of just how much power teachers have in the lives of students and what harm can result when this power is misused.

Louise's story brings to life an important theme that is thickly woven into most postmodern or reconceptualist perspectives on curriculum—the importance of allowing students to have some control over their learning agenda. The importance of choice is a dimension of that theme that rings clear in Louise's piece. The issue of student choice represents a point of tension between traditionalist perspectives, where curriculum flows from the text, and the reconceptualist perspective, where curriculum stems from students' collective experiences and interests. The personal narrative assignment, which asked students not only to recollect early literacy experiences but also to read and respond to them in small and large groups, provided a collective frame of reference—a collection of multiple personal stories—from which the curriculum derived. Since the focus of discussion stemmed from the students' stories, the methods students had a hand in constructing the curriculum.

When we help preservice teachers view the literacy curriculum in autobiographical terms—through the method of *currere*, in which students recollect and script-out past educational experiences, and critique and compare them to the autobiographical texts of others—we help illuminate their passage toward more sophisticated understandings of literacy development and a heightened awareness of the teacher's role in the classroom. This process helps students critically examine their literacy histories for evidence of their existing beliefs about teaching, preparing a more thoroughly examined foundation upon which a modified belief system might be built. To the degree that the methods course helps students understand their preconceptions of teaching, our efforts to help them modify their perspectives about teaching will be more effective.

Summary

In a traditionalist methods course the official curriculum is usually created by an outside authority. Whether it comes from a syllabus written by the professor before the course begins or from a table of contents in a textbook, the course of activities and ideas are dictated from somewhere outside the students' immediate realm of experience. Lectures, assignments, and class discussions are typically based on the official curriculum and run in a linear sequence.

The curriculum in the methods course can be seen as an example of reconceptualism, whereby curriculum is directly linked to the collective personal experiences of the students. The syllabus serves to introduce students to the course framework and goals, but the order of topics and nature of content stems from the specific needs and concerns of students. Concepts and ideas that are discussed stem from the experience of writing and reading personal literacy histories, participating in literacy workshops, and engaging in teacher research activities. Curriculum materials, such as texts and presentations, help to clarify these ideas and concepts as they arise. In that sense, the curriculum can be seen as a collective autobiographical text, and autobiography can be seen as the method of curriculum. Through recollections of personal stories and discussions centering on personal reactions to course content, students construct the methods course curriculum.

Chapter 6

To See the Trees and the Forest at the Same Time: Learning the Art of Responsive Teaching in the Classroom Community

In many schools, teaching is expected to follow syllabi that lay out what students will learn, as well as when and how they will learn it. But in a real classroom, whether kindergarten, graduate school, or the school of life, there are live people with personal needs and knowledge...You have to teach each person, each class group, and each moment as a particular case that calls out for particular handling. Planning an agenda of learning without knowing who is going to be there, what their strengths and weaknesses are, how they interact, prevents surprises and prevents learning. The teacher's art is to connect, in real time, the living bodies of the students with the living body of the knowledge.

(Stephen Nachmanovitch, 1990, p. 20)

For any teacher, the understanding self, of students, and of the unique circumstances that bring about their union is central to the act of teaching. Simultaneously a teacher needs to consider the classroom reality from the perspective of both *self* and *students*. This multidimensional approach to viewing classroom phenomena presents a challenge to both teacher educators and students of education. Instructional approaches that help students work from the *self* to the *subject*, such as the method of *currere* (discussed in chapters 3 and 5), are gaining prominence in all fields of education. For example, Hulse-Killacky (1992) poses the questions, "Who am I?," "Who am I with you?," and "Who are we together?" to her counseling education students in order to help them explore how groups of individuals function and develop together. For a teacher working to promote individual student's learning in a classroom community, searching for answers to these questions can help them understand themselves as teachers, their students as learners, and their classroom community as a learning context. In modified form, these questions will provide the organizing framework for this chapter to make it possible to explore the multiple dimensions of community life and learning in Brenda Power's literacy methods classroom.

Who Am I?: Exploring a New Definition for the Teacher's Role in the Classroom

The category of identity organizes investigations of politics, race, gender, and experience around questions of self...The study of identity enables us to portray how the politics we had thought were located "out there," in society, are lived through "in here," in our bodies, our minds, our everyday speech and conduct. Even when we resist social trends and political directives, we are reconstructing ourselves in terms of those trends and debates and our resistance to them. In studying the politics of identity, we find that who we are is invariably related to who others are, as well as to who we have been and want to become.

(William Pinar, 1994, pp. 243-244)

One primary objective of the methods course was to help students reconstruct their teacher identity in a manner that enabled them to internalize the theories and practices discussed "out there" in class, bringing them "in here," into their own hearts, bodies, and minds.

Developing Perceptions of the Teaching Self Through Classroom Experience

The humanistic phenomenological approach to psychology was pioneered by Carl Rogers (1961). Rogers emphasized the individual potential for growth and the importance of individual perspectives in shaping the developmental course. Central to the humanistic phenomenological approach is the concept of *self*. Rogers believed that development is shaped through aspects of personal experience that can be identified as being oriented with *I* or *Me*. According to this approach, development comes as a result of the choices a person makes. The concept of self is an important factor in the way future teachers develop their sense of themselves as teachers. According to the humanistic framework, the more a student has experiences in the methods classroom that allow her to identify with *I* or *Me*, the more influential instruction and professional development. In order for a student to develop personal teaching constructs, it is essential that she uncover and understand existing teaching constructs. Self-awareness of personal beliefs leads to a more critical understanding of new ideas and their relationship to existing ones. The more self-aware a person is, the better able she is to either adopt or reject ideas and shape personal teaching constructs.

Because traditionalist, scientific-management instructional approaches continue to be commonly used, and basal readers and programmed instruction continue to be the primary reading instructional approach used in many schools, most preservice teachers have had limited learning experiences in student-centered classrooms. They come to the methods course with personal histories characterized by teacher-dominated learning experiences. For most of Brenda's methods students, their understanding of the role of the teacher was often different than the role portrayed in the assigned readings for the course. Throughout the course there were opportunities for them to explore these differences and to understand the role of the teacher in the context of the reconceptualized literacy curriculum.

The methods course was rich with opportunities that enabled students to merge *self* with experience. Structures in the methods course that helped students explore existing and alternative personal teaching constructs included writing assignments, written responses to the readings, classroom visits, and small- and large-group discussions. Descriptions of these structures and illustrations of how they served as opportunities for the methods students to explore the teaching *self* will be described below.

Personal Narrative Because of its power to generate curriculum and course content, the personal narrative was discussed in detail in chapter 5. Briefly I'd like to revisit the assignment and discuss its relevance to the discussion of identity and its function in assisting the methods students in shaping their perceptions of themselves as teachers. The personal narrative assignment and writing response groups parallel *currere*, the method of curriculum introduced by Pinar and Grumet (1976) discussed in chapters 3 and 5. This method enables "students of curriculum [to] sketch the relations among school knowledge, life history, and intellectual development in ways that might function self-transformatively" (as cited in Pinar, Reynolds, Slattery, and Taubman, 1995, p. 515). The act of writing personal narratives and discussing their meaning among a community of future teachers helps the methods students construct or redefine their identity of themselves as teachers.

Group Discussion The structure of group discussion provided a time and place for curriculum to be created. Discussions allow students the opportunity to relate new concepts to pre-existing frames of personal experience. During group discussion students were free to bring up concerns, questions, and opinions relating to the readings and assignments. Opportunities for small- and large-group discussion took place during each of the course segments described in chapter 2 and listed below for reference.

Literacy Workshop (first hour)
- Opening of class with student reading (three-five minutes)
- Silent writing or reading (ten minutes)
- Small response groups for drafts and literature response (twenty-five minutes)
- Whole class sharing (twenty minutes)

Presentation on a Theme by Instructors (second hour)

Reading Seminar (third hour)
- Discussion of readings and related activities
- Close class with student reading (three-five minutes)

During the first hour of class in literacy workshop, students read drafts of their papers in response groups of five or six people. This gave them the opportunity to practice listening and giving feedback to fellow writers. The experience of hearing their peers' narratives also allowed methods students to survey the range of personal experiences that relate to literacy learning. The personal narrative assignment was an opportunity to explore, reconstruct, and articulate their past learning experiences, providing an arena for the classroom community to explore their collective images and opinions of teaching. Perhaps through this experience, and the heightened awareness of the power that experience has in shaping learners' attitudes toward school and learning, preservice teachers will be more sensitive to the quality of interactions they will eventually have with their students. They might better recognize that those interactions will determine, to some degree, the quality of their future students' personal learning narratives, and that these narratives will have the potential to generate either positive or negative attitudes toward school and learning, depending on the quality of classroom interactions.

Group discussion was also a feature of the second hour of class when Brenda or Janice gave presentations on themes or topics related to literacy development and instruction. In these cases, group discussion was another means for students to explore the nature of the teacher's role in the classroom. I'll describe one example of how group discussion unfolded around the issue of basal readers and the role of the teacher in the reading curriculum.

Perhaps nowhere is the role of the teacher more controversial than it is in the debate over the use of basal readers in the elementary classroom. A word unknown to the typical college-age student—basal—is defined as follows: of or at the base of something, or fundamental or basic (Flexner, 1980). For most of this century, the basal reading series—leveled textbook anthologies of literature with accompanying comprehension questions—have served as the base of the curriculum in most schools. While many teachers nationwide are abandoning basal reading and language-arts programs in favor of literature-based reading programs and writing workshops, the pressure on new teachers to follow the textbook curriculum continues to be a reality in most public schools. Brenda realizes the importance of her students knowing these pressures. In the methods course she structured an experience that allowed students to examine basal readers, from early examples to those of the more recent series which aim to incorporate current perspectives on literacy. She first discussed the history of basal reading instruction and then asked her students to examine sample basal readers and prompted their examination with the questions: (a) What is the role of the teachers in the reading program? (b) What are the sociocultural views presented in the reading? and (c) What do you like or dislike about the program? I have included this excerpt of the class discussion because it illustrates how Brenda guides students to understand and analyze the politics of reading instruction. It also reveals how students articulate their perceptions on how the basal reader influences instructional approaches and the teacher's role in the classroom.

Field Notes excerpt, 11/2/94

Brenda: I have readers from the past 150 years (gestures to table of books). [When you look at them I want you to consider the question:] What's the [prevailing] sociocultural view—is it primarily a nuclear family, Judeo-Christian values? What viewpoint is it transmitting?

Basals came about...relatively recently. They were developed [for widescale use] fifty to sixty years ago at the height of the scientific-management model of instruction. It was a big leap at the time to think if you had the perfect reading program you would have the right kinds of reading development. [That's when behavioral approaches to learning dominated the field of education.]

Skinner's ideas were discredited three decades ago, but the model still persists. Some students ask if basals are so bad, why do they still exist? Over the last ten years [we have gone] from 80 percent of schools in Maine using basals to 42 percent. When I first started teaching, students would go into classrooms where everyone was using them.

What's going on is a lot of money changing hands. To understand that you need to know that folks like me have a lot to do with what goes on in publishing. Not only because we teach you, but because we can consult. Publishing companies like to have faculty on board. [Sometime during the 1980s] the average salary was $60,000 annually for university consultants to basal companies. The top authors earned from $80,000 to $250,000 in consulting from the major publishing companies. It costs about $15 million to launch a program. If basal programs go away then so would the golden egg [for consulting professors]. If you are a researcher, expected to be objective, I believe you shouldn't also make money from basal programs.

Lots of [faculty] won't work for basal companies because of this. But until there is a real statement made that you can't do research and be paid by a basal companies [they will continue to dominate].

Each book was $13 in 1985. Just think of all the [trade] books you could buy for that money.

Often, the school system is required to buy an entire basal series for $60,000 or more. Teachers who want to buy literature have no money to do that.

I think in Maine people can really squeeze a nickel. And teachers have become more savvy. They have been able to say, "Look how much more our money can buy if we spend it on real books instead of basals." Also, the library is sucked dry [when money is spent on basals].

It's our money...taxpayers' money...that goes to buy these books. People are taken on cruises, wined and dined to get them to buy basals, all on the backs of our children...the children are the losers.

When you go out into the schools, trace it back to the money...[I]f you go into a school that's looking at a basal program see if you can't get a committee together in order to present a proposal to buy real books. Present it in terms of how much more you get for your money when you buy real books.

With a partner, make sure you take at least one of the *Impressions* books and one of the other books. Make sure you answer these questions:

1. What is the role of the teachers in the reading program?

2. What are the sociocultural views presented in the reading?

3. What do you like about the program? Dislike?

Students work in groups examining the basal readers and discussing their responses to the questions Brenda posed.

Brenda: First question: What is the role of the teacher in the reading program?

Laura: [I had a] 1910 book...a book of plays. Teacher would read or they'd read to her...we also had [an *Impressions* book]. One had lots of pictures.

Gwen: I liked *Impressions*. Spoke quite a bit about preparing children before literature is introduced. Lot of predicting and inferring. She acted more as a facilitator, steering in the right direction, yet letting them have freedom.

Cathy: I still see going back to the comprehension...students are asked to go back to the book and find the answer. If I had a criticism, that's the one.

Brenda: Yes, it all comes back to you being a reflective professional. And some of the basals tell the teacher what she's supposed to say.

Elisha: I had that one...it drove me crazy!!! It told me what I needed to say and do.

Brenda: I have been in plenty of classrooms where the teacher actually does do that. Teachers have been [trained to follow the book]. There was a concept called teacher-proof basals. The idea is that no matter how stupid the teacher is, she'll be able to use it. Think about what that says about attitudes [toward] teachers and attitudes towards publishers. In the '60s and '70s publishers went to administrators saying you don't need to worry about teachers...this text is teacher proof. Next question, "What are the social views presented?"

Brian: I had [basal title] and it could be anywhere.

Student: I had this one written in 1916. A lot of it is religious based.

Cathy: In ours all the boys are in active roles and the girls wear dresses and bows and stand around. The minorities had Anglo faces with a little tinting.

Brian: Mine talked about training students.

This activity involved hands-on exploration and featured extensive group discussion. It provided an opportunity for students to begin to view curriculum materials critically in order to understand them as political texts. This discussion highlighted issues of race, gender, and religion, and how the dominant cultural views are perpetuated through the use of these curriculum materials. The discussion also focused on the role of the teacher in the context of a textbook-driven curriculum. Teacher passivity and the implicit message that a teacher should rely on the textbook to tell her what to say and do were criticisms of several students. Some new teachers will join the ranks of faculty in schools where the textbook is not the base of the curriculum, and they will be supported by colleagues and administrators. Brenda mentioned that school systems in the state of Maine were coming away from the exclusive use of basal readers; in most Maine schools the use of literature as a basis of the reading curriculum will be commonplace. But for some beginning teachers who take their first jobs in schools where the traditionalist perspectives still dominate and the basal readers are the basis of the curriculum, pressure to use basals will be hard to overcome. Their limited base of professional knowledge and experience will be cause for self-doubt, as well as administrative and collegial skepticism toward the use of alternatives to the textbook. But in either case, regardless of the materials available or administrative mandates, a critical understanding of the basal reader is necessary and enables new teachers to proceed more thoughtfully and cautiously.

Reading Seminar Reading seminar groups were another opportunity for students to connect the *I* or *Me* aspects of their experience with issues that came up in the textbook readings. Seminar groups were a regular segment of each class session that occurred during the last hour of class. During seminar, students circulated their typed one-page responses to the reading assignments. Seminar discussion gave students an opportunity to discuss their own points of view concerning the theoretical and practical literature they were reading. This experience centers on the students' concept of *self* in relation to theory and practice. Questioning, extending, and analyzing the readings gave them the opportunity to search for elements of the texts that students could identify with *I* or *Me*. In one of her reading responses, Cathy (10/12/94) commented:

> I felt somewhat relieved to read about the beliefs of Holdaway, Cambourne, and the author. While they all are firmly convinced that the whole language approach to teaching is most effective in terms of student learning outcomes, they all approach the model for these beliefs in a different manner. I equate this to an "all you can eat buffet." I can choose the items that appeal to me, sample those that are foreign but intriguing, but I don't have to partake of items I don't like. The best part of this analogy is that I can go through the line as often as I like. I guess it will

take several years, or "trips," before I'll know which ideologies mesh best with my students and my beliefs about how children learn.

Quick-Write Journals Over the course of the semester, students have many opportunities to go through the line, trying a little of this and a little of that. Students sample from a vast table and file away recipes for future use when their day in the classroom finally arrives. They begin to imagine themselves as the cook, sampling a variety of strategies and techniques to accommodate their individual tastes. The quick-write journals serve as a place to record informal and spontaneous reactions to items sampled during class. In the quick-write dialog journal excerpt which appears below in Figure 6.1, Gwen illustrates *sampling process*. She is exploring the use of journals in her future classroom.

Figure 6.1. Excerpt from Gwen's Dialog Journal

Gwen's Entry	Brenda's Response
11/21/94: I really liked the idea of teachers keeping a journal. Even if students are not encouraged or required to keep a journal, I feel that as a teacher, I need to keep a journal. This comes as a surprise to me because I've crabbed about these journal writes as a pain! I really do think that they are especially valuable and a good source of discipline in organizing, rethinking, and synthesizing my understanding of a reading experience within the classroom (in school) and within connections of my life and the world around me (outside of school). As a first year teacher, I see the daily journal as an invaluable tool for data on lesson plans, reactions, what worked well, what bombed, specific problems some students have, special insights, valuable tangents and offshoots. As things occur in the classroom, whether	It helps me think through class issues in a deeper way. It sounds like you are a budding teacher researcher, whether you realize it or not.

it is management or informa-
tional input, little hints and
reminders can keep these issues
alive and one can come back,
rethink, extend, or shift as the
dynamics within the class-room
change from day to day A great
tool to improve teaching—a
good habit for everyday life. A
terrific, insightful tool. Gwen

For Brenda's students, the methods course experience was a journey in meaning-making at many different levels. Individually, students composed meaning as they read texts and wrote about their experiences and opinions. In groups students shared their insights, which were further shaped and modified through the process of hearing the opinions of others in the classroom community. One-on-one, Brenda conversed with students through the daily quick-write journals. This was another level of communication that enabled students to move through individual courses of learning. Students had a range of opportunities within the structures of literacy workshops, presentations, and reading seminars to construct and share their own understandings about teaching. This process helped them form a personal interpretation of who they are as teachers.

Who Controls the Classroom?

When I was a beginning elementary teacher I was continually reminded to maintain *control* of my students and I was evaluated according to how effectively I *managed* this task. Terms like *control* and *management* help define the role of the teacher within the scientific-management/behaviorist model of instruction. According to this tradition of instruction, the teacher assumes center stage in the classroom by planning and delivering instruction, assigning work, monitoring and documenting accuracy of performance, and managing behaviors. But from a postmodern perspective, upon which reconceptualized views of literacy instruction are based, the focus shifts from manipulating and controlling student behavior to maintaining conditions that will foster individual development and allow students to meet their potential. Within a postmodern instructional framework, terms like control and management cease to be significant. In fact, using that sort of terminology limits and restricts the possibility of viewing teaching in anything other than technical and mechanical terms and, as Pinar (1994) suggests when he paraphrases Huebner, it "displaces ethical and aesthetic modes of teaching and conceiving curriculum" (p. 67).

Like all future teachers, Brenda's methods students were concerned about classroom management. They expected to have management issues explicitly addressed in the course curriculum, and their concerns emerged in classroom discussion. For example, after reading a chapter in *Full Circle* (Chase and Doan, 1994), an overview of a team-taught, multiage classroom from the teacher's perspective, Laura commented, "I was disappointed with *Full Circle's* chapter 4. I think it is too idealistic..." (Journal entry, 9/21/94). Also, during a group discussion about *Full Circle*, a student expressed her desire to see the "real" side of the multiage class-room—some of the problems and difficult issues. She felt that the book made everything sound perfect. Brenda explained that it is not unrealistic to expect the classroom to run smoothly. If something isn't working, it's important to evaluate the possible reasons in order to make modifications. But she also recognized that classroom life isn't always quite as orderly and predictable as the literature sometimes leads one to believe. She commented:

> A problem in the whole language or workshop literature is that there aren't a lot of problems discussed. When we get into Jane and Penny's class you'll get to see those students and some of the problems. (Field Notes excerpt, 9/12/94)

Preservice teachers who are just beginning to explore this new landscape of a vastly different approach to teaching, without an understanding of the sophisticated skills that teaching involves, often think dualistically. They imagine "going with the flow" as an absence of control and structure, or chaos. Most of these concerns were brought up early in the semester. As their fears and anxieties were alleviated, through readings, visits to real classrooms, and small- and large-group discussions, questions about classroom management disappeared from the classroom conversation.

When literacy development is seen as a self-sustaining, naturally evolving process, the role of the teacher is transformed from director to facilitator. In this role, the teacher's skill as an astute observer of children is vital in order to be aware of the progress the child is making and to know where and how to foster learning. *Kidwatching* (Goodman, 1978), the ability to observe children and understand their thinking, is a skill that preservice teachers need to acquire. The issue of what action should be taken based on classroom observations is a matter of debate. Should teachers intervene? Or should they allow nature to take its course with minimal intervention? Goodman (1991) stresses a distinction between intervention and mediation, and underscores the importance of limiting the teacher's role. He writes:

> There is a vital difference between mediation and intervention. In an intervention the teacher takes control of learning, knows with great certainty in advance what learning will be acceptable, and thus undermines the learners' confidence in themselves as learners; the teacher becomes the determiner of social conventions (1991, p. 207).
>
> [G]ood teaching involves a delicate balance: knowing how much support to give without taking control of learning from the learner. That's why intervention is an inappropriate term for any kind of teaching strategy. (1991, p. 215)

Goodman makes an important point. Teachers shouldn't "undermine" learning; they should strive to strike a "delicate balance" between support and control. But to some preservice teachers, still bound to traditionalist conceptualizations of the role of the teacher, Goodman's statements could be interpreted to mean "hands off." If they are to meet the developing needs of their future students, the laissez-faire instructional approach isn't always the best choice. Both terms, *intervention* and *mediation*, have a range of meanings and a range of acceptable applications.

The term *intervene* has four definitions (Flexner, 1980),

1. to come between, as in action.
2. to occur between other events or periods.
3. to occur incidentally so as to modify.
4. to interfere, especially with force or a threat of force.

The term *mediate* has four definitions (Flexner, 1980):

1. to settle (disputes, etc.) as an intermediary between parties.
2. to act between parties as an intermediary.
3. to occupy an intermediate position.
4. acting through or involving an intermediate agency.

Accepting the third definition of intervene to describe the teacher's role, whereby a teacher offers instruction incidentally so as to modify a student's understanding, it is entirely appropriate and compatible with reconceptualist perspectives. On the other hand, the first definition of mediate might have controlling over-tones when it is used to describe a situation in which a teacher pro-vides the final, arbitrary judgment concerning a classroom matter. General statements about the teacher's role in a learning situation need to be made with care; and, where possible, should be qualified and related to the unique conditions of specific learning situations. In line with holistic, child-centered instructional approaches, where the teacher is expected to respond to individual needs of students and is continually negotiating responsibility for learning with students, the teacher is continually moving between multiple roles. Each learning situation will issue a unique set of circumstances and call for a specified approach in light of those circumstances.

In their book, *Through Teachers' Eyes*, Perl and Wilson (1986) explore how six teachers perceive their role in process-oriented classrooms. These teachers expressed their reactions to the idea of whether they should "get out of the way" of their students. Perl and Wilson wrote, "each teacher had to find his or her own balance between imposing judgment and allowing for students' spontaneity, between controlling students' actions and offering free rein" (1986, p. 256). One of the teachers in their study commented:

> I don't know about "getting out of the way." Yes, get out of the way in terms of thwarting or limiting kids, don't be the reason they can't grow, but I don't want to be out of the way. I want to be with them on the way. I like the image of partnership better than the image of the teacher collecting dust in the corner while the students merrily do their thing. (1986, p. 256)

The role of the teacher in setting the limits and boundaries in a classroom is an issue future teachers need to explore. Like public-school teachers, teacher educators can be with their students on the way to learning. As teacher educators, we need to help them develop instructional strategies that allow them to be with their students *on the way* to learning. The methods course experience needs to provide rich opportunities to closely examine the complex-ities of the teacher's role within the reconceptualized framework of curriculum. The question of control versus freedom is an important dimension of that exploration.

Brenda wants her students to develop their ability to think on their feet and to assess and respond to classroom phenomena as they occur. To accomplish this, she brings elementary students and their literacy into the classroom by way of overhead transparencies of elementary students' writing samples and video-tape segments of elementary students involved in acts of literacy in real classrooms. Using these examples, discussion about the role of the teacher can be contextualized and the terms used to describe the teacher's role can be qualified. As Brenda shows these examples, she poses questions that help her students think critically about how they might respond as teachers in these situations. This allows them to articulate their own definitions of the teacher's role and make their own decisions about the degree to which they would mediate or intervene. These discussions help them enact instructional decision making. Opportunities to play the role of teacher help methods students gain confidence as they begin to trust their developing instincts about the nature of literacy development. It also gives them an opportunity to apply theory to practice in hypothetical instructional situations. As teacher educators, it is important to help our students explore the subtle, yet important, nuances between the numerous ways the teacher's role might be defined.

Yetta Goodman (1993), a scholar in the field of literacy education, has voiced her concern that whole-language theorists and practitioners are continually being pressured to define the whole language movement; she reasoned that whole language can't be defined, because it's always changing and evolving. In one sense, she is right. When a system of belief is frozen in static terms, it runs the risk of being reduced to dogma. This is often the case with the traditionalist curriculum that is written by committees or administrators and mandated for use in classrooms. Absent are the voices of teachers and students in those situations. The result is a document that lacks relevance for the individuals it was intended to assist. The deliberation involved in defining a philosophy or an approach is an essential element of its growth; and discussion about the nature, purpose, and philosophy of whole-language, or for that matter any other movement within the field of curriculum, functions to allow discussants a voice in the process of transformation. It is through one's participation in the dialog—a dialog that is embellished with terms that define a belief system— that one grows and develops as a professional. The whole language movement, viewed as an example of reconceptualization in the field of literacy education curriculum,

> is fundamentally a dialectical relation among knowers, knowing, and the known. Its thematic character must and will be identified and constructed through the discourse and scholarship of its participants. To imagine it a

finished product, a doctrine, is to miss its point. What is essential about the reconceptualization—as the literal definition of the word denotes—is its constant redefinition. (Pinar, 1994, p. 73)

The dialectic nature of the debate surrounding the definition of the whole-language movement will help insure that its approaches are always in a state of transformation, constantly adjusting to meet the needs of those who embrace the philosophy. A heightened awareness of one's beliefs about teaching and curriculum, including the philosophical and intellectual traditions that serve as their foundation, can help one remain self-critical and reflective. Also, in order for the whole-language movement to assist in professional development, those practitioners more accustomed to traditionalist instructional approaches, definitions, terms, and labels will be essential. In his discussion on post-formal thinking in relation to vocational education, Kincheloe (1995) expresses ideas that are relevant here. He writes:

Our conception of self, world, and work...can only become critical when we appreciate the historicity of its formation. We are never independent of the social and historical forces that surround us—we are all caught at a particular point in the web of reality. The post-formal project is to understand what that point in the web is, how it constructs our vantage point, and the ways it insidiously restricts our vision. (p. 197)

A primary role of the teacher educator is to help guide students to become critical thinkers who are able to define their practice in terms of the standards, conventions, and philosophical underpinnings that are understood within the larger community of teachers in the field. The process of deliberation is especially important for preservice teachers who need to understand how a new teaching approach is similar or different from one that might be more familiar.

If the methods classroom can capture some level of this discourse, then preservice teachers might join the ranks of an emerging generation of teachers who are critical, competent, and articulate. The teaching workforce will benefit from a new generation of teachers who, from the beginning of their careers, are critical and confident enough to assert their voices and be a part of the continuing debate over what practices best benefit schoolchildren.

Who Are You?
The Importance of Knowing One's Students

My belief in response-based teaching started from working with professors who spent hours responding to my work. But it grew when I became a faculty member because I was so needy myself. When I first began to teach, those long letters [in response to students] were a challenge to students to tell me what I needed to know to help them. Many of the students were amazed and overwhelmed by my responses, and they rose to the challenge by teaching me—about their culture, about their school experience, about the kinds of classroom activities that helped them and those that didn't.

(Brenda Power, 1995, p. 16)

In the excerpt above, Brenda explains how an important aspect of her role as teacher is to learn about her students, for her sake as well as her students. During a large-group discussion about multiage grouping, several students expressed anxiety because they felt they weren't being given enough answers. Brenda accepted their frustrations, explaining she understands how they might feel, but stressed the need to remember that most things won't be clear until they get to know their students.

Field Notes excerpt, 10/17/94

Brenda: Who has one issue for the group.

Gwen: [In reference to multiage grouping] I believe in it, but don't feel we're getting enough information...I'm frustrated. When I go in for one day, it looks like a mess...like a jumble...I need to see how to begin, how to plan. I think a lot of stuff is missing.

Brenda: Other responses?

Student: I agree, it's like a jigsaw puzzle. I need to see the whole. It's difficult to tell from the pieces.

Cathy: I think a lot has to do with the approach.

Dave: We went to observe. We're doing [our field experience] in reverse. I got put into a traditional first-grade class. There was a multiage next door. In the end I went to talk to the teacher. She said the toughest thing was providing a spectrum of instruction to meet the needs.

Brenda: I really do understand your frustration.

Brian: I was in one [multiage class] for four weeks. It was only two years so the first year she had K, the next year she had first and second, next is second and third. If you can teach whole language and process teaching, you set it up to teach multiage. Are all multiage classrooms whole language?

Brenda: Multiage is one of those new things. It's being mandated in some places and some traditional teachers set it up the same as they always have. When I first began to teach, I did know the structures, and I did know the activities. What I did not realize then, and I do realize now, is that you need to know your students. It's like preparing yourself to be a tailor when you don't have a clue who the person is you're going to make the suit for. Your criticisms of multiage are valid. But I do think the most important thing is knowing your students. I had no idea at the beginning of this semester I would let you run your own literature circles. I read in your journals how some of you were scared you would fail. So I thought as a teacher, "How can I set up a structure so that you could try?" My plan came from working with you as students and providing what you need.

Teachers do need to follow the instructional practices they have learned, employ classroom structures that have worked in the past, and draw on the ever-increasing body of knowledge they acquire about teaching theory and practice in order to engage in the art of teaching. This training and skill is essential. But what future teachers cannot fully understand before they have had a chance to teach is that the most important variable in any learning equation is what the teacher knows about the learner. Integrating those personal understandings with pedagogical knowledge and theory constitutes the essential art of teaching.

As discussed in chapter 5, teacher research was a method of curriculum that enabled students to critically examine literacy-related issues. But teacher research also served as a pedagogical tool for Brenda in her role as instructor. Her teaching was based on a continual cycle of inquiry in which she collected data, analyzed and interpreted it, and made instructional decisions as a result of her conclusions. In this section I will describe some of the kinds of data Brenda referred to in order to learn about her students so that she could adjust and modify her own instructional practices.

Structures built into Brenda's class served the purpose of helping Brenda achieve a level of presence with her students. Daily quick-write journals supplied Brenda with personalized snapshots of what each of her students was thinking on any given day in class. Her roving visits to reading and writing response groups allowed her to assess how groups were functioning, to model instruction, and to assist groups in their development. Biweekly individual conferences helped Brenda develop relationships with students, which gave her more data from which to make instructional decisions, and one-page typewritten responses to the readings helped her understand what ideas students were taking away from the assigned readings and what questions were left unanswered. These are the data that Brenda monitors and uses to guide the curriculum.

Brenda sets in place some classroom structures before the semester begins. She writes the grading criterion, the daily class structure and schedule, what texts will be used, and how many papers will be assigned. But most of the curriculum evolves from students' particular needs. For example, when several of the students expressed concern and anxiety about implementing literature circles in their own classrooms, Brenda organized a literature circle assignment that allowed each student to plan, facilitate, and critique a small-group discussion around a children's picture book. Below are summaries of examples of the data points I mentioned that help Brenda understand who her students are and what their particular needs are.

Journals Students write each day in the quick-write journal. It is specifically designed to be "...A quick, gut reaction to ideas from class, concerns—a way to connect each week." (Quick-write response to Laura, 9/21/94). About the journals, Brenda writes,

> Lately I've enjoyed using quick-write dialogue journals in many classes. I take manila folders and staple lined paper inside. Students draw a line down the middle, and write to me on one side at some point before, during, or after class. I write back before the next class. They never take these journals home, and neither do I. It's a wonderful way to do a gut check of what is and isn't going well in the class, and they help me as a teacher researcher of my own students. Students use these journals to take care of minor questions and concerns in the class, to respond to something I've said or written, or to expand on ideas or issues in their work.

> (Brenda Power, 1995, p. 21)

Methods students' journal topics range from complaints about the cost of texts or the amount of reading required, to how much they enjoyed an activity or group discussion, to strictly personal, nonschool-related issues (if there are such things). Some examples appear in Figure 6.2.

Figure 6.2. Examples of Types of Dialogue Journal Responses

Panicking: "Today was somewhat overwhelming—not in a bad way. It was just a lot of activities that we'll be doing throughout the semester. In the span of a semester the work required will be manageable—I just have a habit of panicking." (Kirsten, 9/7/94)

Apologizing: "I have just been so busy and afraid that I had bitten off more than I can chew. And this is a journal, so I felt free to pour out all my feelings. Including my negative feeling. I'm sorry if I took everything out on you." (Laura, 9/14/94)

Personal Issues: "Could I be any more ecstatic! I doubt it. I have gotten almost all of the classes that I need, only one more to go. My plans were altered from going to school in Colorado to suddenly being at U. Maine again. I suppose it is the best because going to a new school is hard and I transferred here from [the University of Southern Maine] and from there to out of state. (Brian, 9/7/94)

Questions about theories and instructional approaches: "I still am confused as to what exactly whole language is. How is it used in the school as age and developmental level increase? (Karen)

Personal connections with ideas that came up in class: "The video today really got me thinking—about kids who have trouble starting a topic in writing. I worked with a student who had a very difficult time deciding what to write—and when he did write—it was always on the same topic. It made me think about how much I pushed him to try to come up with something he was interested to write about. His teacher really wanted him to write about something other than his family, and his new house. In thinking back, I really think if we had concentrated more on what he was writing and how—rather than whether he was writing on an "appropriate topic." It's such a fine line—between pushing a student to do something new and allowing him to do what is comfortable. (Elisha, 9/19/94)

Self Reflection: "I have taken to heart your comments about the few students that seem to dominate the conversations. It is my nature to be forthright and I must admit—I'm not as comfortable with the silences as you are. So perhaps a behavioral objective of mine would be to listen more to those around me and learn what they have to offer." (Cathy, 9/12/94)

During the final class meeting, the issue of using journals with students came up in the group discussion. Brenda reiterated how important they were in helping her monitor the health of the community. One of the students explained how the journal would have served well as a self-evaluation tool during the semester. This excerpt illustrates the modification-in-action potential of student/ teacher dialog.

Field Notes excerpt, 12/14/94

Laura: I really liked the journals. I want to do that when I teach. It is personal and individualized.

Brenda: If you're hearing from five people that their groups aren't working, then you know exactly who those five are. You get a sense of who the groups are working for as well. I like being able to look back over your work too.

Gwen: I found I would have liked to have my journal in front of me [during evaluation time]. I couldn't see my progress. I had to try to remember.

Brenda: I could do something like they do for evaluation conferences. I could let you have them for a few days during evaluation period, then get them back so I have them over the weekend.

Conferences Brenda believes that before she can meet individual needs of students, she needs to understand their individual issues that might either deter or foster learning. Individual conferences satisfy this need. She uses a range of conference approaches in the methods course. During writing-workshop response groups she circulates among groups, and participates in the writing-response process, as well as monitors how the groups are functioning.

Also required are individual, out-of-class conferences with her students every two to three weeks. The focus of these conferences changes over the course of the term. Initially, she uses them in order to learn students' names, to answer questions, and to get to know students. Later in the semester they provide a chance to discuss writing assignments and progress in the course. About the value of conferences, Brenda writes:

> I try to meet with every student for a quick conference every two weeks, with the first conference the first week of class. I need to know what's going to get in the way of their learning over the semester—a struggle to find day care for a child that isn't resolved, a too-heavy class load, financial problems that may cause a student to drop out. These quick initial conferences resolve so many small problems before they blow up. It's also hard to care about students before you know them. These conferences help me to know my students better fast. I schedule them for ten or fifteen minutes during my office hours. I will be in my office at these times anyway, so the conferences fit into my quest for a balanced life and reasonable work hours. I only do these conferences every two weeks, because I couldn't sustain the intensity of the experience every week. I am exhausted after the days when I have had long hours of student conference after conference, but I have learned so much.
>
> (Brenda Power, 1990, p. 19)

Reading Response Papers. The one-page, typewritten responses to assigned readings also provided valuable data for Brenda to consider. They gave her first-hand feedback about the value of texts and provided a survey perspective about the degree to which students understood the material. Brenda always circulates during response-group discussions, spending about ten minutes with each group. During this time students can ask questions that they might hesitate to bring up in the larger group. Brenda reads and responds to each paper outside of class. Prior to the next class she writes a brief comment to each student in which she addresses questions or comments that weren't addressed previously during in-class group work. Brenda learns a great deal about students over the course of the semester by reading their biweekly response papers.

Who Are We Together?: Exploring the Power and Process of Community Life

Throughout the semester the methods students had a variety of opportunities to explore the process of group work and community building. In mid-September the students analyzed results from the Burke Reading Interview (Burke, 1980), a tool widely used by teachers of reading in order to understand students' preconceived notions about what it means to be a good reader and in order to understand the strategies students believe they use while reading. The methods students had been asked to complete the interview on three individuals and bring the results to class. In small groups they analyzed responses to interview questions; and in the large-group discussion that followed, the class as a whole made conjectures about the role of reading in the culture of their respondents. But the interview exercise was more than a data-analysis exercise. It was an opportunity for students to work collaboratively through a task. Brenda gave the class open-ended directions, they would be responsible for analyzing the interview results—coming up with categories and somehow diagramming the results. Students in the small groups were left to puzzle through the process, which involved outlining a plan of action, analyzing and categorizing results, and presenting the results in diagram form to the rest of the class. Each group went about the process in unique ways. These were my notes from the process.

Field Notes excerpt, 9/14/94

The ways the students went about organizing the project of making a bar graph was very different. One group set out by establishing categories. Then they cut the chart paper into four pieces and each tallied the categories. Another group had one person keep track while the other called out categories.

Janice (the teaching assistant) commented to me how differently each of the groups approached the task. One group skipped the task of making a tally sheet, but ended up making a rough draft of the graph. Janice also noticed how each group handled dividing responsibility. In some groups one or two people took over, and others in the group ended up not doing anything. Before getting into the data-analysis stage of the activity, Brenda asked the class to consider how they functioned as a group.

The methods students had a follow-up discussion to the Burke interview activity. Not only did they discuss the results of the interview-analysis process, they also commented on their group working processes.

Field Notes excerpt, 9/19/94,

Brenda: [We'll begin] by talking a bit more about the Burke interview process we did last week. Any responses about the process?

Student: Ours was a very democratic process. We cut up the chart paper and divided the workload.

Brenda: What are some other ways you handled it?

Student: We made categories and double-checked to make sure we were right.

From the first day of class students were expected to work in small groups. Initially students worked in writing response groups formed on the first day of class. As the semester progressed and once they had become accustomed to the process, the methods students were invited to think about the process of group work. Toward the end of the semester the writing workshop evolved into a literacy workshop where students had a choice between reading or writing. They also had the opportunity to reorganize into self-selected groups. Brenda explained to her students that she wanted to structure integrated, social learning opportunities in the methods course that paralleled in principle the kind of teaching approaches suggested in the assigned texts. Before students were given the opportunity to regroup, Brenda reminded them to consider the conditions that would best foster their own working process.

Field Notes excerpt, 11/14/94

Brenda: We only have five workshops left. What I tried to do is give you some structure, but also some freedom. What I hope is that you're ready to decide for yourself how you'll work with others in a way that will meet your needs. If you don't, it's something to think about. If your group doesn't work, then you should be thinking about what isn't working for you yet in terms of literacy instruction. If it's hard for you to work in groups now, then I think it will be really hard in one year when you're teaching.

Opportunities to reflect on the process of working with others were interwoven into group activities and discussions. They came about naturally in a relevant context. Addressing group process issues in the context of authentic experiences is something Brenda wants her students to be able to do with their students in future classrooms.

Learning to Facilitate Community Living

> It is poor use of the teacher's time and effort to assume responsibility for jobs and routines. If students aren't good at doing them, it is up to the teacher to help students perceive the value of the work, practice doing it, and receive feedback from the group. In taking charge of identifying what jobs need to be done, planning and doing them, and evaluating results, students use language in authentic situations to accomplish important work. That is, more is accomplished than getting the jobs done.
>
> (Ralph Peterson, 1992, p. 63)

Student-centered classrooms require extensive planning and organizing. Brenda wants her students to be aware of just how important planning is to a smooth-running classroom community. She stresses how important it is for the teacher to delegate some responsibility to students. Brenda shows how jobs can be delegated to her students by asking them to sign up for chores. On the first day of class she circulated a page of white adhesive labels, each with a different chore listed. These included: pick up VCR, return VCR, snack, opening reading, and closing reading. Students were asked to take an adhesive label and stick it inside their notebook as a reminder. Lists of chores were passed around every few weeks, during which time students were reminded to take one they hadn't done before. Taking part in tending to the needs of their own classroom community helps students understand the way community might function in their own future classrooms.

Democratic communities need members who are willing and able to be problem solvers. If school is to be a place where children learn and develop, they need real opportunities to work through genuine predicaments. In traditional, teacher-directed classrooms, it is usually the teacher who solves routine problems that arise. The kinds of problems children are typically asked to solve stem from the prescribed curriculum and appear in the form of artificial problems. When the curriculum is based on children's issues, when they have the freedom to work and talk among peers and to choose writing and reading topics that are relevant to their own lives, real-life problems become the focus of community concern. And life's real problems are confounded by complicated circumstances that are all relative to the individuals involved. With a reality-based curriculum, teachers need to be listeners, helping children use their voices to identify real-life issues and find workable solutions. They must also be flexible, able to build in discussion time when the need arises. As they solve problems together, children learn personal and community responsibility. They have opportunities to use their own experiences to sort out problems while they also benefit by learning from others. Laura expresses the importance of shared responsibility in the following excerpt

> I like the group community feeling I get from this class. Sharing responsibilities such as snack, reading before and after, I feel like I am learning a lot about what is important to future teachers which I realize are also important to me. (Laura, 9/19/94)

Students have another opportunity to see how responsibility is delegated to students in a real-life classroom when the watch the video *One Classroom: A Child's View* (Whitney, Hubbard, and Miller, 1988) from *The Writing and Reading Process* video series. In the video, Johanna, a child in a second-grade classroom, takes the viewer on a tour of her classroom, explaining the procedures and practices the students follow. Brenda prompts her students to keep a running list of all of the responsibilities students have in the classroom. The excerpt of the class discussion appears below.

Field Notes excerpt, 9/12/94

Brenda: As I read through your responses, I saw that many of you focused on what your rooms will look and feel like. And that's natural since you read about real classrooms in [the texts]. So I want to give you a chance to take a look at a classroom. What you need to do is keep a running list of everything the children seem to be responsible for, from everything as mundane as sorting the books to something as implicit as asking someone permission to read their draft. Workshop teaching is very time consuming. So you want to give as much responsibility to the children as you can.

(Viewing of video)

Brenda: Do you have any questions about the tape? Let's just have groups of three or four, your choice. What comes up in common on your lists? What responsibilities do the children have in this class.

(Small-group discussions for fifteen minutes, followed by large-group discussion:)

Brenda: Any comments?

Kirsten: I was surprised how the kids coded the books. It's just something I didn't think they could do.

Brenda: There are a lot of things the kids can do with just a little preparation. One thing I like that they do in Benton (a nearby school) is the bus drivers collect the lunch money.

Student: Delegating responsibility isn't easy.

Brenda: Yeah, there are a lot of kinks in the beginning. But usually after the initial weeks things run themselves. Same thing with your children. Ask yourself, what do students need most from you? What's the best use of your time? What are other responsibilities that surprised you?

Student: That the kids were responsible for publishing.

Brenda: We'll talk about that later. But you can use parents to help in the publishing process.

Student: In several places I noticed there were instances of asking permission—asking permission to share something. A respect for privacy.

Brenda: Moment by moment you as a teacher do things that either show or don't show respect.

Student: I like the way students asked the questions about their writing.

Brenda: And that's a big part of the records you keep. If you choose to write down what students are saying rather than talking all the time, it shows what you value. It establishes a classroom tone at a lot of different levels.

Gwen: I think the way a lot of the children behaved. If you expect children will misbehave, they will. If you expect them to behave, they will.

Brenda: Right, and it works.

Good teaching is improvisational. Sometimes plans just simply don't work. The ability to learn from mistakes, to come away from an experience asking the questions, "What went wrong?" "How can I improve next time?" is a skill that helps improve teaching over the course of one's professional career. Delegating responsibility is often a case of trial-and-error. If things don't initially work, they can easily be modified.

Communication in the Community: Interpreting Language Structures and Patterns

Successful classrooms are safe communities where students are willing to take risks and offer opinions, where they respect their peers and the teacher, and in return are equally respected. Teachers have an important role in guiding children to use language to establish these communities. But often as teachers we rely on our own past experiences to shape how we interact with students. Those who were never given opportunities in their own elementary years to help construct classroom democracies rely in part on past experiences to shape teaching behaviors. For those teachers who haven't looked critically at their own histories and have never had the opportunity to see how alternative classroom language structures function, it is easy to fall into the traditional teacher mode, using language mostly to control and regulate student behaviors. In these classrooms students are expected to mold their language to conform with teacher expectations. And when this happens, children are silenced.

Classroom discourse is one dimension of classroom life that concerns issues of power and control. In a community, it is important that speaking rights are observed and that teachers monitor language patterns and safeguard against negative habits that might jeopardize those rights for individual students. The methods students had a chance to explore speaking rights through speaking turns. Brenda gave each student several popsicle sticks. They were to use one stick each time they took a talking turn. She prompted her students to look critically at their own speaking patterns, if they were usually big talkers, they should only briefly talk, and if they were typically small talkers, they needed to say more than usual. The point of this activity was to bring about a greater awareness of the balance of particip ants' contributions to classroom discussion. Brenda's explanation and the group discussion follows.

Field Notes excerpt, 11/2/94

Brenda: We didn't really get to debrief from the activity of the popsicle sticks.

Cathy: I loved the activity. Because I liked hearing from others and didn't feel I needed to speak...I think I'm uncomfortable with silences and need to change that.

Brenda: I taught a couple classes where there were two students who were really dominant. They didn't like the activity because they ended up doing the same amount of talking.

There are people who have a lot to say, like Cathy, but they also have good social skills. There are others who like to mull things over and need some think time.

What didn't you like about the activity?

Student: I thought it was interesting but I don't think it made any difference. I was more conscious, and I thought that was good.

Brenda: A fair amount of time isn't the same as an equal amount of time. You can do some really artificial things to try to make things equal, but you begin to find that things aren't necessarily fair. You don't want to set up artificial activities like this for every class session whenever literacy topics are discussed. You do want to catch any negative patterns that might be beginning. But to make it so that students pick up their token before any discussion about books or writing isn't a good idea—that's not what real readers and writers do.

The stick activity allowed the students an experience-based opportunity to analyze talking patterns in their group. This is an important skill for teachers who face continual problems and challenges associated with the human side of teaching. The unpredictable glitches that cloud successful teaching, such as interpersonal conflict, are rarely covered in college methods courses. Discussions like these that focus on talking patterns in the group help future teachers begin to develop a sensitivity to classroom language issues.

Learning How to Respond in a Community

> If you are a teacher, holding a conference with a writer is not easy. The problem is twofold. Authors break easily, and teachers tend to criticize. Authors, especially authors who happen to be children, do not want advice right away. Authors want readers to tell them they've done a good job. Recently a fourth grader put it rather simply: "I want people to say, 'Oh, that's excellent.'"
>
> (Ruth Nathan, 1991, p. 19)

Learning to give meaningful response to writing is a skill that Brenda values and one she wants her students to value. Sharing a piece of writing is risky business for those who feel insecure about their writing. One of Brenda's primary concerns is helping her students learn to be supportive, friendly critics so that the group can develop a sense of trust. Each day students have the opportunity to respond to peers' writing in small and large groups. Throughout the course, she builds a scaffold for the response-giving process with comments and modeling. During the first few days of class, she offers comments that serve to direct the focus of the writing workshop.

Field Notes excerpt, 9/7/94

Brenda: I don't believe in quizzes and tests. But reading and responding as a community of readers and writers is important for seeing if you're comprehending. Also, [my teaching is] about getting to know you as individuals through conferences.

Field Notes excerpt, 9/14/94

Brenda: OK, we need to meet back together as a large group. Let's talk for a few minutes, rather than having large group share, about your group process. I think we're getting to know each other better so we can be more critical about our writing. Some of you wrote in your dialog journal how you want more critical feedback. It takes time to get to know each other.

The value and importance of sharing writing came up in a class discussion during writing workshop after Brenda had shared an excerpt from the book she was writing. Because they experience the pleasure and pain of hearing responses to their writing during the workshops, it doesn't take long before students can articulate the importance of knowing how to respond to a writer in a conference. But many of the students in the class resist sharing with the large group. The class is discussing one of the assigned readings: "Effective Teacher-Child Conferences, the Importance of Writing Yourself," by Ruth Nathan (1991). In the discussion, Brenda issues a challenge for her students to push themselves to take the risk of reading to the large group.

Field Notes excerpt, 9/19/94

Student: I especially connected to the part about the importance of humane response to my work.

Brenda: I do think it comes down to your own writing and sharing your writing with others. I recall in college how some of my professors who were reviewers for journals would just laugh at some of the manuscripts that were submitted. And these were professors that didn't publish—it was like they got tenure and died. They never wrote. It is only through being a writer yourself that you can understand what it means to be a writer, and how it hurts to get cruel response.

Student: I had a professor last semester who, it was an ENGLISH Class, found everything wrong with your piece. If it was OK, you'd get it back blank. Another class member and I stayed after and explained it would help if we could get constructive comments. He sort of reminded us that it wasn't too late to drop the class.

Student: Let us all remember that. Our students won't be able to drop out of our classes.

Brenda: And it is probably the case that most professors are the kind of teachers that they had when they were students. It's partially because that is the kind of role assigned to English teachers in our culture. When I tell people I'm a literacy professor, they say, "Oh, I'll have to watch my grammar around you." And I know it's the case that I don't get letters or thank-you notes from people sometimes and it's the case that people feel I will evaluate and criticize their writing. They don't know the way I teach and that that's not what I believe. It's important not to focus on mistakes.

Now, try to gather up your courage. The next class might be a good chance to share your writing with the whole group. You'll have had some time in groups to get response so that your piece will be where you want it to be.

Through the daily practice of reading and responding to texts, Brenda believes her students will develop skills as thoughtful listeners and supportive critics. She explains her hopes for each student in the excerpt below.

> I want students to reach the point where they can respond incisively, thoughtfully, and tactfully to their peers' work. But many have never been in a writing-response group. They are overwhelmed at the thought of reading their work to someone else...I give them a structure for response. The writer will read her work, and the responders will think about what they would have underlined as a favorite part. If time permits, they can also talk about what they want to learn more about from the writer.
>
> (Brenda Power, 1995, p. 10)

In order for her students to reach the level of skill she hopes for, Brenda realizes her students need practice and good examples. Her role during small-group conferences was to circulate among groups, giving response to the texts she heard her students read. Students were able to learn from her example. During one sharing session, one of the students had written a draft about her brother who was diagnosed with a debilitating disease which nearly took his life. Brenda's response follows.

Field Notes excerpt, 9/19/95

Brenda: It's such a powerful incident that you could almost cut some of it. There is a place where you begin reading his attributes. I think that's clear to the reader that he has these qualities just by what he accomplished. Another thing, could you read the first line:

Student: "The phone call I received was terrifying."

Brenda: How about if you just write, "The phone call terrified me." Remember the discussion about verbs? You want to grab the reader.

Invariably, sensitive issues come up in writing workshop. Whenever students write about real-life events, their pieces reflect all levels of emotion. When students aren't accustomed to responding to sensitive pieces, they often find themselves in uncomfortable and awkward silences. Brenda helped the group explore the issue of responding to sensitive issues as a classroom teacher, offering insights and strategies.

Field Notes excerpt, 9/28/94

Brenda: I wanted to mention that a lot of you seemed uncomfortable about orally responding to those two pieces that were sensitive [during the last writing workshop]. But in your journals, a lot of you wrote about it. Does anyone want to add anything?

Student: I went home and told my roommates.

Cathy: I just lost my cat (one of the pieces was about a pet cat who died).

Gwen: I think when you feel like that, anything you say is pointless and trivial. I didn't have anything worthwhile to say.

Kim: Because it was so close, nothing anyone could say would be trivial. My roommate told me I was psychotic.

Brenda: So much of what happens in class is artificial and set up not to communicate. So when anything real happens in class, you almost don't know how to react. Because classrooms are so artificial.

Student: I was thinking that responding to the mechanics of it would be so awful.

Brenda: Yes, and a lot of teachers do that with the best of intentions.

Brenda comments, "In all of my response to students, I try to remember these words from Donald Murray, the father of the conference approach to teaching...especially when I don't know how to respond:"

How should we respond to student writing? How should we respond to a look, a piece of blackberry pie, a kiss, a death in the family, a joke, to the sneaky warmth of the winter sun when it touches a hand?

As a human being. As a human being who also writes. As a human being who writes and wants to help.

To me a draft is a living thing. It is a piece of human communication—an embryo of understandable experience—that deserves its own life. It must be respected for its own possibilities. It must be nurtured, cultivated, cared for, delighted in.

There can be no way—no single, correct, pre-conceived way—for one human being in the dynamic, ever changing context of a human interaction to respond to another human being.

(Donald Murray in *Power*, 1995, p. 18)

Conversations in the methods classroom served as the building blocks of students' learning about themselves as writers, readers, and teachers. Brenda recognizes the power of conversation; that's why most of the class consists of opportunities for students to talk. She commented, "It is true that even if you only meet with a group for a few months, you carry those voices with you into the future" (Field Notes excerpt, 9/21/94). Those voices become your partners in a continuing dialog that generates new learning. Brenda's belief in the importance of conversation to learning was illustrated in her 11/14/94 reading response (see Figure 6.3).

Figure 6.3. Brenda's Response to Heath's (1991) "A Lot of Talk About Nothing"

When I first read Shirley Brice Heath's work when I was in graduate school, I can honestly say it changed my life. Up until this point, I know I believed deep down that everyone learned to talk and read in basically the same way. Any deviances from these norms were deficiencies. It wasn't until I read Heath's research that I learned people in different cultures learn things in different ways, and these differences must be known and respected by teachers.

Heath's work really made me respect the value of talk in learning. My husband will finish his undergraduate degree here next semester. I am appalled at how little room there has been for talk as part of his course work. Even relatively small classes are built around lectures. I know from research and experience that students need to "talk through" concepts to learn and understand them.

This doesn't mean that a talk-centered curriculum always progresses smoothly. Some of you have loved the small-group work in here, some of you have found it to be an enormous challenge. But being able to work with others is an essential part of almost any profession, and to work with others you need to learn how to converse with them. Even many factories have gone to a "worker empowerment" model, where line workers have a say in governance and product design.

You will find it challenging to implement a talk-centered curriculum in your own classroom. Heath's work makes you realize you do need to accept that students will have a wide range of backgrounds and talk norms. Even at the college level, I have students who stubbornly refuse to think about issues of what it means to be "on task" or how they might support others in small groups.

But for every student who finds little value in small-group work, there are five who find it is the best part of the class by the end of the semester. They have learned much about framing criticism tactfully, considering the needs of others, and knowing when it is best to talk and when it is best to be silent. There are many lessons available during these groups. I can't know what they all are, and they will be different for each student.

I know I could never teach in a classroom where students spent most of their time listening to me lecture, dutifully taking notes. The ideas in here become new to me each semester as I listen to you talk about them, challenge them, nod in agreement at tangents your classmates bring up. Talk-centered teaching is an eternal challenge, but after reading Heath's work it was a challenge I became committed to for the duration of my teaching career.

The methods students converse on paper as well as in person during each class session as they share response papers. The conversations that surround these texts help them construct their learning experience. Brenda comments about the power of these response-group discussions.

> Discussions are richer in these groups because students have already thought about the materials. Over time, they begin to have "a few good voices in their head"—a continuing conversation with their classmates as they complete these papers class after class. I always write a response, too, and this keeps me involved in all the discussions. It also keeps the assigned readings fresh for me. I'm rereading each semester as a member of a different community." (1995, p. 24)
>
> The written responses allow every voice to be heard, and different voices to emerge. Some students who are very shy, even in a small group, will write eloquently and passionately in these papers. Other folks with strident voices find they can't help but temper their views as they anticipate group reaction. I write a response to each of these brief papers on a post-it, and return the assignment during the next class session.
>
> (Brenda Power, 1995, p. 24)

Elisha, one of the methods students whose narrative we read earlier, also commented on the power the group discussions had in clarifying her beliefs and opinions.

> One of the greatest things about our reading-response group is having the opportunity to discuss our opinions. Last class someone else wrote on the same topic/reading—and we had different opinions on its value. It is so irritating sometimes to have to discuss something you disagree about with another person—but I realize it's the only way you can really grow firm in what you believe.
>
> Conflict is the best way to question yourself and what you believe. You really have to evaluate what you find is true—and what you disbelieve. It always amazes me that not everybody thinks exactly like I do. (Elisha inserts a smiling face)—this will be good for me! (9/14/94)

The methods students began to make personal connections with their peers on the first day of class when they were asked to work in groups of three and respond to their peers' writing. Over time, these groups were the basis of developing friendships and close personal involvement. Laura expressed the value of groups on two occasions.

> Group today was helpful. They let me be open and sensitive without fearing rejection. You have no idea how much these groups are helping me. I'm getting more and more confident about my writing abilities. (9/19/94)
>
> Gosh, I really love my first group. We are getting to be good friends. (9/21/94)

Summary

In her class, Brenda used an assortment of strategies in order to help herself and her students answer the questions "Who am I?," "Who are you?," "Who are we together?" Writing workshop, writing-response groups, and teacher-research activities provided students with opportunities to develop the skills they will be asked to use as teachers, skills that will enable them to most successfully respond to the specific needs of individual students who will someday compose their elementary classroom communities. Through these strategies, groups and individuals interacted and shared beliefs and ideas. These interactions helped shape the classroom community, and the community was central to learning in the methods classroom.

Chapter 7

Knowing a Place for the First Time: Implications and Conclusions

Stories of literary merit, to be sure, are about events in a "real" world, but they render that world newly strange, rescue it from obviousness, fill it with gaps that call upon the reader...to become a writer, a composer of a virtual text in response to the actual. In the end, it is the reader who must write for himself what he intends to do with the actual text...literary texts initiate "performances" of meaning rather than actually formulating meanings themselves.

(Jerome Bruner, 1986, pp. 24-25)

It was nearing the end of the reading methods course I was teaching last summer term when two of my students lingered after class. They approached me hesitantly and after a minute or two of small talk, one of them asked, "When are we going to start learning how to teach reading?" Initially I was speechless and puzzled, then I began to feel a little irritated. I felt like asking, "Where have you been the last several weeks?" Instead I calmly and courteously explained how the process of teaching reading can't be distilled into an algorithm, that it stems from a number of cultural, social, and developmental factors that are interrelated, complicated, and not entirely knowable until one gets to know one's students. The issues we had addressed throughout the course were all relevant to the process of teaching reading. I felt ambivalent about the question—it had made me feel frustrated, concerned, and a little defensive about my teaching approach. But my students meant no harm. They were genuinely concerned about that time in the not-too-distant future when they would enter the classroom and begin the challenging job of teaching their students to read.

"When are we going to start learning how to teach reading?" is a question that reveals a student's uncertainty in her stage of intellectual development—it's another way of saying, "I'm unsatisfied with the complexities and uncertainties of what I'm learning. I want to be told what to do and how to do it. I want straightforward answers in clear-cut terms. I want to be told what to do and how to do it."

This simplistic approach to problem solving is indicative of a stage in human intellectual development known as *dualism* (Perry, 1970). According to Perry's classic model of cognitive development, college-age students move through stages of intellectual development. Initially they think in bipolar terms, believing there are right and wrong answers and clear-cut solutions to problems. Ambiguity is more-or-less inconceivable and causes frustration. As they develop, young adults begin to understand that there are multiple perspectives on issues, and often more than one right answer. Eventually they are able to understand that decisions must be made in context, weighing wide-ranging variables. In the final stage of development, what Perry calls *relativism*, the individual is committed to the benefits of relativistic thinking, understanding that multiple perspectives bring richness and wholeness to any given situation, that there is rarely one right answer, but rather a range of possibilities. For students like the two who approached me after class, ambiguity is viewed as a source of frustration. The notion that there are multiple perspectives on issues, and often more than one right answer, isn't satisfying to students who have been accustomed to being told in what pace and manner they should progress through segments of a given subject in order to achieve mastery of the whole.

While Perry's model of cognitive development was based on his work with undergraduate male students, most teachers will recognize dichotomous, dualistic thinking as a trait common to learners of all ages and both genders who are exploring new ideas for the first time. As Perry explains, thinking patterns develop at different rates throughout life. Getting older doesn't automatically insure that one will progress from dualistic thinking to relativistic thinking. What's more, educators, including college teachers, can facilitate and support intellectual development, but they can't make students develop (Perry, 1970).

The introduction of Perry's theory coincides with the early stages of reconceptualism, when the field of education was beginning to embrace postmodern perspectives. Postmodernism, after all, represents an effort to embrace relativism and the notion of multiple realities or multiple versions of reality. Like the theories discussed in chapter 3, Perry's ideas of dualism and relativism have implications for the way we understand approaches to college teaching.

Are We Encouraging Relative Thinking?

Reconceptualist approaches have tremendous implications for college teaching. The idea of designing learning experiences that are responsive to the unique and specific needs of students has the potential to transform educational practice at the college level. But in order for reconceptualization to occur, measures need to be taken in classrooms at the college level to help college teachers develop their teaching. As it is, there is a conspicuous absence of support for professional development at the college level. College teachers receive virtually no pedagogical training. In his survey of college-level teaching in the United States, Finkelstein (1995) writes[2]

> Virtually all faculty received advanced training in an academic discipline or a professional field; virtually none received any pedagogical training. Nor did many come to their first full-time academic appointment with prior teaching experience except perhaps for a graduate teaching assistantship that did not involve full responsibility for a course. While some groups promoted reforms, most novices still began their teaching careers armed with memories of an influential teacher and little else.[15] It must all be learned "on the job."

While many colleges and universities have voluntary mentorship programs that connect new faculty members with veteran faculty members who serve as mentors, these programs are usually only minimally effective. Typically all the demands of a new job are so consuming both in terms of time and energy, that professional development ends up being one of the last concerns of new professors. Colleges and universities should do more than talk about quality teaching. Action speaks louder than words—and gets better results. One option would be to grant reduced teaching loads to new faculty members in exchange for their participation in structured training programs. Until colleges and universities demonstrate their commitment to professional development, significant changes in the quality of college teaching will never occur.

Experience taught me that simply accumulating graduate-level credits in my discipline didn't necessarily prepare me to teach that

---

[2] The reference to no. 15 in Finkelstein's quote corresponds to Finkelstein, 1984. See the reference section for full citation.

discipline to adult students. Almost everything I learned about teaching stemmed from deliberate efforts to learn about the art of effective college teaching while I was involved in the experience of teaching. As a beginning teacher I also discovered that I, like any learner, needed guidance and support in my learning process. I needed strategies that would help me build classroom structures that foster learning. I needed techniques to help build classroom learning communities in which I could get to know each of my students on a personal level. I was fortunate to have had the assistance of a mentor during those needy beginning teaching experiences. For me, the learning experience of beginning teaching, the experience of solving the mystery of good teaching and developing an awareness of its essential elements, was a revelation. I began to understand how my evolution as a college teacher has many connections to larger issues of how college faculty learn to teach, or, in many cases, never learn how to teach.

The typical initiation into the college teaching culture is usually a lonesome, trial-by-fire experience. Conway (1989) describes her experience in the following way.

> The morning of each lecturing day, I woke up with a hollow feeling in the pit of my stomach and set out for the university like a prisoner headed for the guillotine...At night I had nightmares of standing naked before laughing audiences, or of losing my notes and standing on the platform in terrified silence...Slowly, cured by exhaustion and frequent exposure, I began to be able to walk toward the lecture hall without my knees knocking together, or becoming sick to my stomach with nervous anxiety. (pp. 219-220)

My experiences are similar to Conway's. In my recurring teaching nightmares, I too stood mute in front of a class of students. My nervousness and insecurity sabotaged my self-esteem. Conway's story and my own are representative of the general experience new faculty have during their first years of college teaching. Finkelstein (1995) comments on the general experience of new faculty members when he writes[3]

---

[3] References in Finkelstein's quote correspond to the following authors. See the reference section of the book for complete citations.
16. Sorcinelli and Austin, (1992),
17. Boice, (1991),
18. Carnegie, (1989); Boice, (1993); Olsen, (1993);
19. Boice, (1991).

Recent research focused on the first years of a college teaching...[depict] an intense period of stress.[16] Overwhelmed by the demands of preparing a host of courses for the first time—often including courses outside their area of expertise, fearful of student disapproval, and of appearing to need help—new faculty tended to be highly structured and lecture oriented, to over prepare, and to teach "defensively." That is, to strive to avoid error and adverse student reaction[17]...New faculty members found that teaching made inordinate time demands, provided few intrinsic rewards at the novice's skill level, and counted little towards promotion and tenure.[18] By the third or fourth semester, many new faculty members established a negative teaching orientation and style that persisted throughout their careers. They "wrote off" teaching.[19] (1995, pp. 35-36)

The Limitations of the Transmission Model

Conventional wisdom concerning college-level teaching falsely assumes that because a professor has earned a degree in her field she is automatically qualified to teach. This assumption is based on the belief that knowledge and skill are transmitted from one source to another—a traditionalist assumption that is not compatible with the postmodern learning theories described previously. Without the aid of pedagogical training that emphasizes reconceptualized instructional approaches, beginning college teachers are left to rely on personal teaching constructs. As a new college-level teacher, I focused on content alone as I prepared for my classes, paying little attention to issues of classroom structure or community. My own preoccupation with content in the process of course preparation is not uncommon. Preoccupation with content, without an equal consideration of the learner, leads to over-reliance on the lecture. Finkelstein (1995) reports.[4]

Eighty percent of a sample of undergraduate arts and sciences faculty, reported a recent study, lectured during all or most of their classes.[10] When queried about their propensity to lecture, faculty members noted the lecture's usefulness in facilitating student understanding by simplifying an ever-expanding volume of complex material. (1995, p. 35)

The philosophical school of thought driving instruction in the typical college-level classrooms aligns with the behaviorist, essentialist, and traditionalist educational philosophies described in chapter 3.

---

[4] The reference in Finkelstein's quote corresponds to the following author. See the reference section of the book for complete citation: 10: Thielens, 1987,

Most college teachers would probably say that they hope their students will acquire integrated thinking skills. They probably hope that their students will learn the principles and skills of their discipline well enough to be able to apply them in real-life circumstances. But courses that follow a straight lecture format restrict the curriculum to teacher-defined content, leaving little room for students to set the learning agenda. The word "lecture" has two definitions (Flexner, 1980).

1. A *discourse read or delivered before an audience or class, especially for instruction.*
2. A *long, tedious reprimand.*

While 80 percent of college teachers probably believe that their discourse is contributing to students' intellectual development, many college students probably identify with the latter definition of lecture and other transmission approaches to teaching, and put up with it because they have had experience with so few alternatives. With roots in the scholastic traditions of the Middle Ages, the lecture has a sanctified, time-honored tradition in Western education. This was an appropriate means of conveying information at a time when texts were hard to come by and bodies of knowledge grew only incrementally over decades or centuries. Many teachers know no other alternative to standing at the front of the class talking. But throughout the last century the hallowed lecture tradition is being discredited on all fronts—new epistemologies, such as those described in chapter 3, challenge the positivistic, reductionist perspective upon which the lecture approach is founded. Knowledge in all fields grows not incrementally but exponentially. Students of every discipline need to be assisted in developing skills that will enable them to deal with vast amounts of information. The lecture as an instructional approach was never intended to achieve such an end.

As college teachers, we need to ask ourselves: "Are we encouraging dualistic thinking through our teaching approaches?" I wonder if the majority of college-level teachers aren't condoning dualistic thinking, even promoting it, by employing instructional practices that are themselves dualistic. The field of higher educa-tion is engaged in an extensive debate over lecture effectiveness (ERIC lists over 1,300 citations under the subject "lecture effective-ness"). Most people accept that in some cases under certain conditions the lecture is effective. There are occasions when the didactic approach is most efficient and effective, and lectures and presentations have their place in the classroom. But perhaps it is time to move past the *effective* versus *ineffective* debate and begin to ask the harder questions: How do my students learn? What instructional approach would best suit both the course objectives and my students' learning styles? How can I change my teaching accordingly? What message do we convey to students when we stand in front of the class and lecture? The lecture rules out the possibility that the construction of knowledge is a dialectical process. Instead it implies that the version of truth being put forth is incontestable, regardless of the meaning the student brings to that body of information; that the content is determined solely by an outside expert who organizes and interprets ideas into the correct form, that knowledge is received rather than constructed, that the world the student brings to the learning situation is irrelevant. Where does this leave the student? In many disciplines where the literary canon was developed and dominated by scholars and thinkers representing perspectives of the dominant mainstream culture, such as history or literature, the lecture approach marginalizes students whose perspectives and cultural backgrounds differ from mainstream perspectives. These students are often left feeling alienated, disaffected, ambivalent, and sometimes hostile. In an age when educational psychology plainly acknowledges the correlation between attitude and emotion to performance and achievement (Goleman, 1995), teachers of students at all levels need to continually monitor their students' intellectual and emotional involvement while they invite their contribution to classroom discourse. Didactic instructional approaches don't allow for this kind of complex interaction or monitoring. Moreover, because they encourage passivity and conformity, they disregard the need for students to become reflective and critical thinkers. Implicit in the very idea of a lecture as singular educational method is the notion that the mind of a student is a vacant space, waiting to be filled. This approach trains young, developing minds to accept a mind-set of obedience and conformity: "You, the authority, will tell me everything I need to know." Ironically, it is precisely this mind-set that Perry and others urge educators to help our students move past.

As college teachers, we need to help our students move through the right/wrong mind-set of intellectual dualism toward a way of thinking that values multiple perspectives. But first it might be necessary to break out of the pedagogical dualism to which many of us have been socialized. Constructivist and social learning theories suggest that students need learning opportunities that allow them to translate new concepts and ideas into personal beliefs and behaviors through active and social learning experiences. Knowledge is constructed through mediated involvement in meaningful learning situations; and in these situations the assistance of more experienced and knowledgeable mentors guide and monitor student development. Within this framework the teacher spends more time amongst students instead of in front of them. Rather than talking from the podium or overhead projector, the teacher sits at their sides, observing, assessing and instructing, and helping them through the process of constructing knowledge.

Overcoming Dualism:
Reconstructing the Role of the College Teacher

I wonder if we as a profession are in the dualistic stage of our zone of development. We embrace new ideas and, through words, emphasize them in our classes; but in our classrooms we cling either deliberately or subconsciously to the traditional role of teacher as all-knowing expert, telling our students what they need to know. Our field is at a consensus of opinion concerning suggested pedagogical techniques for teacher-education courses. Almost a decade ago, the Coalition of English Associations issued a statement on teacher education, suggesting that courses should emphasize how to do English rather than what English is, and should emphasize learning rather than teaching (Lloyd-Jones and Lunsford, 1989). Research and theories offered in our methods instructional textbooks are based on new paradigms, including phenomenological perspectives, constructivist and social learning theories, and references to whole language and workshop approaches to instruction. But even with our newer, more powerful theories, we haven't quite convinced ourselves. The prevalent model of instruction in the classroom follows a linear progression through content. We present ideas, allow for discussion, and move on to new ideas. While we believe that it is important to expose students to progressive practices, and incorporate them if possible, they resemble the add-ons that are a feature of teaching in the classrooms of the newly converted elementary-school teachers. We, like the classroom teacher who has not yet made the leap of faith, make room for writing workshop two or three days a week, as long as we leave enough time for spelling and grammar drill. We are still stuck in the dilemma of dualistic thinking—we incorporate newer practices, but feel we are doing so at the risk of covering content. It seems to me that unless we are willing to go out on a limb with our students, to demonstrate through our practice the principles we preach, to have confidence in the benefits that experience-based learning will bring about, how can we expect that our students will do the same?

We need to convince ourselves of our own practical theories, comparing our practices to our beliefs, and to work to close the gap. We can't continue to teach in a traditional mode and expect our students to do otherwise. Our students will practice teaching in the manner of those who served as their mentors, not in the manner of those abstract models presented in textbooks and trade books. We need to enter the stage of relativism in our own teaching practice. Our methods classes need to allow students to experience best classroom practice as well as hear and read about it. We need to realize that the success of our instruction depends on our knowledge of individual students, that learning is relative to their needs and perspectives, and that we can't know how to address their needs until we meet them. Before preservice teachers can grasp an instructional idea in the abstract, they must be familiar with the idea in the concrete; and, therefore, learning experiences in the methods course need to be embedded primarily in the realm of present experience. We need to develop teaching practices that match the theories of our reconceptualized teaching paradigm.

At a professional level we seem to be on a dualistic search for one right answer. Our debates center on the search for the one right theory that would serve as the basis for one adequate theory concerning the teaching of English education. In his report concerning the status of English language-arts teacher education, O'Donnell cites Henry (1986) on the nature of English education:

> In sum, English education is composed of an "English" never sure of the nature of its substance, and an "education" uncertain of the soundness of the kind of science it believes English teaching needs. Under these conditions the foremost role of research in English education is to help explore this very paradox, and it is the role of English to point out to science where to spade. But only a large philosophical theory—such as transactionalism, phenomenology, the drama of conflict in a Universe of Discourse—can put the two in tandem. To date, such a philosophy has never been summoned up by a science of education alone or by English alone. (p. 32)

In reference to Henry's comments, O'Donnell stresses that until we find a large philosophical theory we will be unable to find "an adequate unifying theory of teacher education." Lacking that, we cannot expect "persuasive research evidence of what the indispensable elements of an ideal program for preparing teachers of English might be" (p. 715). I question whether there is such a unifying theory. The discourse of modern philosophy, after all, demonstrates the impossibility of such a feat (Tarnas, 1991). Even if there were such a philosophy, I question whether it would be appropriate to apply it to the field of English education. After all, there is not a singular, unified *English*; rather, there are multiple versions of it. By definition, a unifying philosophy is also a philosophy that marginalizes and minimizes heterogeneous elements. A philosophy of diversity, plurality, and relativity, rather than a theory of totality, would better serve our purposes. Perhaps as teachers we should be embracing the philosophies that best serve our unique needs as teachers of specific kinds of students. Philosophy is too vast and we compromise the power of our practice when we attempt to be all things to all people. It's unrealistic, even dualistic, to believe we can, or should, ever agree on one unifying theory. Different paradigms promote different ways of teaching and learning. The field of English education can't afford to wait for a global philosophy or a globally adequate theory of teacher education to be developed. Instead, each teacher should become aware that the philosophy she alone embraces is the theory of education for the particular group of students she teaches. Instead of looking outward for a unifying theory, teachers should look inward in order to discover the sources of our own personal and individual philosophies. Perhaps, then, a more realistic and generative goal would be to begin to acknowledge and validate the rich knowledge that stems from our professional experience, to use that frame of experience in order to define a personal philosophy, and then to consider how that philosophy fits with our teaching practices. In this scenario, the practice of self-study will bring about an awareness of the power each teacher has to shape and influence her own teaching beliefs and practices.

This study offers one possibility toward the resolution of the paradox between *education* and *English*. More studies that focus on other versions of classroom reality are needed. Once they exist, these different versions of classroom reality portraying a broad range of perspectives will serve as models for college teachers who are striving to meet the unique demands of their own classrooms.

Reconciling Our Practices with Our Theories: Embracing Relativity

It is often difficult for preservice teachers to embrace the notion that teaching decisions are made in the context of an ever-changing classroom dynamic, and that as teachers they will need an ability to weigh wide-ranging variables and understand multiple perspectives. Each of our students is at a different stage of intellectual development. Since they are familiar with the traditionalist approach to teaching, which most of them experienced as students, many will see teaching in dualistic terms, wanting right answers, steps, and procedures. While an acceptance of alternative viewpoints is initially challenging for some students, the ability to embrace multiple perspectives is also liberating because it gives one permission to trust her instincts in order to think and act independently. Some students will understand the rich potential of relative thinking, realizing specific teaching actions will need to be based on unique circumstances that can't be entirely understood until the complex phenomenon of classroom life brings them into being. These students will more easily accept current theories of teaching and learning that stress multiple realities of the classroom and the importance of basing instructional decisions on those realities. Classroom learning experiences should be supportive of both types of learners. The challenge for preservice teachers, then, is to acquire a basic understanding of teaching practices that are responsive to the individual needs of students, and to have classroom-based opportunities to practice these techniques. The methods-course experience should be transformational as well as educational in order to help future teachers begin to acquire strategies that will enable them to meet the demands of holistic, child-centered teaching approaches, which have become the standard in English education (National Council of Teachers of English Elementary Section Steering Committee, 1996).

If not the lecture, then what? As a new college teacher I felt deeply that something about my own teaching was lacking—but at the time I was at a loss to know what it was. If I am no longer to stand at the front of the room and tell my students what they need to know, where am I to be? What are my students and I to be doing? The approaches discussed in the previous chapters offer several alternatives. Brenda believes that future teachers need to experience writing and reading in the methods course in order to understand and discuss how it is taught. When I first sought advice from her about my teaching, she recommended: "Get them started writing—first thing." She suggested I begin each class with a workshop so that students could learn about teaching practices through their own experience. Admittedly, it seemed like the wrong approach at the time. I couldn't justify "wasting" precious time on frills, and there was so much to cover. My reaction was similar to the student's who asked me, "When are we going to learn how to teach reading?" I wondered, "When am I going to teach them how to teach reading and writing?" I was desperate and willing to try anything—I took a leap of faith. While initially I felt very insecure in trying something so new and foreign to me, and also a little guilty and afraid that my students would feel like they weren't learning the "basics," my initial reservations gave way to a clear understanding of what my students were learning about themselves as readers and writers, as well as methods of teaching. I developed confidence in the power of the new approaches I was using.

My initial reservations reveal a dualistic mode of professional thinking. I thought, "If I don't cover it, they won't learn it." I couldn't yet understand the messy ambiguity of a process approach to literacy methods instruction, and I didn't understand that the process of learning about teaching methods is relative to the nature and identity of the student involved in the learning experience. Those insecure, conflicting thoughts I had when I first began to try new approaches—the feeling that if I practice what I preach, I do so at the risk of sacrificing content—is a sentiment that other college teachers share. For example, Henney (1990) reported her experiences of teaching a six-credit literacy methods course in which students had first-hand experiences with whole language. She concluded that, while the course was successful in many ways, perhaps the greatest shortcoming was that students didn't learn as much as they might have in a lecture-recitation class. I believe the sentiment Henney describes—that something good had happened, but that it had happened at the expense of covering the official curriculum—is similar to the feelings many classroom teachers have when they begin writing or reading workshop. Initially, these structures are seen as "add-ons," taking time away from the traditional subjects of spelling, grammar, literature, and composition. It seems to take an initial leap of faith to dramatically change classroom practice. As teacher educators, we need to trust in the learning process of our young-adult students, just as we suggest they trust in the language-learning processes. It might take more than an initial leap of faith; it might require looking within ourselves and examining our biases and assumptions. Self-study and autobiography offer powerful methods of helping to bring about a conscious examination of those biases and assumptions. It might also be important to critically examine the philosophical ideas that support our formal understandings. An examination of the ideas of reconceptualism and the tenets of postmodernism would be an important place to begin that journey. Teacher-education programs should incorporate courses or course work that help students explore these philosophical movements and their relation to teaching.

Literacy Education and Pedagogical Challenges

For the past twenty years the fields of English and literacy education have struggled to define a new set of beliefs and practices that are compatible with reconceptualist ideas. English-teacher educators have voiced their commitment that education students should experience effective models of instruction as well as learn about them; they should have opportunities to practice effective teaching throughout the course of their teacher preparation experience; they should have opportunities to critique the nature of effective teaching; and they should do these things in ways that will make them lifelong students of effective teaching (National Council of Teachers of English, 1986). Our educational philosophies emphasize the importance of learning experiences that are active, social, and personally relevant. But as members of a rapidly changing profession, we are often trapped into continuing along more traditional courses of instruction by the inertia of experience, habit, and tradition. As is the case with practitioners in other professions, our ideas speed ahead of our practice. Without the benefit of having experienced alternative instructional models ourselves, we resort to teaching in the ways we have been taught. (Squire 1977) explained two decades ago that, in spite of continued efforts to improve the preservice and inservice education of teachers of English, changes have generally occurred only in what content is taught or emphasized; the manner in which it is taught has remained the unchanged. This scenario has changed somewhat as college teachers have made efforts to incorporate more active, experience-based learning opportunities into their courses (such as those discussed in chapter 3). But as Anderson explains (1988), a gap still exists in most preservice teacher-education courses between the talk about good teaching and the development of a working knowledge and problem-solving expertise that characterizes good teaching. The typical teacher training experience doesn't include the principles of modeling, coaching, scaffolding, articulation, and reflection—elements that would help bridge that gap.

Models of instruction for literacy education methods courses that include active, experienced-based learning opportunities are needed. As I explained in chapter 3, Anderson offers three examples of teacher training experiences that do promote these qualities, including Reading Recovery, the Kamehameha Early Education Program in Hawaii (KEEP), and Reciprocal Teaching. Based on findings in my study, I would like to suggest that several additional instructional models can be added to Anderson's list. The structures that Brenda used in the methods course—literacy workshops, teacher-research activities, and reading seminar groups—had many of the elements of learning that Anderson claims are needed. Over the duration of the course, the frameworks of these approaches provided experiences in which teaching practices were demonstrated. Methods students were assisted through learning experiences in which they practiced instructional techniques, solved problems, and reflected on observations and experiences. Brenda modeled best practice as she coached her students' performance. Workshop, teacher research activities, and reading seminar groups were not "add-ons" to the curriculum; rather, they were the curricular framework intended to be vehicles for helping methods students learn pedagogy as well as theory. As writers of personal narratives, poetry, memoirs, and reflective essays, students explored the theory and practice of writing composition. As they planned, facilitated, and participated in literature circles in which they read Caldecott award-winning literature, students learned about reader response theory and how to apply it to the classroom. Students read Rosenblatt's (1978) views on efferent and aesthetic reading while, simultaneously, they were reading texts from efferent and aesthetic stances. Presentations and instruction were given, but were done in the context of practical, experience-based learning situations.

Learning to Know Ourselves Through Mentor Study

As a beginning college teacher I held certain beliefs about learning. But as I reconstructed my early teaching experiences I realized my practices conveyed something other than my beliefs. It was important for me to reexamine my beliefs, and then to take deliberate steps to bring my practice in line with them. In order to do that, I studied the practices of an exemplary teacher.

Gregory Bateson's statement, "It takes two to know one," affirms my research experience. Through the study of my mentor, I was able to develop a more critical understanding of my own teaching beliefs practices. I set out to answer questions I had about teaching; these questions were set against a backdrop of my beliefs and experiences about learning and teaching. My systematic examination of Brenda's classroom practices helped me chart out my own personal theory of education. Through a process of learning about her teaching beliefs and practices, and crossing her creative teaching style with ideas about my own, I have arrived at a more versatile personal teaching theory.

Vygotsky's zone of proximal development (ZPD) is typically applied to the cognitive development of children. But the ZPD can also be used as a metaphor for teacher development. As teachers, we can begin to explore our unknown zones in order to begin to move through them. Our mentors can be our companions on the journey, mediating our professional learning experience. The field of education, at the elementary through college levels, is in desperate need of knowledgeable, skillful, and experienced mentors—teachers who are able to offer their assistance in helping the novice practitioner reach higher levels of expertise. Vera John-Steiner (1985) talks about the importance of "distant teachers" to creative development. They are those special people who have influenced our thinking in indirect ways. In my role as a classroom teacher, Nancie Atwell (1987) and Bobbi Fisher (1991) were my distant teachers. Indirectly, through their books, they served as my mentors. I adopted and adapted the practices they described, and developed as a teacher.

During my earliest and most angst-filled days of college teaching, I would have devoured teacher research accounts by scholars and teachers I admire such as Donald Graves, Ken Goodman, Shirley Brice Heath, and Marie Clay, among others. These influential figures, together with teacher researchers such as Nancie Atwell

(1987), Carol Avery (1993), and Mary Mercer Krogness (1995), to name only a few, have made vast contributions to the development of knowledge of theory and practice in literacy education. There is an increasing demand by elementary and secondary teachers for books written by teachers for teachers. Publishing companies are responding to this need and each year additional titles appear on the market. However, college-level teaching has yet to undergo a transformative era similar to that which has influenced elementary teaching practices. There is a serious absence of this teacher research at the college level, and few books written by college teachers are available that describe in detail pedagogical approaches and teaching philosophies. Perhaps it is time for teacher educators to begin to look more critically and systematically through teacher research accounts. The resulting findings would benefit the larger society of teacher educators. This research project has helped me see the power in descriptive accounts of exemplary teaching practice. Hopefully, other college teachers will begin to explore their own teaching, and college teacher researchers' accounts will begin to satisfy the need for personal accounts of best teaching practice at the college level. This study of Brenda's teaching provides a close examination of one teacher's approach to college-level teaching and has the potential to make such a contribution. But one is not enough; more studies containing the rich, contextualized, local detail of exemplary practice at the college level are needed.

The power of mentorship in teaching is often overlooked as a method of professional development in favor of more technical, theoretical approaches. Each year teachers gather for inservice programs where outside "experts" are invited to offer advice. During five years as an elementary teacher and one as a college teacher, I recall attending these programs. I remember hearing about cooperative learning, whole language, and experience-based science instruction, but I've forgotten the focus of the remaining sessions. This approach to professional development exemplifies how the field of education is continually searching for single solutions to multiple problems. Somehow administrators believe they will achieve sweeping reform or systemwide improvement through infrequent workshops. Professional development is a much more involved, extensive and long-term process. For teachers who want to reinvent their personal teaching constructs, it is necessary to search out mentors who can share teacher lore and with whom they can form lasting, collaborative relationships that nurture the process of

professional transformation. Because it is personal and individualized, working with and learning from mentors offers a realistic and
powerful professional development possibility.

Finkelstein (1995) confirms the importance of mentors when he
explains, "most novices still began their teaching careers armed
with memories of an influential teacher and little else." First-year
teacher studies paint a gloomy picture of professional disappoint-
ment. Beginning teachers report that they find their jobs "intellectually and physically arduous" (Cooper, 1989). They feel a lack of
control and power, pressure to use specific texts and methods, and
pressure to compromise alternative instructional approaches
learned about in college in favor of traditional ones used by veteran
teachers (Hensley, 1989). Once teaching at all levels is transformed
from lecture-recitation structures to more student-centered ones,
being armed with memories of good teaching mentors could be a
powerful tool for new teachers.

Just as beginning college teachers need mentors, so do beginning elementary teachers. Often times, socialization into the school
culture is characterized by new teachers feeling a lack of power and
the pressure to compromise their own beliefs in favor of school traditions (Hensley, 1989). As teacher educators, we need to help beginning teachers through their own zones of proximal development
during the critical entry years into the profession. Perhaps if beginning teachers can maintain relationships with university mentors
through their first, second, and third years of teaching, some of the
negative pressures that characterize beginning teaching might be
alleviated. We need to acknowledge that learning the art and craft
of teaching takes many years. On the simplest level, we might help
new teachers move from what they can do by themselves to what
they can do with the assistance of more knowledgeable others who
help them establish professional connections. Just as Brenda was
my mentor, helping me develop as a teacher and as an academic
professional, she also served as a mentor to her undergraduate students. For example, in the place of purchasing one textbook, she required her students to become members of the National Council of
Teachers of English (NCTE). Also, she required attendance at the
New England Reading Association (NERA) conference which took
place in Portland, Maine. Brenda recognizes the limitations of one
course experience. The literacy methods course, or any other course
for that matter, is only a brush stroke in the portrait of a teaching
career. But she believes that her efforts to connect future teachers to

professional networks will sustain their continuing professional growth and increase the impact of the literacy methods course experience.

Theorizing Within the Realm of the Practical

Traditionalist instructional practices continue to dominate in schools; and reconceptualism has only begun to influence how some teachers practice. A major task for the next generation of educators and teacher educators will be to apply and incorporate the currently accepted theories of reconceptualism (constructivism and social learning theory, for example) into the practical instructional repertoire of the majority of teachers. The question of how theory can best be applied to practice will continue to be a primary concern in the field of education. Some scholars have argued that scholars and theorists should maintain distance from the practical worlds of students and schools. For example, Pinar writes:

> The theoretical wing of the reconceived field aspires to ground itself not in the pressured everyday world of the classroom but in worlds not present in schools, in ideas marginal to the maximization of corporate profits, and in lived experience that is not exclusively instrumental and calculative…Theory must create spaces apart from the pressurized sphere of practical activity, spaces in which the demands of the state and of the principal, parents, and students can be viewed, understood and reframed as questions posed to oneself. By living in worlds apart from the everyday and the taken-for-granted, we might participate in the daily world with more intensity and intelligence. (1991, p. 241)

Others have maintained that scholars and researchers are in the best position to help advance practice in schools and have an obligation to do so. For example, Moll (1996) explained that grand theoretical constructs often cannot be directly applied to practice; instead they require intermediate concepts that are immediately applicable to classroom pedagogy. Moll reasons that researchers who are familiar with the theoretical realm of their field and who are also connected with the real worlds of classrooms are in the best position to help teachers utilize the cultural resources of the students in order to help them develop students' thinking. If researchers and scholars intend to study the real issues and problems of real students, they need to work with real classroom teachers (Moll, 1996). Moll and Pinar both make important points. The main objective of theory and practice is to enhance the potential for learning in schools. On the one hand, in order to be free of the tyranny of tradition, theorists must necessarily be free to conceptualize viable alternatives to the status quo. Educational researchers need time and space to theorize. But theorizing ultimately should apply to the reality of the classroom in as much as it can offer a possible way to improve or transform it.

Teacher research and classroom-based inquiry offer important means of merging the theory/practice dichotomy. Teacher education programs should begin to help preservice and in-service teachers understand the power and importance of theorizing as it relates to practice. Teacher research can help transform classrooms in a number of ways. First, many teachers manage to carve out time away from the pressure-filled, everyday world of the classroom by forming teacher research networks with other colleagues. School districts could acknowledge and support teachers' efforts for this type of professional development by reducing contact hours in the classroom in order to allow participation in teacher research networks. Second, undergraduate education programs will demonstrate a commitment to the development of pedagogy that is both practical and theoretical by incorporating teacher research into the official curriculum of education courses. This can be accomplished at the undergraduate level by including teacher research activities in the methods course curriculum as Brenda did (see chapter 5 for a discussion of teacher research). At the graduate level, courses in teacher research or classroom-based inquiry could be a requirement for those working toward an advanced degree in education. The University of Maine has always required a research course for the master's degree in literacy education. Students were required to choose from statistics or traditional qualitative research courses until several years ago when a new course called Teacher Research was developed. Now students learn about research approaches while they are assisted in the process of doing their own classroom-based research. Third, teacher research could replace the ineffective model of in-service education currently practiced in most school districts. Teachers could be required to work with a team consisting of a university professor and other teachers on inquiry projects as a means to satisfy continuing education requirements.

Reconstructing Teaching: Autobiography and Research

Self-study, or autobiography, helps us revisit all that has happened in our past to better understand what is happening now. By writing personal history, we can clarify what we believe. Writing my research story convinced me that teacher development needs to begin with self-examination. It has helped me understand that personal development is recursive—past experiences shape present ones, which form the basis of how the future proceeds. Autobiography can help solidify experience by capturing it permanently in ink on paper. We can take fragments of experience and write them into a whole (Clandinin and Connelly, 1994). Self-knowledge is powerful; in the process of composing one's history, one gains control of destiny.

Incorporating my teaching narrative into my research gave me a starting point for my explorations of Brenda's classroom, and also helped determine how my research developed. My experience parallels what Clandinin and Connelly (1994) explain: autobiography opened me up to the rich and seemingly endless range of possible stories; it prepared me to follow leads in many directions and to hold them all in inquiry context as my project proceeded. The stories I chose to give life to in my research text concerned the questions I had from my standpoint as a teacher. My own experience shaped what questions I sought to answer while I researched Brenda's teaching.

The composition of my own personal teaching narrative has served as a tool for making sense of my life. I have tried to identify themes in my own teaching that help explain my beliefs, my failings, and my growth in order to find a starting place for my research. As I complete this project I see how important the combination of self-study with the empirical research process has been in my development as a researcher and as a teacher educator.

Future Research Possibilities: Channels of Inquiry into Unknown Zones

My research agenda was personal. I set out to identify and describe the elements of college-level teaching in a literacy methods courses. My intention was not to assess whether, how much, or what, the methods students learned. That question was beyond the scope of this study, though it clearly is a question that needs to be explored. Possible follow-up studies might include longitudinal accounts of methods students, tracking their professional development and teaching practices one, two, and three years after the methods experience. Also, we need more descriptive studies of different models of methods instruction and studies that determine their effectiveness.

Hopefully the descriptions and interpretations of exemplary college teaching described in this study will serve as an alternative point of view to another beginning college teacher, also searching for a distant teacher or a mentor. If college teaching practices are to improve, and if beginning college teachers are to have the mentors they need, more case studies of exemplary college teachers need to be done. Mentor studies by students of exemplary teachers, or collaborative teacher-research studies, might be incorporated into research/teaching assistantships as a method of educating beginning college teachers. These efforts could provide a potential method of professional development for beginning and veteran teachers alike.

Epilogue

Often we look at ourselves and feel that *everything* is lacking! It is in this gap, this zone of the unknown, where we feel most deeply—but are most inarticulate.

(Stephen Nachmanovitch, 1990, p. 67)

When faced with unfamiliar situations or confronted with the unknown, we are often at a loss for words. At those times, when we find ourselves in unknown zones, there is a brief period of muteness while we struggle through the uncomfortable silence. As a doctoral student and beginning college teacher, I continually found myself in the mute territory of unfamiliar ideas, struggling to find terms that would lend a voice to the inarticulate places where I feel most deeply. Acquiring a language to explain my experience as a teacher has been the work of my recent life as both a student and beginning professor.

Before I began graduate school, I spent four years as an elementary-classroom teacher. Those four years of teaching taught me to value my students' perspectives and provide instruction based on their needs. They also made me realize that children learn best through experience, and that they need to be given ample opportunities to choose the pace and direction of their learning. I saw my role in the classroom as being that of a guide, helping students engage in integrated learning experiences. But when I began my doctoral studies and what would become a new career of college teaching, I found myself unwitting in a zone of the unknown. While the emphasis of my literacy education courses included the constructivist and social learning theories I believed and practiced, my instructional practices were based on a traditional framework. I was lost—I felt deeply about my convictions regarding how people learn, but I also felt "inarticulate"—I had not yet learned to practice approaches to instruction that reflected my beliefs.

When I left my elementary teaching job five years ago in order to begin my doctoral studies in literacy education, I had a vague sense that I would be putting my teaching career on hold while I learned, among other things, how to do research. But five years of learning, teaching, and researching have helped me realize that my teaching identity and my research identity are tightly meshed. Their interrelatedness has become increasingly clear to me through this research project.

The previous chapters are a chronicle of the research that documents my discoveries about Brenda's teaching beliefs and practices. In addition to offering a new model for my own teaching, the process of observing, describing, analyzing, and interpreting Brenda's teaching helped me find a language for my own teaching practices and beliefs. As I engaged in the research experience, I simultaneously cycled through a process of deconstructing, reconstructing, and modifying my own teaching beliefs and practices. As I emerge from my research experience, I realize that in order to help future teachers acquire teaching pedagogy and knowledge, they need experience-based learning opportunities in the college classroom. I have a better understanding of how I can implement classroom structures that will serve as a basis for exploring the content of educational theory and practice. Finally, and perhaps most importantly, I realize that my students should inform my instructional practices. It is my primary role to forge strong relationships with my students so that I am able to structure personalized learning phases for them.

Though my research project was a case study of another teacher, unexpectedly it also became a personal case study. I learned as much about myself as I did about Brenda. While I began in a zone of inarticulate silence, over time I have acquired a rich language for my own newly developed teaching behaviors and beliefs.

> We shall not cease from exploration,
> And the end of all our exploring
> Will be to arrive where we started
> And know the place for the first time.
>
> T. S. Eliot ("Little Gidding," in Four Quartets, [1941] 1952)

Methodological Appendix

Exploring Where the "Self" and "Study" Intersect: A Reflection on Method

As thought without sensation is empty, so is sensation without thought blind. Only in conjunction can understanding and sensibility supply objectively valid knowledge of things.

(Richard Tarnas, 1991, p. 345)

All experience is the product of both the features of the world and the biography of the individual. Our experience is influenced by our past as it interacts with our present. Thus, not only must a certain kind of competence be acquired in order to perceive the qualities of form in the objects available to us, but the nature of our experience with these forms is influenced not only by the form itself but by our past.

(Elliot Eisner, 1985, pp. 25-26)

My original purpose for employing an autobiographical research approach in conducting this study was to build a coherent and credible research text. But the writing process has helped me discover that the tools of qualitative research and autobiography have helped me construct a better understanding of myself as both a teacher and researcher as much as they have helped construct a better research text. Ernst Gombrich said, "The painter does not paint what he can see, he sees what he is able to paint" (cited in Eisner, p. 27, 1994). As I engaged in self-study as a framework for my investigation of college-level literacy methods, I was more able to see what I was painting. Reflecting on my own life as it related to college teaching, while at the same time observing, documenting, and interpreting the teaching and learning phenomena in the literacy methods course, helped me see more clearly the picture of meaning I was in the process of composing. In this chapter I will summarize my research process, elaborate on issues of concern in the study, and describe the relationship of autobiography to my research process.

Locating the "Self" Within the "Study"

> Nature is not mute. It eternally repeats the same notes which reach us from afar, muffled, with neither harmony nor melody. But we cannot do without melody...It is up to us to strike the chords, to write the score, to bring forth the symphony, to give the sounds a form that, without us, they do not have.
>
> (Francois Jacob, 1988, p. 274)

Empirical-analytical research, the dominant mode of inquiry in research on curriculum and teacher education (Schubert, 1989), presents the views of others and then explains how they all have limitations and that their shortcomings are thus and so, and that the reported findings offer a better version of truth. But in the context of this study, I examined Brenda's teaching practices not with an eye toward discovering what they failed to accomplish, but with the desire to see one method of teaching more clearly so that I could better understand myself as a teacher. Because of my own position in the study and my close relationship to the person under study, I realized from the outset that subjectivity might be an issue of concern. Critics might ask, "Is this study reliable?" After all, Brenda and I shared a strong rapport before I began my research study. My relationship with her extends to the spring semester of 1992 when I took a graduate course that she taught, and subsequently had her as my professor for three other courses. Through the course of my doctoral experience she became my friend, mentor, and research advisor. The nature of our relationship took on different dimensions throughout the study. While I was collecting data for my study, she was conducting her own research in her classroom and writing a book about her teaching. During that time we had frequent, informal discussions about our respective projects. My role during those discussions shifted between student, protégé, researcher, co-researcher, and colleague.

Confidence, trust, and respect characterized our relationship. But these are the very qualities one hopes to foster in a classroom and in one's teaching. Rather than labeling them as bias, I believed it was necessary for these qualities to be cultivated and acknowledged in the research. Because of the subjective nature of my study—the examination of the teaching practices of my mentor under her guidance and direction—I began to understand how

autobiographical inquiry would provide the necessary epistemo-
logical foundation for my study. Glesne and Peshkin (1992) explain
that formalist standards for qualitative research caution against
friendships between the researcher and researched because there is
a risk of bias. They summarize one school of thought in qualitative
research that cautions against friendships between researcher and
subject.

> When a distinction between rapport and friendship is made in qualitative
> literature, the overwhelming tendency is to warn against forming
> friendships because of the hazards of sample bias and loss of objectivity.
> These hazards are likened to over identification, also called "over-
> rapport" and "going native." (p. 98)

These cautions seem to apply to a research situation where the
"alien" researcher is seeking to know "native" populations and is
concerned with results and content rather than methods of learning
and the nature of relationships between learner and teacher, which
need to be experienced and entered into on a personal level. The
native/alien dichotomy didn't apply to my research world. I had
already *gone native*. For two years I had been an apprentice to the
teaching and research perspectives and practices of Brenda and
other faculty members in the College of Education at the University
of Maine. In fact, a primary concern driving my interest in the study
was to *go native* all the way. I wanted to study the practices of my
mentor in order to improve my own practices—a very subjective
endeavor, indeed! Surely, I thought, there are research models that
won't discredit my study on the grounds of subjectivity. After all,
unless I understood myself in relation to the study, I had no basis for
judging alternatives, initiating change, and responding to students'
needs in the learning process.

I was looking for a research methodology that would free me to
find answers to personally relevant questions. These questions were
subjective, based on my personal causes and experiences.
Traditional qualitative research paradigms, those Glesne and
Peshkin refer to in the passage above, seem to adhere to what
Jerome Bruner describes as the paradigmatic mode of thinking. He
describes it this way:

> The paradigmatic or logico-scientific [mode of thinking] attempts to fulfill
> the ideal of a formal, mathematical system of description and
> explanation. It employs categorization or conceptualization and the
> operations by which categories are established, instantiated, idealized,
> and related one to the other to form a system ...The logico-scientific mode

deals in general causes, and in their establishment, and makes use of procedures to assure verifiable reference and to test for empirical truth. Its language is regulated by requirements of consistency and noncontradiction. Its domain is defined not only by observables to which its basic statements relate, but also by the set of possible worlds that can be logically generated and tested against observables—that is, it is driven by principled hypotheses. (1986, p. 12)

The paradigmatic mode of thinking is useful in its power to attain high levels of abstraction in order to make broad generalizations. This mode of thinking is compatible with the conventional positivist social-science research perspectives that have traditionally been applied to qualitative as well as quantitative research. But these standards have been found to be lacking in their ability to support research for which the relationships between researched and researcher are the basis of interpretation and meaning making (Lincoln, 1995a). Denzin and Lincoln (1994) describe the standards for conventional social science research and their shortcomings.

Conventional positivist social science applies four criteria to disciplined inquiry: *internal validity*, the degree to which findings correctly map the phenomenon in question, *external validity*, the degree to which findings can be generalized to other settings similar to the one in which the study occurred, *reliability*, the extent to which findings can be replicated, or reproduced, by another inquirer, and *objectivity*, the extent to which findings are free from bias. [These views] have recently come under considerable attack. [On the grounds that] these paradigms are unable to deal adequately with the issues surrounding the etic, emic, nomothetic, and idiographic dimensions of inquiry. Too many local (emic), case-based (idiographic) meanings are excluded by the generalizing (etic) nomothetic, positivist position. At the same time, the nomothetic, etic approaches fail to address satisfactorily the theory- and value-laden nature of facts, the interactive nature of inquiry, and the fact that the same set of "facts" can support more than one theory. (p. 100)

The problems I had identified were personal. My research questions centered on my specific interests in the unique circumstances of Brenda's methods classroom. The conventional standards for social-science research, including internal validity, external validity, reliability, and objectivity, couldn't apply to my study. In fact, I was relying on my subjectivity in order to interpret my observations and make meaning from them. If in the end my study contributed to general knowledge about college-level teaching, it would be all the better. But I realized from the outset that I could not make generalizations from my study to other classrooms.

I explored research methodology literature that would validate my study. I reasoned that my subjectivity wouldn't confound the study. It would define it. Hullfish and Smith (1961) articulated a sentiment I share.

> A problem is always a personal affair...The individual, whether in school or out, faces no problem until he stakes out a claim to it. When he does this, he acts as if he had shouted for all to hear, "This is mine! Let me get at it." The simple fact is that individuals become involved in only those problems they accept to solve. Inevitably, therefore, their biases, knowledge, values—in short, their personalities—are vital factors in the reflection they carry on in problem situations. (p. 107)

The statement, "This is mine! Let me get at it," mirrored my position. There was no doubt that my research question was shaped by my values and biases, and I was personally invested in the study. So instead of viewing my bias as detrimental, I began to see it as a dimension of the study that should be explored and understood. I also felt that any interpretation of what I was seeing in the methods classroom would be richer as a result of my unique standpoint. I realized that I needed to explore qualitative research standards that recognize and build from the close relationships that develop between the researcher and the researched. Lincoln (1995b) explains that increasingly the criteria for qualitative research isn't found in set standards, but rather in an array of traits, unique for each particular study, that serve to state what the research should be like. The criteria has the effect of creating space for "shared discourse and compelling dialog" between the researcher and the researched (Lincoln, 1995b). Lincoln (1995b) describes emerging qualitative research standards that serve as an alternative to the conventional social science research standards described above. These include an awareness that issues that stem from the relationships between the researcher and the researched are often the basis for meaning making. Lincoln's description of standards for qualitative research appear in Figure 8.1.

Figure 8.1. Lincoln's "Qualitative Research Standards"

Positionality (*or* standpoint epistemology)—The study must explicate the researcher's grounds and standpoint.

Community—The research takes place and is addressed to a community. Objectivity can deter community, and can be anti-communal. Any form of knowing *is* relational. The new epistemologies create relational knowing.

Neighborliness—Is a kind of "praxis"—a practical activity having a theoretical base. "Praxis" is based in critical theory and action-research traditions.

Voice—Issues concerning who speaks, how, and why are important to the study. This creates praxis.

Reflexivity—Is a critical subjectivity. Reflexivity is a high consciousness or awareness to understand others in order to move to create personal and social transformation.

Reciprocity—Is the recognition that persons are always in relations. The researcher must understand relations of subjects and include them in research. Trust, respect, and mutuality between researched and researcher are of primary importance.

Sacredness—The researcher must have a deep respect for the researched.

Sharing of the Perquisites of Privileges—It is the debt we owe to the lives we portray. Questions concerning who owns the lives we use, and the realization that most research is consumed by ourselves are central to the issue of perquisites.

Cautions—Deciding which criteria to use at which stage is something the researcher needs to consider. All criteria are relational. Valid knowledge "is a matter of relationship." Research methods are ethics (dissolution of boundaries between ethics and methods).

Source: Lincoln, Y. (April, 1995b). Emerging Criteria for Qualitative Research. Paper presented at the meeting of the American Educational Research Association, San Francisco, CA. See Also: Lincoln, Y. S. (1995). Emerging criteria for qualitative research. Qualitative Inquiry. 1 (3).

I found additional research standards that were more akin to my study in the literature on classroom-based action and teacher research methodology. As a classroom teacher I had conducted a research study of the writing processes of my kindergarten students—children with whom I had relationships that could also be characterized by the subjectivity-laden terms of affection, respect, confidence, and trust. I found wisdom and relevance in the words of a leader in the teacher research movement, Dixie Goswami, who, in an interview with Tim Gillespie (1994), responded to his question "Well, what's the value then? What's the use if these teachers are all studying singular and personal questions that can't be generalized to other classrooms?" Goswami responded by saying "I don't engage in that argument any more. We all need criteria by which to judge our work, but other kinds of researchers have different purposes, different training, different agendas, different questions" (p. 98). She went on to list questions that teacher researchers ask in order to maintain high standards for their research. These questions appear in Figure 8.2.

Figure 8.2. Goswami's Standards for Teacher Research

"**Is it ethical?**" Does inquiry exploit anyone, especially students and parents?

"**Does it improve the quality of learning in my classroom?**" Does inquiry help establish a rich environment for students and teachers to learn.

"**Is it valid?**" [or, rephrased] "**Is it meaningful for us?**" Does it make sense to participants?" [To assess validity] "I would ask people who participated in the study if it seems accurate and if it makes sense in light of what they know from experience to be true. Those involved in the study have to find it meaningful and useful.

"**Is it replicable?**" Is the inquiry systematic and intentional as I described it in my narrative or my report or my journal, so the readers will know what I did, how I did it, and why I did it? It's not going to be replicable in the sense that I've controlled variables and there they are and we can do it exactly the same way next year, but I have a deep obligation to tell you what we did, how we did it, and why, so that we can keep on doing it. That's where I'm going to get my answer to the question whether the case study is replicable.

"**Is it generative?**" That is, does it generate good questions? We need to ask if our inquiry raises questions from us as teacher researchers and questions for others. If we claim to have the last word...forget it! If it generates more questions to keep us excited and happy, if it lets us see how complex teaching and learning are, that's great.

Source: Gillespie, T. (1994) An Interview with Dixie Goswami. Teacher Research, 1 *(2). 97-100.*

I realized that subjectivity would influence my study and recognized the importance of monitoring it throughout the research process. Given my inherent bias, I knew I would need to continually explore my subjectivity. Glesne and Peshkin (1992) point out the importance of exploring subjectivity in a research project.

> How you pursue your own subjectivity matters less than that you pursue it; the means can be as idiosyncratic as the special, personal twist that all researchers give to the standard methods that they adopt to conduct their research. Reading, reflecting, and talking about subjectivity are valuable, but they are no substitute for monitoring it in the process of research. (p. 106)

I incorporated a range of strategies into my research process that helped raise self-awareness of opinions and conclusions that I was forming. For example, I discussed my findings with Brenda several times a week. We met for a half hour after each class in order to talk about the preceding class session. Other measures that helped me pursue my subjectivity were built into my research approach. They are as follows:

> Note taking: In an effort to be an objective observer, I scripted my notes for the duration of the class sessions. Most of the notes I took were verbatim, eliminating opportunities to put value terms into the text. I added my personal and theoretical notes after the fact.
>
> During the data collection period I was also collecting data for another research project in a first-grade classroom, a study in which I was also looking at the teacher's instructional practices. The first-grade teacher's practices and perspectives about teaching and learning were similar to Brenda's in many ways. Yet they differed significantly in many ways as well. I was able to balance what I was observing and analyzing from one research site with an alternative view. This bifocal view provided a built-in calibration function, allowing me to test out the merit of the theory I was developing.
>
> I had four readers outside my committee who offered helpful questions and comments about the content and surface features of my text. They included fellow students in a course I was taking at the time.

The respect I had for Brenda as a teacher, and the desire I had to learn more about her teaching, were already based on evidence I had internally and informally "gathered" throughout the years that I had known her. But in order to justify my research interest for the purposes of a formal study, I included data from other sources that supported her credibility and authority as a college-level literacy instructor. For example, the quality of Brenda's teaching had been recognized by others. She was nominated for a University teaching award in the spring of 1994 by a committee of peers in the College of Education. She has consistently had exemplary student evaluations since she began teaching at the University in 1990. In a letter to the teaching award committee, the dean of the College of Education wrote,

> I don't recall ever seeing statistical summaries of student evaluations with mean scores so high (1.00 being high) and standard deviations so low. For example, for all classes combined on Question #13, "Overall, how would you rate the instructor?" an astonishing 91 percent (353 out of 389) of the ratings had a ranking of "1" or Excellent; 8 percent (16 our of 389) of the ratings had a ranking of "2"; and 1 percent (5 out of 389) were "3." There were absolutely no ratings of "4" or "5." Student evaluations representing this kind of unanimity over time and across so many classes is a first in my experience. (Letter to the Members of the Selection Committee for the President's Outstanding Teaching Award, February 25, 1995.)

> Brenda co-edited a textbook on literacy education, *Literacy in Process* (1991), which is now in its fourth printing, used at over 200 colleges nationwide. The text is a reader that includes research and conceptual pieces on major issues in the field of literacy education. She also co-wrote an accompanying teaching guide to assist college-level literacy-education instructors. Thus, she had credibility from the larger community of publishers and teacher educators.

> Brenda is the co-author of a best selling videotape series about writing and reading instruction, *The Writing and Reading Process: A Closer Look* (1988).

> Brenda is the author of a manuscript on working with methods students (1995).

As I engaged in the process of uncovering my own subjectivity in relation to the study, I became interested in the way other researchers were treating the issue. Even purely positivistic scientific inquiry is subjective according to the research paradigm of the researcher (Kuhn, 1970). Regardless of the intention to break free from the confines of one's subjectivity, a researcher's perspective is influenced by her own particular standpoint in relation to her study. Phillips (1990) writes:

> [I]nquirers always work within the context of a paradigm...All inquirers are trapped within their own paradigms; they will judge certain things as being true (for them) that other inquirers in other paradigms will judge as being false [for them]. (p. 33)

Even scientific hypotheses have their beginnings in the realm of intuition and personal reasoning. In his book, *In the Palaces of*

Memory, author George Johnson (1991) tracks the theory-making process in the field of brain research by investigating the research perspectives of several researchers from various disciplines. He discovered these researchers had vastly different hunches, governed by experience and training, that led to their respective experimental courses: "The question of what science is and why it is so successful comes back to memory and the way brains convert experience into knowledge" (p. xii). The long-held boundaries between the sciences and the humanities are collapsing (Lincoln, 1995a). Lincoln (1995a) points out that this collapse can be witness-ed through the scholarly work stemming from wide-ranging disciplines. She explains, for example, how the distinction between fact and fiction is increasingly blurred in the ethnographic novels and essays that have moved from the social-science tradition into the rhetorical tradition. Also, there is a blurring of the genres of research and scholarly writing wherein the lines between sociology, anthropology, and art, for example, are increasingly less clear. Lincoln (1995a) points out that interpretation of any kind is historically and culturally situated and can be reflected by social markers such as sex, race, and economic background of the researcher/writer.

The biographer Phyllis Rose (1994) articulates how interpretation is a personal construction in her work. She explores the influence of her own subjectivity on her research and writing, arguing toward a role for subjectivity in the larger arena of biographical writing approaches.

> If you believe in the myth of objective fact and objective biography, the self is not supposed to be in biography at all. Journalists and other positivists who turn to biography tend to regard any uncertainty about truth, any concern with subjectivity, as academic waffling. Of course the truth can be known! Of course it exists apart from the perceiving self! It exists in hard little nuggets that are to be dug up from the surrounding matter, arranged in chronological order and presented in as great numbers as possible. This is the ideal of one school of biography, what I'd call the objective school...
>
> Another school, which I call the school of literary biography, whether or not the subject is a literary figure, sees all facts as artifacts, and context and argument as copartners of fact. (p. 72)

The Research Process

Prior to beginning data collection I knew mine would be a study of teaching and learning processes focusing on the instructional practices and beliefs of a college methods teacher. The study would be relevant in answering the questions I had as an emerging college instructor. I also knew I would use the qualitative case study as the mode of inquiry. I sketched out preliminary plans for data collection and analysis. But, as qualitative research tends to do, my study changed shape as it developed.

The eventual purpose of the study evolved into an evaluation and action-research project designed to describe and understand one model of undergraduate literacy-methods instruction. The clarity of my research purpose became more focused after I read about the wider range of research methods and their capacity to address different needs. Patton's (1990) description of the broad range of research methods, featured in Figure 8.3, helped me understand that action research would be the best methodology to help me answer my question, "How can I improve my teaching of undergraduate literacy methods?"

Figure 8.3. Research Methodology and Purpose

Basic Research is used to contribute to fundamental knowledge and theory,
Applied Research is used to illustrate a societal concern,
Summative Evaluation is used to determine program effectiveness,
Formative Evaluation is employed to improve a program,
Action Research is used to solve a specific problem.

Source: Patton, M.Q. (1990) Qualitative evaluation and research methods. London: Sage Publications, p. 150.

I planned to be in the classroom for every class, from the beginning to the end of the semester, in order to collect data. During class I would take notes, collect students' work samples, and interview the teacher and students.

I collected data throughout the fall semester of 1994, which lasted from September 1994 through December 1994. I observed every class during the semester (with the exception of field trips). Class met twice weekly and lasted from 9:00 A.M. to 12:00 P.M. The common predicament of coming into or going out of the research site midstream was not an issue with my study because I was able to observe the entire course.

The plan for data collection was simple. I would be in the classroom for every session, from the beginning to the end of the semester. While the class was in session I would take notes, collect work samples, and interview the teacher and students. The data I collected included.

- Transcriptions of classroom language including the instructor's presentations and large-group discussions.

- A variety of notes, including contextual notes, personal notes, theoretical notes, and field notes.

- Copies of students' written assignments, including papers, responses to readings, and self-evaluation forms.

- Excerpts of literature read to the class by the instructor.

- Texts written by the instructor, including two published books and one unpublished monograph.

Patton (1990) distinguishes between the length of time needed for basic research in the social sciences and evaluation and action research. The former requires a participant observer to

> [S]pend six months at a minimum, and often years, living in the culture being observed...to unveil the basic complexities and patterns of social reality. The social scientist engaged in the conduct of basic research hopes to generate and verify theoretical truths and empirical generalizations. (p. 213)

Whereas the purpose of the action researcher is "more modest: generating useful information for action. To be useful, evaluation information must be timely" (p. 213). The purposes of action research fit my needs. A lengthy duration in the field was not necessary because I was already somewhat familiar with the culture I would be studying. I had studied and worked with Brenda, I had taught five sections of the undergraduate literacy methods course, and I had been a resident director in a campus dormitory for the previous two years, an experience which had made me very familiar with the culture of students I would be studying. Moreover, my unique circumstances paralleled those of other evaluation and action researchers—I was working within a tight timeline with limited resources.

On the second day of class Brenda offered me the use of her laptop computer. With the aid of the computer, I scripted my notes, typing as fast as I could in order to capture everything I heard and observed. These scripted notes provided me with raw data. After the class I read over and reflected on my notes, incorporating additional notes having to do with theory, methodology, or personal impressions. I coded the additions I made during the "cooking" stage with the following recording conventions (Schatzman and Strauss, 1973):

FN: Field Note—A note that describes events or interactions at the data-collection site. I didn't use this code often. All of my raw notes began as field notes. Because they served as the primary source, and they were so great in volume, I rarely coded my raw field notes.

MN: Methodological Note—A note that pertains to my research methodology, including notes on procedures. These notes had to do with issues of research methodology. I used them in order to remind myself to incorporate another step into the collection process or to put a research idea on the record.

TN: Theoretical Note—A note that refers to a theoretical explanation for an event or interaction observed. I used these notes frequently. They helped me incorporate theory into what I was observing. Theoretical notes provided organizing points, which helped later in the data analysis process when I was looking for themes and patterns.

PN: Personal Notes—A note pertaining to personal feelings or opinions. These notes allowed me a chance to incorporate my personal reactions and ideas into the data. Labeling these elements as "personal" helped me separate my personal bias and opinions from the data.

I employed a range of qualitative research methods to analyze my data and to develop grounded theory (Schatzman and Strauss, 1973), including coding of data, triangulation and constant comparison of data, and creation of analytic files and indexes. I used the process of constant comparison (Glaser and Strauss, 1967) throughout the collection period to develop conceptual and theoretical structure. Early in the study I began reading my notes with an eye to linking specific examples in the data to my research question. Initial categories emerged, developed, and often merged with other categories. I considered how the emerging categories were linked to the larger issues in my study which were becoming clearer through my autobiographical writing, which I'll describe below. The coding of data according to the conventions described above helped me identify patterns and themes as they emerged, and facilitated categorization. I triangulated my notes with other sources, including the book Brenda had written about college-level teaching, as well as journal responses and papers by the students, and mid-term and end-of-term student self- and course evaluations. Examining these additional sources of data confirmed, repudiated, or extended my ideas, lending structure to my findings. This helped me relate what I saw in the data to my research questions, which stemmed from my classroom teaching experiences. This process helped me identify the themes of Classroom Structures, Course Content, and Classroom Community. I then created an index based on those categories. With the word processor I copied excerpts in my notes that referred to any of the three categories. The indexing process helped me narrow my focus.

Throughout the course of data collection, analysis, and writing, I wrote a series of six research memos to my committee members. These memos summarized my progress and outlined subsequent steps in my process. I often wrote them when I was feeling unclear or unproductive. The process of revisiting what I had accomplished and casting my mind to the end of my research journey lifted my spirits and gave me energy.

The Writing Process

> We dream in narrative, daydream in narrative, remember, anticipate, hope, despair, believe, doubt, plan, revise, criticize, construct, gossip, learn, hate and love by narrative.
>
> (Barbara Hardy, 1986, p. 5)

My study is a research narrative—its purpose and scope relate directly to my experience and personal needs. In fact, my intention was to endow my experience with meaning (Bruner, 1986). The more I read about the multitude of possibilities for research, the more I discovered that the narrative mode of thinking (and, by extension, writing) would best satisfy my purpose.

As the study progressed it became not simply an observer's account of another teacher, but a self-reflective and open-ended research narrative. But that was not the genre of research writing I had originally intended. The style of writing and the purpose of the study both evolved throughout the writing process. A month after I had completed data collection, I began writing about some of my findings. I assumed the standpoint of an outsider trying to describe the teacher's role in the classroom. But after several hours of writing

I realized I was getting nowhere. I was unable to hit my stride. I decided to back up, out of the data, and begin again by writing about my personal experience as a college teacher and my connection to the study. It was unplanned, stream-of-consciousness writing which allowed me to discover, through the act of writing, more about my purpose. What was written became a way to connect with the subject. I was able to clarify the purpose of my research and focus my data-analysis approach.

This discovery enlightened my study. Jerome Bruner writes, "Narrative deals with the vicissitudes of intention" (1986, p. 17). This statement seemed particularly relevant to my experience. Through the act of writing my teaching autobiography, I was able to clarify the purpose of my research and focus my data-analysis approach. My findings hadn't changed, but their meaning and significance had. As I began to write my story, my reconstructed experience helped identify the central themes in my data.

Bruner explains the narrative mode of thinking. He writes:

> The imaginative application of the narrative mode leads instead to good stories, gripping drama, believable (though not necessarily "true") historical accounts. It strives to put its timeless miracles into the particulars of experience, and to locate the experience in time and place. Joyce thought of the particularities of the story as epiphanies of the ordinary. The paradigmatic mode, by contrast, seeks to transcend the particular by higher and higher reaching for abstraction, and in the end disclaims in principle any explanatory value at all where the particular is concerned. (1986, p. 13)

While I wanted my interpretation to be as closely linked to "truth" as possible (according to definitions that are applicable to my purpose), I realized that I wanted to understand the "particulars of my experience, to locate them in time and place." As a classroom teacher, when I read research reports that reached ever higher for abstraction, leaving behind any explanatory power, I was left uninspired and unenlightened. I preferred studies that were written from a perspective I could relate to and understand. That is why I chose to write this report from a teacher's perspective. I preferred to focus on "epiphanies of the ordinary" in the methods course data— the particulars that could potentially guide my development as a teacher educator.

In writing my research findings, I have taken the advice of Don Graves, which was given to him by Donald Murray: "Write research to be read" (personal communication, 1/29/95). Referring to his recent book, Graves explains, "I tried to make *A Fresh Look At Writing* sound like one long, gossipy letter—teacher to teacher." (personal communication, 1/29/95). The literary genre of research writing had its beginnings in the work of Donald Graves, and I decided prior to beginning my study that a challenge to myself during my program was to improve my writing—not solely for the writing's sake, but for pedagogical reasons. I believe that in order to be an effective teacher of writing, one must write. A continued personal goal has been to be a good model for my students. I felt that writing a traditional research report, laden with the high jargon of empirical research in my field, would be a cop-out. I intended to write in a voice that could reach other teachers.

I realized my study had the potential to contribute to my professional knowledge, to extend my understanding of teaching practices and their theoretical rationale, as well as expand my knowledge of instructional content. I knew my findings would be specific to my experience and not generalizable in the sense that scientific research can be generalized. But the theoretical principles of constructivism and social learning strongly influence my field of discipline. My findings had the potential to be of interest to other teacher educators who, like me, are interested in using instructional practices in their classrooms that mirror the content of what they teach. Though my question was personal, I knew enough about my future profession to understand that I wasn't doing research in a vacuum. I could foresee my research being relevant to other teacher educators and wrote with the intention to eventually submit my study for publication. Patton (1990) helped justify my research methodology and writing focus. He explains:

> Basic and applied researchers publish in scholarly journals, where their audience is other researchers who will judge their contributions using disciplinary standards for rigor, validity, and theoretical import. In contrast, evaluators and action researchers publish reports for specific stakeholders who will use the results to make decisions, improve programs, and solve problems. (p. 150)

Donald Graves and his colleagues from the University of New Hampshire have been influential in establishing trends in process-oriented research approaches and literary, "readable" texts that explain research findings. Early (1991) explains that the focus of these studies shifted from writing product to writing process, and this shift "in studying learning was accompanied by changes in methodology from empirically-based analyses to descriptive, anecdotal, and example-filled documentation, more like reportage than research and, consequently, more readable. And they exemplify the profession's mounting concern for the role that teachers play in the learning process" (p. 149). Early also explains on what grounds the New Hampshire studies were criticized and how that criticism was addressed:

> Hillocks criticizes the reports on the grounds that, although their points are illustrated with anecdotes, the authors provide no means to confirm that the anecdotes are typical of what they observed...they make inferences about cause-effect relationships without considering alternative explanations and without controlling for instructional variables...but that [other researchers, in defense of the methodology] depends on how broad a definition one gives to research. (p. 149)

I had the opportunity to ask Graves (personal communication, 1/29/95) how he responds to Hillocks's attacks. He explained:

> These publications are reporting research to teachers. We had the data behind our findings, especially about how children actually went about composing. We were fully accurate in reporting what children actually did...A mixture of story and anecdote does not negate the quality of the research one iota.

I agree with Graves. The research and scholarly writing that has the greatest influence on my teaching practices and beliefs are studies that are realistic, personal, persuasive, and readable. Figure 8.4 summarizes Van Maanen's description of the range of styles that are employed by ethnographic writers. I have deliberately written in a first-person voice and at various points in my report I have used some of the literary and rhetorical devices described by Van Maanen. During the writing phase of my study I sought response to my drafts from friends, colleagues, and authors whose writing styles I admired. Their feedback helped me know whether my prose was successful in conveying my intended ideas.

Figure 8.4. Styles of Writing Ethnography

Realist Tales—Those in which "a single author typically narrates the realist tale in a dispassionate, third-person voice. On display are the comings and goings of members of the culture, theoretical coverage of certain features of the culture, and usually a hesitant account of why the work was undertaken in the first place. The result is an author-proclaimed description and something of an explanation for certain specific, bounded, observed (or nearly observed) cultural practices. Of all ethnographic forms discussed [in Van Maanen's book] the realist tales push most firmly for authenticity of cultural representations conveyed by the text" (pp. 45-46).

Confessional Tales—"The distinguishing characteristics of confessional tales are their highly personalized styles and their self-absorbed mandates." It is often an "attempt to explicitly demystify fieldwork or participant-observation by showing how the technique is practiced in the field" (p. 73). Stories of fieldwork incidents and how the fieldwork affected the researcher are common features of the fieldwork confessional style of ethnographic writing.

Impressionistic Tales—Impressionistic ethnographic writing, like impressionist paintings, are "out to startle their audience. But striking stories, not luminous paintings, are their stock-in-trade. Their materials are words, metaphors, phrasings, imagery, and most critically, the expansive recall of fieldwork experience. When these are put together and told in the first person as a tightly focused, vibrant, exact, but necessarily imaginative rendering of fieldwork, an impressionist tale of the field results...[They] present the doing of fieldwork rather than simply the doer or the done. They reconstruct in dramatic form those periods the author regards as especially notable and hence reportable" (pp. 101-102).

Critical Tales—Studies that consciously select a strategically situated culture to study. The intention is to explore larger social, political, symbolic, or economic issues through the eyes of the culture being studied.

Formal Tales—These studies are designed to "build, test, generalize and exhibit theory." The researcher derives generalizations "through inductive and inferential logic...Representations of persons, places, activities, belief systems, and activities, when not the specific target of study, are limited and used only to provide a context for the textualized data under review" (pp. 130-131).

Literary Tales—A style of ethnographic writing in which the researcher borrows literary conventions to tell the story. They feature "dense characterization, dramatic plots, flashbacks (and flashforwards), and alternative points of view" (p. 132).

Jointly Told Tales—Jointly authored texts, by the fieldworker and the native, tell the tale in a way that reveals "the discursive and shared character of all cultural descriptions." The researcher "provides space for the natives to tell their own tales without the undue interference and wanton translation of the fieldworker" (p. 136).

Source: Van Maanen, J. (1988). Tales of the field: On writing ethnography. Chicago: The University of Chicago Press.

Conclusion

In his book *To Teach: The Journey of a Teacher* (1993), Bill Ayres compares teaching to Stanislavsky's method acting. He writes:

> Any part must be learned anew, day by day, moment by moment, and year by year... Great acting is always in search of better acting, always beginning again... Greatness in teaching, too, requires a serious encounter with autobiography: Who are you? How did you come to take on your views and outlooks? What forces helped to shape you? What was it like for you to be ten? What have you made of yourself? Where are you heading? An encounter with these kinds of questions is critical to outstanding teaching because teachers, whatever else they teach, teach themselves. Of all the knowledge teachers need to draw on, self-knowledge is most important. (p. 129)

For me, autobiography has been a link between theory and practice in my dual roles as teacher and researcher. The study wouldn't have happened if I hadn't been thinking about the process of becoming a creative educator. While I was describing, interpreting, and analyzing data I collected, I was coming to terms with and describing the process of my own development as a teacher. I studied Brenda's teaching so I could find out what is unique to me and where I am situated in the society of teachers.

Autobiography was also an ethical dimension of the study in which Barbara Finkelstein said "we have to care about interpretive meanings associated with fact. Interpretation means to intrude" (1995). When the data have to do with people, the researcher needs to be self-reflective in order to explore and explain, in the most honest terms possible, the links that are being made between subject and conclusion. These links shape and determine the research findings. I examined my mentor's self-reflective teaching practices as a self-reflective researcher. Autobiography played a role, not simply by allowing me to recount my experience, but to make sense of it after the fact.

The story I have just told hasn't ended. What I learned from this research—the importance of classroom structures that provide space and time for students and teacher to inquire, explore, and reflect— continues to be a reality of my teaching approach. For me, autobiography is the essence of my understanding of curriculum and teaching. Questions, concerns, and interests I have had through my years of teaching determine my present research agenda, which in turn influences the issues I bring into the classroom. I place a great emphasis on self-awareness in my teaching, and this influences what I do as a teacher. The activities I use and issues I present in the classroom are determined by ongoing assessment of my students. I try to help cultivate in my students an awareness of the importance of autobiography to the act of teaching—I use the structure of writing workshop in which my students write personal narratives of learning experiences that have been memorable to them. These narratives become the curriculum of the course and a vehicle for connecting with the theories and practices we read about. My students conduct case studies on elementary students— they analyze data including notes from observations and interviews. They learn to develop their own awareness of how autobiography plays a role in their lives as teachers and the lives of their students as learners.

In simile, a research text is like a work of art—a creative and aesthetic construction. At the hands of the creator, it serves as a work for others to admire and appreciate. At that point it becomes something for readers to take up and introduce to others or to incorporate into their own autobiography. Autobiography plays a central role in the way I approach research and scholarship. I recognize the power of narrative to convey ideas and information and, with awareness and intention, have employed the autobiographical approach throughout this text.

Bibliography

Anderson, R. C. (1989). *A modest proposal for improving the education of reading teachers* (Report No. 487). (ERIC Document Reproduction Service No. ED 333674)

Andrews, S. V. (1990, November). *Tracing the effects of reflective classroom practice.* Paper presented at the annual meeting of the National Reading Conference, Miami, FL.

Atwell, N. (1987). *In the middle: Writing reading and learning with adolescents.* Portsmouth, NH: Heinemann.

Avery, C. (1993). *... And with a light touch.* Portsmouth, NH: Heineman.

Ayres, W. (1993). *To teach: The journey of a teacher.* New York: Teachers College Press.

Bean, T. W. (1989). Using dialogue journals to foster reflective practice with pre-service content-area teachers. *Teacher Education Quarterly, 16,* (1), 33-40.

Bernstein, D. A., Clarke-Stewart, A., Roy, E. J., Scull, T. K., & Wickens, C. D. (1994). *Psychology* (3rd ed.). Boston: Houghton Mifflin Company.

Boice, R. (1991). New faculty as teachers. *Journal of Higher Education, 62,* 150-173.

Boice, R. (1993). Primal origins and later correctives for mid-career disillusionment. In M. Finkelstein & M. LaCelle-Peterson, (Eds.), *Developing senior faculty as teachers, new directions in teaching and learning,* (pp. 33-42). San Francisco: Jossey-Bass, 1993).

Brazee, P. E., & Kristo, J. V. (1986). Creating a whole language classroom with future teachers. *The Reading Teacher, 39,* (5), 422-428.

Brooks, J. G., & Brooks, M. G. (1993). *In search of understanding: The case for constructivist classrooms.* Alexandria, VA: Association for Supervision and Curriculum Development.

Brown, A.L., Armbruster, B.B., & Baker, L. (1986). The role of metacognition in reading and studying. In J. Orasanu (Ed.), *Reading*

Comprehension (pp. 49-75). Hillsdale, NJ: L. Erlbaum Associates.

Bruner, J. (1986). *Actual minds, possible worlds.* Cambridge, MA: Harvard University Press.

Burke, C. (1980). The reading interview: 1977. In B. P. Farr & D. J. Strickler, (Eds.), *Reading comprehension: Resource guide.* Bloomington, IN: School of Education, Indiana University.

Butler, D., & Clay, M. (1979). *Reading begins at home.* Portsmouth, NH: Heinemann.

Calkins, L. M. (1986). *The art of teaching writing.* Portsmouth, NH: Heinemann.

Calkins, L. M. (1991). Mini-lessons: An overview, and tools to help teachers create their own minilessons. In B. M. Power & R. Hubbard, (Eds.), *Literacy in process* (pp. 149-173). Portsmouth, NH: Heinemann.

Cambourne, B. (1988). *The whole story: Natural learning and the acquisition of literacy in the classroom.* Auckland, New Zealand: Ashton Scholastic Limited.

Campbell, J. (1993). A paper on a paper. *Teacher Research 1,* (1), 104-105.

Carnegie Foundation for the Advancement of Teaching. (1989). *The condition of the professoriate: Attitudes and trends.* Princeton, NJ: Carnegie Foundation.

Chambers, A. (1985). *Booktalk: Occasional writing on literature and children.* New York: Harper & Row.

Champagne, A. B., & Klopfer, L. E. (1986). *Effecting changes in cognitive structures among physics students.* Pittsburgh, PA: Learning Research and Development Center, University of Pittsburgh.

Chase, P., & Doan, J. (1994). *Full circle.* Portsmouth, NH: Heinemann.

Clandin, D. J., & Connelly, F. M. (1994). Personal experience methods. In N. K. Denzin & Y. S. Lincoln, (Eds.), *Handbook of Qualitative Research* (pp. 413-427). Thousand Oaks, CA: Sage Publications, Inc.

Clay, M. M. (1987). *Writing begins at home.* Portsmouth, NH: Heinemann.

Clay, M. M. (1991). *Becoming literate.* Portsmouth, NH: Heinemann.

Coles, R. (1989). *The call of stories: Teaching and the moral education.* Boston: Houghton Mifflin Company.

Conway, J. (1989). *The road from Coorain.* New York: Alfred A. Knopf, Inc.

Cooper, M. G., & Morey, A. (1989). *Developing thoughtful practitioners through school/university collaboration.* (ERIC Clearinghouse for Higher Education. ERIC Document Reproduction Service No. ED 306 871).

Corsaro, W. (1985). *Friendship and peer culture in the early years.* Norwood, NJ: Ablex.

Curtis, J. P. (1995). *Autobiographical understandings: Writing the past into the future.* Manuscript submitted for publication.

Daiute, C. (1988). "Let's brighten it up a bit": Collaboration and cognition in writing. In B. Rafoth & D. Rubin. (Eds.), *The social construction of written communication.* Norwood, NJ: Ablex.

Denzin, N. K., & Lincoln, Y. S. (Eds.). (1994). *Handbook of qualitative research.* Thousand Oaks, CA: Sage.

Dewey, J. (1933). *How we think, a restatement of the relation of reflective thinking to the educative process.* Boston: Heath and Company.

Dewey, J. (1944). *Democracy in education.* New York: Macmillan Company.

Dillard, A. (1989). *The writing life.* New York: Harper & Row Publishers, Inc.

Doll, Jr., W. (1993). Curriculum possibilities in a "post-future." *Journal of Curriculum Supervision, 8* (4), 277-292.

Donaldson, M. (1978). *Children's minds.* New York: W. W. Norton & Company, Inc.

Dyson, A. H. (1988). Unintentional helping in the primary grades: Writing in the children's world. In B. Rafoth & D. Rubin, (Eds.), *The social construction of written communication* (pp. 219-248). Norwood, NJ: Ablex.

Early, M. (1991). Major research programs. In J. Flood, J. M. Jensen, D. Lapp, & J. R. Squire (Eds.), *Handbook of Research on Teaching the English Language Arts* (pp. 143-158). New York: Macmillan Publishing Company.

Eisner, E. (1985). Aesthetic modes of knowing. In E. Eisner, (Ed.), *Learning and teaching the ways of knowing: Eighty-fourth yearbook of the National Society for the Study of Education* (pp. 23-36). Chicago, IL: University of Chicago Press.

Eisner, E. (1994). *Cognition and curriculum reconsidered* (2nd ed.). New York: Teachers College Press.

Eliot, T. S. (1952). Four quartets. In *The complete poems and plays, 1909-1950*. New York: Harcourt, Brace & World.

Emig, J. (1977). Writing as a mode of learning. *College Composition and Communication 28*, (2) 122-128

Farr, R., & Tone, B. (1994). *Portfolio and performance assessment*. New York: Harcourt Brace College Publishers.

Finkelstein, M. J. (1995). *National education association's 1995 almanac*.

Finkelstein, M. J. (1984). *The American academic profession*. Columbus, OH: Ohio State University Press.

Fischer, C. W., & Bullock, D. (1984). Cognitive development in school-aged children: Conclusions and new directions. In W. A. Collins, (Ed.), *Development during middle childhood: The years from six to twelve* (pp. 70-146). Washington, DC: National Academy Press.

Fisher, B. (1991). *Joyful learning*. Portsmouth, NH: Heinemann.

Fishman, A. (1988). *Amish literacy*. Portsmouth, NH: Heinemann.

Fletcher, R. (1990). *Walking trees*. Portsmouth, NH: Heinemann.

Flexner, S. B. (Ed.). (1980). *Random house dictionary*. New York: Ballantine Books.

Freire, P. (1970). *Pedagogy of the oppressed*. New York: Continuum Publishing Company.

Gage, N. (October, 1989). The paradigm wars and their aftermath. *Educational Researcher*, 4-10.

Gallagher, T. (1983). My father's love letters. In S. Berg, (Ed.). *In praise of what persists* (pp. 109-124). New York: Harper & Row, Publishers.

Gillespie, T. (1994). Interview with Dixie Goswami. *Teacher Research 1*, (2), 89-103.

Glaser, B., & Strauss, A. (1967). *Discovery of grounded theory: Strategies for qualitative research*. Chicago: Aldine Publishing Co.

Glesne, C., & Peshkin, A. (1992). *Becoming qualitative researchers*. White Plains, NY: Longman Publishing Group.

Glick, J. (1995, April). *Vygotsky Centennial: Directions for the Future*. Panel conducted at the annual meeting of the American Educational Research Association, New York, NY.

Goleman, D. (1995). *Emotional intelligence: Why it can matter more than IQ*. New York: Bantam Books.

Goodlad, J. I. (1984). *A place called school*. New York: McGraw-Hill.

Goodman, K. (1986). *What's whole in whole language?* Portsmouth, NH: Heinemann.

Goodman, K. (1991). Whole language: What makes it whole? In B. M. Power & R. Hubbard (Eds.), *Literacy in process* (pp. 88-95). Portsmouth, NH: Heinemann.

Goodman, K. S., Goodman, Y. M. , & Bird, L. B. (1992). *The whole language catalog supplement on authentic assessment.* New York: SRA.

Goodman, Y. M. (June, 1978). Kidwatching: An alternative to testing. *National Elementary Principal, 57,* (4), 41-45.

Goodman, Y. M. (1986a). Discovering children's inventions of written language. In Y. M. Goodman (Ed.), *How children construct literacy: Piagetian perspectives* (pp. 1-11). Newark DE: International Reading Association.

Goodman, Y. M. (1986b). Children's knowledge about literacy development: An afterword. In Y. M. Goodman (Ed.), *How children construct literacy: Piagetian perspectives* (pp. 115-123). Newark, DE: International Reading Association.

Goodman, Y. M. (1993). *Whole language open forum.* Annual Conference of the National Council of Teachers of English.

Graham, R. J. (1992). Currere and reconceptualism: The progress of the pilgrimage 1975-1990. *Journal of Curriculum Studies, 24,* (1), 27-42.

Graves, D. H. (1983). *Writing: Teachers and children at work.* Portsmouth, NH: Heinemann.

Grumet, M. (1976). Psychoanalytic foundations. In W. Pinar & M. Grumet (Eds.), *Toward a poor curriculum* (pp. 111-146). Dubuque, IA: Kendall/Hunt.

Hardy, B. (1986). Towards a poetics of fiction: An approach through narrative. *Novel, 2,* 5-14.

Harp, B. (Ed.). (1993). *Bringing children to literacy: Classrooms at work.* Norwood, MA: Christopher Gordon Publishers, Inc.

Harste, J., Woodward, V. A., & Burke, C. L. (1984). *Language stories and literacy lessons.* Portsmouth, NH: Heinemann.

Harste, J. & Short, K. G. (1991). Literature circles and literature response activities. In B. M. Power & R. Hubbard (Eds.), *Literacy in process* (pp. 191-202). Portsmouth, NH: Heinemann.

Heath, S. B. (1983). *Ways with words.* Cambridge: Cambridge University Press.

Heath, S. B. (1991). A lot of talk about nothing. In B. M. Power & R. Hubbard (Eds.), *Literacy in process* (pp. 79-88). Portsmouth, NH: Heinemann.

Heinemann (1995). *Heinemann: Books for teachers K-8.* Portsmouth, NH: Heinemann.

Henry, G. H. (1986). What is the nature of English education? *English Education, 18,* (1), 4-41.

Hensley, R. (1989, November). *Instructional choices in language arts: Reality or Illusion.* Paper presented at the annual meeting of the National Reading Conference, Austin, TX.

Holdaway, D. (1991). *Independence in reading* (3rd ed.). Portsmouth, NH: Heinemann.

Hubbard R., & Power, B. M. (Eds.). (1991). *Literacy in process.* Portsmouth, NH: Heinemann.

Hubbard, R., & Power, B. M. (1993). *The art of classroom inquiry: A handbook for teacher researchers.* Portsmouth, NH: Heinemann.

Hullfish, H. G., & Smith, P. G. (1961). *Reflective thinking, the method education.* New York: Dodd, Mead & Company.

Hulse-Killacky, D. (1992). Who am I? Who am I with you? Who are we together? *Maine perspective: A publication for the University of Maine.* Orono, ME: University of Maine.

Jackson, P. (1992). Conceptions of curriculum and curriculum specialists. In P. Jackson (Ed.), *Handbook of research on curriculum,* (pp. 3-40). New York: Macmillan.

Jacob, Francois. (1988) *The statue within.* New York: Basic Books.

Johnson, G. (1991). *Palaces of Memory.* New York: Basic Books.

John-Steiner, V. (1985). *Notebooks of the mind.* Albuquerque, NM: University of New Mexico Press

Kelly, G. A. (1955). *The psychology of personal constructs.* New York: W. W. Norton.

Kliebard, H. M. (1985). A perspective on twentieth-century curriculum reforms. In E. Eisner, (Ed.), *Learning and taching the ways of knowing: Eighty-fourth yearbook of the National Society for the Study of Education* (pp. 23-36). Chicago, IL: University of Chicago Press.

Kincheloe, J. L. (1995). *Toil and trouble.* New York: Peter Lang Publishing.

Krogness, M. M. (1995). *Just teach me Mrs. K.* Portsmouth, NH: Heinemann.

Kuhn, Thomas S. (1970). *The structure of scientific revolutions* (2nd ed.). Chicago: University of Chicago Press.

Lincoln, Y. (April, 1995a). *Fact, truth, and interpretation*. Paper presented at the meeting of the American Educational Research Association, San Francisco, CA.

Lincoln, Y. (April, 1995b). *Emerging criteria for qualitative research*. Paper presented at the meeting of the American Educational Research Association, San Francisco, CA.

Lloyd-Jones, R., & Lunsford, A. A. (1989). *The English coalition conference: Democracy through language*. New York: Modern Language Association.

Mehan, H. (1979). *Learning lessons*. Cambridge, MA: Harvard University Press.

Ministry of Education, Wellington, New Zealand. (1985). *Reading in junior classes*. Katonah, NY: Richard C. Owen Publishers, Inc.

McGowan, J. (1991). *Postmodernism and its critics*. Ithica, NY: Cornell University Press.

Moll, L. (April, 1996). *Vygotsky centennial: Directions for the future*. Panel conducted at the annual meeting of the American Educational Research Association, New York, NY.

Mooney, M. (1990). *Reading to, with, and by children*. Katonah, NY: Richard C. Owen Publishers, Inc.

Murray, D. M. (1991). Getting under the lightening. In B. M. Power & R. Hubbard (Eds.), *Literacy in process* (pp. 5-13). Portsmouth, NH: Heinemann.

Nachmanovitch, S. (1990). *Free Play*. New York: Putnam.

Nathan, R. (1991). Effective teacher-child conferences: The importance of writing yourself. In B.M. Power & R. Hubbard (Eds.), *Literacy in process* (pp. 19-20). Portsmouth, NH: Heinemann.

National Council of Teachers of English, Standing Committee on Teacher Preparation and Certification. (1986). *Guidelines for the preparation of teachers of English language arts*. Urbana, IL: National Council of Teachers of English.

National Council of Teachers of English, Elementary Section Steering Committee. (1996). Exploring language arts standards within a cycle of learning. *Language Arts, 73*, (1), 10-13.

New York University Reading Recovery Project. (1995). *Program Description* [Brochure]. School of Education, New York University.

New Zealand's Department of Education. *Reading in the junior classes: With guidelines to the revised ready to read series*.

Wellington: School Publications, 1985. Distributed in the United States by Richard C. Owen Publishers, Inc.

North, S. M. (1987). *The making of knowledge in composition.* Upper Montclair, NJ: Boynton/Cook.

O'Donnell, R. C. (1990). English language arts teacher education. *The Handbook of Research on Teacher Education.* New York: Macmillan Publishing Company.

Ohio Stae University, The (1996). *Reading recovery executive summary.*

Olsen, D. (1993). Work satisfaction and stress in the first and third year of academic appointment. *Journal of Higher Education, 64,* 453-477.

Panofsky, C. P. (April, 1996). *Vygotsky centennial: Directions for the future.* Panel conducted at the annual meeting of the American Educational Research Association, New York, NY.

Patton, M. Q. (1990). *Qualitative evaluation and research methods.* London: Sage Publications.

Perl, S., & Wilson, N. (1986). *Through teachers' eyes.* Portsmouth, NH: Heinemann.

Perret-Clermont, A. N. (1980). *Social interaction and cognitive development in children.* London: Academic Press.

Perry, W. G. (1970). *Forms of intellectual and ethical development in the college years: A scheme.* New York: Holt, Rinehart, and Winston.

Peterson, R. (1992). *Life in a crowded place.* Portsmouth, NH: Heinemann.

Phillips, D. C. (1985). On what scientists know. In E. Eisner (Ed.), *Learning and teaching the ways of knowing: Eighty-fourth yearbook of the National Society for the Study of Education* (pp. 23-36). Chicago: University of Chicago Press.

Phillips, D. C. (1990). Subjectivity and objectivity: An objective inquiry. In E. W. Eisner & A. Peshkin (Eds.). *Qualitative research in education: The continuing debate* (pp. 19-37) New York: Teachers College Press.

Piaget, J. (1926). *The language and thought of the child.* London: Routledge & Kegan Paul.

Piaget, J. (1952). *The origins of intelligence in children.* New York: International Universities Press.

Piercy, M. (1991). Starting support groups for writers. In B.M. Power & R. Hubbard, (Eds.), *Literacy in process* (pp. 14-18). Portsmouth, NH: Heinemann.

Pinar, W. F. (1994). *Autobiography, politics and sexuality.* New York: Peter Lang Publishing.

Pinar, W., & Grumet, M. (1976). *Toward a poor curriculum.* Dubuque, IA: Kendall/Hunt.

Pinar, W., Reynolds, W., Slattery, P., & Taubman, P. (1995). *Understanding curriculum.* New York: Peter Lang Publishing.

Pollard, A. & Tann, S. (1987). *Reflective teaching in the primary school: A handbook for the classroom.* London: Cassell Educational Limited.

Power, B. M. (1995). *Long roads, short distances.* Manuscript submitted for publication.

Reading Recovery Council of North America. (1995). *Reading Recovery Executive Summary, 1984-1995.* [Brochure]. Ohio State University, Columbus, OH: Author.

Renwick, W. L. (Director-General of Education, Ministry of Education, New Zealand). (1985). *Reading in junior classes.* New York: Richard C. Owen Publishers, Inc.

Rhodes, L. & Dudley-Marling, C. (1988). *Readers and writers with a difference: A holistic approach to teaching learning disabled and remedial students.* Portsmouth, NH: Heinemann.

Rief, L. (1992). *Seeking diversity.* Portsmouth, NH: Heinemann.

Rogers, C. R. (1961). *On becoming a person.* Boston: Houghton Mifflin.

Rogoff, B. (1996, April). *Vygotsky centennial: Directions for the future.* Panel conducted at the annual meeting of the American Educational Research Association, New York, NY.

Rogoff, B. & Wertsch, J. V. (Eds.). (1984). *Children's learning in the zone of proximal development.* San Francisco: Jossey-Bass.

Rose, P. (1995). Confessions of a biographer. *Civilization, 2,* (1), 72-74.

Rosenblatt, L. M. (1938). *Literature as exploration.* New York: Modern Language Association.

Rosenblatt, L. M. (1978). *The reader, the text, the poem: The transactional theory of the literary work.* Carbondale, IL: Southern Illinois University Press.

Rosenblatt, L. M. (1991). The reading transaction: What for? In B. M. Power & R. Hubbard, (Eds.), *Literacy in process.* (pp. 114-127). Portsmouth, NH: Heinemann.

Roth, W., & Roychoudhury, A. (1993). The development of science process skills in authentic contexts. *Journal of Research in Science Teaching, 30* (2) 127-152.

Routman, R. (1991). *Invitations, changing as teachers and learners K-12*. Portsmouth, NH: Heinemann.

Sadker, M. (1991). *Teachers, schools, and society* (2nd ed.). NY: McGraw-Hill.

Schatzman, L. & Strauss, A. (1973). *Field research: Strategies for a natural sociology*. Englewood Cliffs, NJ: Prentice-Hall.

Schon, D. (1983). *The reflective practitioner: How professionals think and act in action*. New York: Basic Books.

Schon, D. (1991). *The reflective turn: Case studies in and on educational practice*. New York: Teachers College Press.

Schubert, W. H. (1989). Reconceptualizing and the matter of paradigms. *Journal of Teacher Education, 40* (1), 27-32.

Schubert, H., & Ayres, W. (1992). *Teacher lore: Learning from our own experience*. White Plains, NY: Longman.

Shannon, P. (1990). *The struggle to continue: Progressive reading instruction in the United States*. Portsmouth, NH: Heinemann.

Short, E., Willis, G., & Schubert, W. (1985). *Toward excellence in curriculum inquiry: The story of the AERA special interest group on creation and utilization of curriculum knowledge: 1970-1984*. State College, PA: Nittany Press.

Shunk, D. H. (1991). *Learning theories: An educational perspective*. New York: Macmillan.

Sims, N. (1984). *The literary journalist*. New York: Ballantine Books.

Smith, F. (1985). *Reading without nonsense*. New York: Teachers College Press.

Smith, J. W. A., & Elley, W. B. (1994). *Learning to read in New Zealand*. Katonah, NY: Richard C. Owen Publishers, Inc.

Sorcinelli, M. D., & Austin, A. E. (1992). *Developing new and junior faculty, new directions for teaching and learning*. San Francisco: Jossey-Bass.

Sowers, S. (1991). Six questions teachers ask about invented spelling. In B. M. Power& R. Hubbard (Eds.), *Literacy in process.* (pp. 174-179). Portsmouth, NH: Heinemann.

Squire, J. R., (Ed.). (1977). *The teaching of English*. Chicago: University of Chicago Press.

Stanfield II, J. H. (1994). Ethnic modeling in qualitative research. In N. K. Denzin & Y. S. Lincoln (Eds.), *Handbook of qualitative research* (pp. 175-188). Thousand Oaks, CA: Sage Publications, Inc.

Stenhouse, L. (1985). *Research as a basis for teaching: Readings from the work of Lawrence Stenhouse.* Portsmouth, NH: Heinemann.

Tarnas, R. (1991). *The passion of the western mind.* New York: Ballantine.

Temple, C., Nathan, R., Burris, N., & Temple, F. (1988). *The beginnings of writing.* Boston: Allyn and Bacon, Inc.

Tharp, R. G., & Gallimore, R. (1988). *Rousing minds to life.* Cambridge: Cambridge University Press.

Thielens, W. (1987). *The disciplines and undergraduate lecturing.* Paper presented at the annual meeting of the American Educational Research Association, Washington, D.C.

Tomkiewicz, W. C. (April, 1991). *Reflective teaching and conceptual change in an interdisciplinary elementary methods course.* Paper presented at the annual meeting of the National Association of Research in Science Teaching, Fontana, WI.

Tyler, R. (1949). *Basic principles of curriculum and instruction.* Chicago: University of Chicago Press.

University of Maine. (1995). Course number: Physics 497-002; Course Title: Physics by Inquiry.

Van Maanen, J. (1988). *Tales of the field: On writing ethnography.* Chicago: University of Chicago Press

Vukelich, C. (1993). Play: A context for exploring the functions, features, and meaning of writing with peers. *Language Arts, 70* (5) 386-392.

Vygotsky, L. (1956). *Selected Psychological Investigations.* Moskow: Izdstel'sto Adademii Pedagogicheskikh Nauk SSR. (Eds.). Cambridge, MA: Harvard University Press.

Vygotsky, L. S. (1978). *Mind in society: The development of higher psychological processes.* (M. Cole, V. John-Steiner, S. Scribner, & E. Souberman, Trans.). Cambridge, MA: Harvard University Press.

Vygotsky, L. (1986). *Thought and language,* (A. Kozulin, Trans.). Cambridge, MA: MIT Press.

Weaver, C. (1988). *Reading process and practice, from sociopsycholinguistics to whole language.* Portsmouth, NH: Heinemann.

Weiner, B. (1986). *An attributional theory of motivation and emotion.* New York: Springer-Verlag.

Wells, G. (1986). *The meaning makers.* Portsmouth, NH: Heinemann.

Whitney, J. (Writer/Producer), & Hubbard, R. (Writer/Producer). (1988). One classroom: A child's view. In Hansen, J. & Graves, D. (Developers) *The writing and reading process: A closer look.* Portsmouth, New Hampshire: Heinemann .

Whitney, J. (Writer/Producer), & Hubbard, R. (Writer/Producer). (1988). Time and choice: Key elements for process teaching. In J. Hansen & D. Graves (Developers), *The writing and reading process: A closer look.* Portsmouth, NH: Heinemann.

Whitney, J. (Writer/Producer), & Hubbard, R. (Writer/Producer). (1988). Writing conference principles: The child learns, the teacher learns. In J. Hansen & D. Graves (Developers), *The writing and reading process: A closer look.* Portsmouth, NH: Heinemann.

Whitney, J. (Producer), Hubbard, R., & Miller, B. (Writers). (1988). Writing and reading conferences. In J. Hansen & D. Graves (Developers), *The writing and reading process: A closer look.* Portsmouth, NH: Heinemann.

Whitney, J. (Producer), Hubbard, R., & Miller, B. (Writers). (1988). Skills and recordkeeping. In J. Hansen & D. Graves (Developers), *The writing and reading process: A closer look.* Portsmouth, NH: Heinemann.

Wickes, F. (1928). *The inner world of childhood.* New York: Appleton-Century.

Willinsky, J. (1990). *The new literacy.* New York, NY: Routledge.

Index

Studies in the Postmodern Theory of Education

General Editors
Joe L. Kincheloe & Shirley R. Steinberg

Counterpoints publishes the most compelling and imaginative books being written in education today. Grounded on the theoretical advances in criticalism, feminism and postmodernism in the last two decades of the twentieth century, Counterpoints engages the meaning of these innovations in various forms of educational expression. Committed to the proposition that theoretical literature should be accessible to a variety of audiences, the series insists that its authors avoid esoteric and jargonistic languages that transform educational scholarship into an elite discourse for the initiated. Scholarly work matters only to the degree it affects consciousness and practice at multiple sites. Counterpoints' editorial policy is based on these principles and the ability of scholars to break new ground, to open new conversations, to go where educators have never gone before.

For additional information about this series or for the submission of manuscripts, please contact:

Joe L. Kincheloe & Shirley R. Steinberg
637 West Foster Avenue
State College, PA 16801